The MAILBOX®
The Idea Magazine For Teachers®
KINDERGARTEN

1996–1997
YEARBOOK

Jan Trautman, Editor

The Education Center, Inc.
Greensboro, North Carolina

The Mailbox® 1996–1997 Kindergarten Yearbook

Editor In Chief: Margaret Michel
Magazine Director: Karen P. Shelton
Editorial Administrative Director: Stephen Levy
Senior Editor: Jan Trautman
Associate Editor: Mackie Rhodes
Contributing Editors: Ada Hanley Goren, Marie Iannetti
Copy Editors: Lynn Bemer Coble, Jennifer Rudisill, Debbie Shoffner, Gina Sutphin
Staff Artists: Jennifer T. Bennett, Cathy Spangler Bruce, Pam Crane, Teresa Davidson, Clevell Harris, Susan Hodnett, Sheila Krill, Rebecca Saunders, Barry Slate, Donna K. Teal
Contributing Artists: Marilynn G. Barr, Lucia Kemp Henry
Cover Artist: Lois Axeman
Editorial Assistants: Elizabeth A. Findley, Mickey Hjelt, Wendy Svartz

ISBN 1-56234-165-0
ISSN 1088-5528

The Education Center®, *The Mailbox*®, *Teacher's Helper*®, *The Mailbox*® *Bookbag*™, *Learning*™, "the idea magazine for teachers,™" and the mailbox/post/grass logo are trademarks of The Education Center, Inc., and may be the subject of one or more federal trademark registrations. All brand or product names are trademarks or registered trademarks of their respective companies.

Printed in the United States of America.

The Education Center, Inc.
P.O. Box 9753
Greensboro, NC 27429-0753

Look for *The Mailbox*® 1997–1998 Kindergarten Yearbook in the summer of 1998. The Education Center, Inc., is the publisher of *The Mailbox*®, *Teacher's Helper*®, *The Mailbox*® *Bookbag*™, and *Learning*™ magazines, as well as other fine products and clubs. Look for these wherever quality teacher materials are sold, or call 1-800-714-7991.

Contents

BULLETIN BOARDS

Bulletin Boards.....................................

Here's an enticing display that kids help create before they even arrive! During your kindergarten screening, take a photo of each child and have him draw a self-portrait. Mount a border of pink paper and yellow dots. Attach each child's photo to the center of a different, construction-paper coconut tree. Mount the tree near his self-portrait. Add a very large, construction-paper coconut tree and a title near the board. And be sure to share the book with your new group of students.

Felice Kestenbaum—Gr. K, Goosehill Primary, Cold Spring Harbor, NY

Happy birthday to you, and you, and you! Decorate, then laminate, a large birthday-cake cutout. Write each child's name and birth date on a different construction-paper balloon. Then mount the cake and the balloons to make this festive birthday display.

Denise Brown—4- and 5-year-olds, America's Children Of Oakmoor, Des Moines, IA

These handsome ghosts serve to reinforce a variety of skills. Provide a bulletin-board length of white butcher paper and black and orange paint. Have each child make one right- and one left-hand print on the paper. Let dry; then give the child markers to turn his hands into a ghost. Don't miss the opportunities to talk about right and left, and the similarities and differences among the ghostly creatures.

Linda Leonard, Mt. Olive, IL

Imaginations and phonics are at work in this Halloween hullabaloo! Have each child make a chain by linking ten paper strips together. Use the chains to form the word "BOO!"; then mount it next to "B is for." Have each child use art supplies to create the seasonal character of her choice and to write the character's beginning letter (or whole name) on a strip of paper. Mount each character and letter (or name) on the board.

adapted from an idea by Kathleen Miller—Gr. K, Our Lady Of Mt. Carmel, Tenafly, NJ

Bulletin Boards ....

Our Little Angels

Adorn your classroom wall or door with this angelic display. Cut out a large construction-paper wreath. Mount the wreath, and add construction-paper holly leaves and a bow. For each child, cut out a white construction-paper angel. Have each child glue a photo of his face on the angel, then decorate his angel using gold and silver crayons, paint pens, pasta, and glitter. Mount each angel on the wreath; then add the title.

Adapted from an idea
by Carolyn Johnson—Gr. K
W. A. Carpenter Elementary, Deer Park, TX

With each element made from recyclable items, this seasonal eye-catcher emphasizes the joy in the season *and* the earth! To make this board, set up art stations as described on page 9. Encourage children to visit the stations during center times to make the projects that make up this holiday display. Youngsters will be amazed to see the results of their cooperative efforts. Merry! Merry!

Allison Prose—Gr. K, Orlando, FL

Art Stations

(For use with the bulletin board on page 8.)

Tree Station

Making this glistening tree causes the art of cooperation to shine out! Cut the tops off a large supply of school milk cartons. Stock a center with these cartons, scissors, green tempera paint (mixed with a bit of dish soap), paintbrushes, white glue, and glitter. When a child visits this center, have him cut out a triangle shape from each side of a milk carton, then paint the carton green. At another time—after the paint is dry—have the child drizzle glue onto his carton, then sprinkle glitter on the glue. When the glue is dry, have him shake off the excess glitter. Encourage children to make as many cartons as they'd like. When you have enough cartons, staple the cartons to a bulletin board in the shape of a tree. (Also paint four cartons brown and use them to make the trunk of the tree.)

Ornaments Station

Children are the creators of these beautiful baubles. Stock a center with a supply of old greeting cards, plastic-tub lids, beads/sequins, scissors, glue, and ribbon. To make an ornament, have a child cut out a picture(s) from a card and glue it to a lid. Encourage her to decorate the edge of the lid with beads/sequins. Glue a loop of ribbon to the back of the lid for hanging. When the glue is dry, hang each ornament on the board.

Candles Station

These brightly blazing candles add that special holiday flair to your display. Stock a center with toilet-tissue rolls, brightly colored wrapping paper, scissors, glue, construction paper, and tissue paper in yellow and orange. To make a candle, have a child cut and glue wrapping-paper scraps around a tube. To make a flame, have the child cut out a construction-paper flame. Direct him to glue tissue paper onto the flame; then glue the flame on the inside of one end of the candle.

9

Bulletin Boards ....

Mrs. Martin's Sweeties

Carly
Pete
Jennifer
Grant
Liz
Josh
Clevell
Brianne
Kevin
Sue

This sweet display can be used as a door decoration or on a classroom wall or bulletin board. Cut out a large, red construction-paper heart. Decorate its edges with doily pieces and fabric scraps to resemble a valentine box of candy. Have each child color a small picture of his face, then cut it out. Glue each child's picture to the bottom of a cupcake liner; then glue the liner to the heart. Write each child's name below his picture; then mount the finished project for a seasonally alluring display.

Adapted from an idea by DeAnna Martin—Gr. K
Hargett Elementary
Irvine, KY

WE ARE A RAINBOW OF EARTH COLORS...

JUST LIKE THE MANY FLOWERS OF ONE GARDEN.

Here's a display to complement your multicultural-awareness studies. In advance, take a close-up photo of each child's face. Have each child cut out a large construction-paper flower, then glue his photo to its center. Instruct each child to construct and staple a paper stem and leaves to the board, then attach his flower. Add the caption, and your garden is complete!

Perry Stio, Martin Luther King School, Piscataway, NJ

Students will sparkle with pride when their names are on your good-as-gold board! Make a 3-D rainbow by arranging, overlapping, and stapling sections of red, blue, and yellow plastic wrap to the board. Mount a pot cutout at each end of the rainbow. Have each child write his name on a piece of construction-paper gold. Attach each child's name to the board as you deem appropriate.

Adapted from an idea by DeAnna Martin—Gr. K, Hargett Elementary, Irvine, KY

Foster self-esteem and keep skills right on track with this board. Mount an engine cutout on a wall or board. Attach the caption to a smoke puff made of batting. For each skill that you'd like to track, add a labeled construction-paper train car. As each child masters or makes progress with a given skill, write his name on the appropriate train car. Keep chuggin' along!

Michele D. Romeiser—Gr. K, Childtime Child Center, Fairport, NY

Bulletin Boards...

With this display, your students—and all your visitors—will know what's up in your classroom! Using an opaque projector, enlarge the bear pattern (page 16) on colored construction paper. Color in details; then cut out and laminate the pattern. Also cut out and laminate several construction-paper balls. Program each ball with a skill or topic that you're currently studying. Mount all the pieces on a classroom wall or board; then use a permanent marker to write a title on the bear's buttons.

Diane Pittman
Tina-Avalon School
Tina, MO

To create this heartwarming scene on a bulletin board, first have children paint a blue sky and staple on paper grass. Add a fence, a finger-painted sun, and a tree cutout. Have students paint cardboard egg cups for tree blossoms and glue on tissue-paper leaves and child-created birds/nests. Have each child make one flower to represent himself, one cut-out drawing that resembles himself, and one caterpillar section on which he writes his first and last name.

Connie DiRienzo—Gr. K, William E. Russell School, Medfield, MA

Here's a convenient showcase for your little artists' masterpieces. Using bulletin-board border, divide a board or wall into sections according to the number of children in your class. (Add extra sections for new students, if desired.) Write each child's name on a sentence strip; then laminate the strips. Mount the names as shown. When each child completes a work of art, she'll know just where to display it.

Diane Joseph—Gr. K, Bayou Vista Elementary, Morgan City, LA

Launch good behavior with this display. Duplicate and personalize a hot-air balloon (page 16) for each child. Then enlarge the pattern and trace it on colorful paper. Cut out all the patterns. Mount the large balloon on a blue background with five rows of clouds. For each day that a child demonstrates good behavior, advance his personalized balloon to the next row of clouds. When a child gets to the top row of clouds, reward him!

Jennifer Woods—Gr. K
Alma Primary
Alma, AR

Bulletin Boards ....

Staple crepe-paper sea plants to a background—then set your kids in motion! Make fish from paper plates; then sponge-paint. Add marker details when dry. For crabs paint cutouts with red/orange fingerpaint; then glue on wiggle eyes. For starfish glue popcorn kernels on tagboard cutouts. Make sea horses by brushing a coat of water-diluted white glue onto cutouts, sprinkling on colored sand, and adding wiggle eyes.

Rosemary Bonelli, Building Blocks, Commack, NY

This board's great for reminiscing with your present class *and* for motivating incoming children who might visit you. Enlarge and trace the lion on page 17. Color, laminate, and mount the pattern. After adding a speech-bubble title, staple on mounted class-related photos. Ask students to dictate a caption for each picture; then record their dictation on the picture mounting. Looks "gr-r-r-eat"!

Tonie Liddle, Central Baptist Christian Academy, Binghamton, NY

This display is child-created all around! To make a border piece, fold a coffee filter so that it resembles a rounded-edge triangle. Dip the pointed end into red-colored water, letting the color seep up to within an inch of the edge. Then dip the rounded edge into green-colored water. Let the filter dry; then open and iron it flat. Cut each circle in half; then add seeds with a marker. Amidst the melons, mount children's illustrations of their summer activities.

Edie Davison—Gr. K, Xenia Nazarene Christian, Xenia, OH

Honor your kindergarten grads with this display. Hang a real graduation robe on a hanger; then attach the hanger to the board. Arrange and pin the flowing robe to the board. Give each child a copy of the graduate and cap patterns on page 18. Have him color the graduate (and cap) to resemble himself, then glue on the cap. Display each proud graduate on the board; then have him write his name near his cutout.

W. L. Harris, St. Petersburg, FL

bear

hot-air balloon
Also use this pattern with "Take Flight!" on page 49.

Graduate Patterns

Use with the bulletin board on page 15.

Arts And Crafts

Arts & Crafts
For Little Hands

Underwater World

Here's an underwater art project that will really make a splash. To make a fishbowl and underwater scene, draw a fishbowl pattern on a sheet of construction paper; then cut it out. Use permanent markers and crayons to draw underwater pictures such as fish, seaweed, coral, and aquarium rocks. Mix a few drops of water and blue food coloring with some white glue. Then brush over the entire fishbowl with the blue mixture. Allow it to dry. There you have it—an underwater art experience.

Melissa L. Mapes
Little People Land Preschool
St. Petersburg, FL

Handprint Sunflowers

Little ones will love this sunflower project hands down! To prepare, mix together yellow tempera paint and a few drops of liquid soap in a shallow pan. To make a sunflower, paint a brown circle near the top of a large sheet of construction paper. Next repeatedly press one hand into the yellow paint, then onto the paper around the brown circle. When the paint dries, glue sunflower seeds to the center of the flower. Draw a stem and leaves on green construction paper; then cut them out. To complete the project, glue the stem and leaves on the paper under the handprints. What beautiful blooms!

Adapted from an idea by Cindy Larson—K–2 Special Education
Western Hills Elementary
Omaha, NE

Here Are My Fingerprints

Each student's fingerprints will give this project a personal touch. In advance, copy the poem (shown) onto white paper; then photocopy a classroom supply. To make a fingerprint project, have each child write his name at the top of a 12" x 18" sheet of construction paper; then have him trace both hands on his paper. Instruct each child to press each finger (including thumbs) one at a time on a stamp pad, then onto the corresponding finger on each hand outline. Direct each student to glue a copy of the poem on his paper. To complete the project, write the date at the bottom of the paper. Here are my fingerprints!

Angie Mrowiec
Niles Park District
Niles, IL

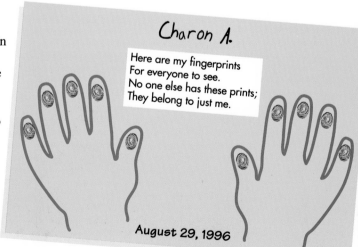

Charon A.

Here are my fingerprints
For everyone to see.
No one else has these prints;
They belong to just me.

August 29, 1996

A Colorful Creation

Youngsters will love this colorful idea. To prepare for this activity, place a classroom supply of red, yellow, and blue crepe-paper strips on a table. Have each child choose two differently colored strips, then place his strips in a glass jar. Assist each student in pouring water in the jar; then have him twist a lid on the jar. Encourage each child to carefully shake his jar and watch a secondary color appear. Place the jars on the center of a table and seat youngsters around the table. Then supply each child with a sheet of light-colored construction paper and a paintbrush. Encourage him to dip the paintbrush into the jar or jars of his choice, then to paint, drip, or splatter a picture or design.

Connie Allen
Immanuel Lutheran
Manitowoc, WI

Spaghetti Art

This activity sure has oodles of noodles. Provide each child with a sheet of waxed paper and some cooked spaghetti noodles. Have him arrange the spaghetti on the waxed paper in the design of his choice. Allow the pasta to harden for a few days. To complete the project, have each student glue his design on colored oaktag. To vary this activity, use differently colored and shaped pasta. A perfectly fun pasta project!

Linda Anne Lopienski
Asheboro, NC

Paper Pictures

Creative and beautiful—that's how these art projects turn out. To prepare for this activity, cut a large supply of small square and rectangle shapes from various colors of construction paper (including many shades of the same color). To make a paper picture, draw or trace the design of your choice on a sheet of construction paper. Glue on the squares and rectangles, overlapping the pieces inside the outline to fill in the picture. Continue in this manner until the entire picture is covered. (You might wish to complete this project in several settings.) What an artistic creation!

Cherie White-Helms
Wendell Phillips Visual & Performing Arts Magnet Elementary
Kansas City, MO

Arts & Crafts
For Little Hands

Spider Wear

Creepy crawlers will be popping up all over when you make these spider hats. Measure and cut a black tagboard strip to fit around each child's head. Staple the ends of the strip together to make a headband. Have each child cut eight strips of black construction paper, then accordion-fold each strip. Staple four of the strips to one side of the headband and four strips to the other. Now your little ones are ready for spider wear!

Cathy Gust—Gr. K
Stiegel Elementary School
Manheim, PA

Jack-O'-Lanterns With Panache

These tissue-paper pumpkins will be nifty additions to any classroom. To make one, bend a hanger into a circular shape. Place the hanger atop a sheet of orange tissue paper so that the hook of the hanger extends past the top of the paper. Glue around the inside and outside edges of the hanger. Place another sheet of tissue paper on top of the hanger and press the two sheets together with the hanger in between. When the glue dries, trim the excess paper from around the hanger. Use construction paper to make facial features for the jack-o'-lantern. Mount the finished projects and construction-paper vines on a wall or bulletin board.

Kitty Bags

Your little trick-or-treaters will be excited to make one of these "kitty" Halloween bags. To make a bag, cut a three-inch strip from the top of a paper grocery bag and set the strip aside for later. Then cut three inches down from each corner of the bag. Fold the tops down to the inside of the bag. Use the three-inch strip to make a handle. Next use black tempera paint to paint the outside of the bag. When the paint dries, use Slick® paint or construction-paper cutouts to make the cat's eyes and nose on the bag. Glue on accordion-folded construction-paper strips to resemble whiskers and construction-paper triangles for ears. "Meeeeeee-ow!"

Carol Bruckner—Gr. K
Oaklawn Elementary
Fort Worth, TX

Autumn Wind Socks

Adorn your classroom with these autumn wind socks. In advance collect a supply of brightly colored leaves, or photocopy the leaf patterns on page 35 onto construction paper; then cut them out. To make a wind sock, glue the leaves onto a 12" x 18" sheet of construction paper. Allow the glue to dry; then staple the sides of the paper together to form a cylinder. Cut crepe-paper streamers into varying lengths and attach them along the bottom edge of the paper. At the top, punch two holes on each side of the sock; then thread string through the holes and suspend the wind sock from the ceiling.

Mary Delak—Gr. K
Washington Elementary School
Ely, MN

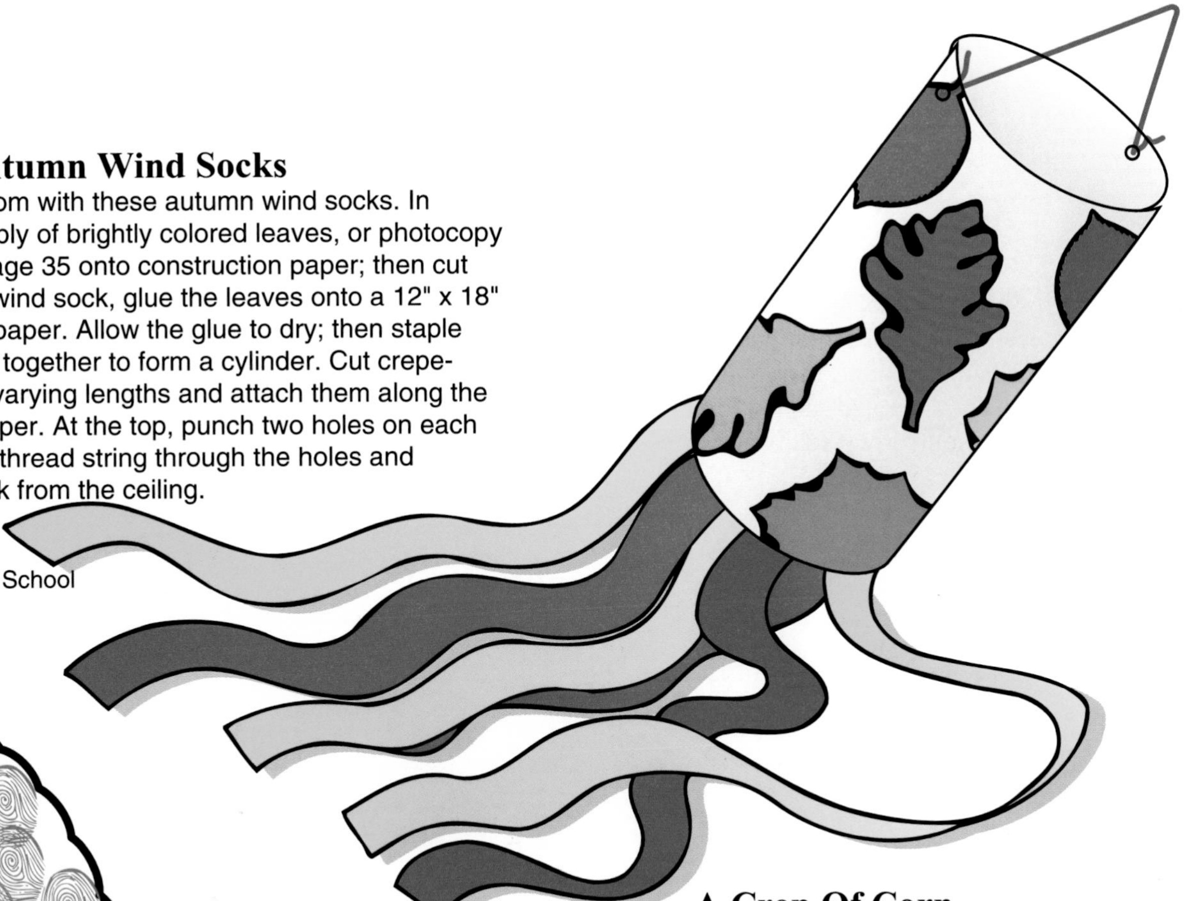

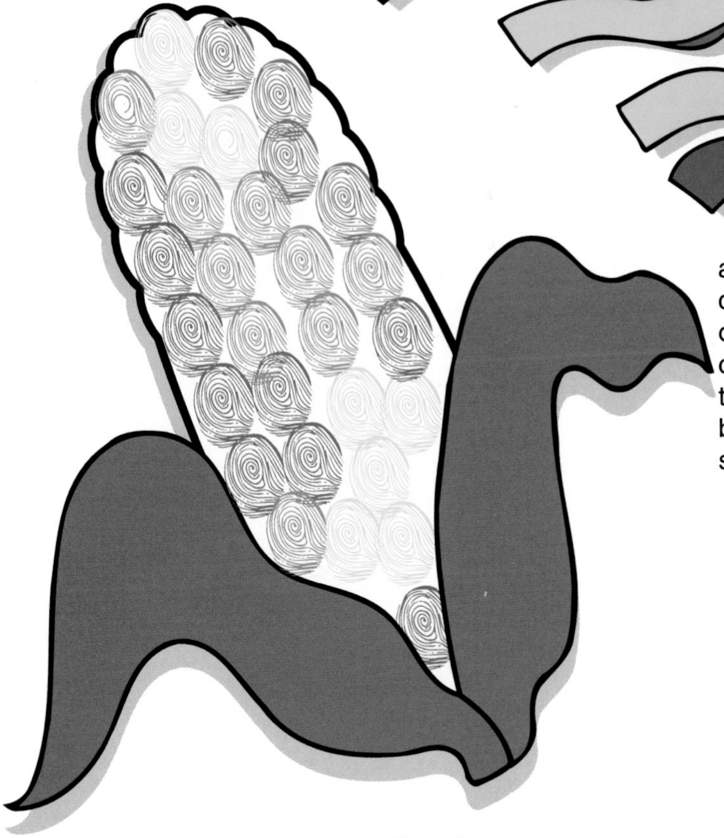

A Crop Of Corn

Harvest a crop of Indian corn with this fun activity. To make an ear, reproduce the corncob pattern on page 36 onto white construction paper; then cut it out. Dip your finger into red, orange, yellow, brown, or black tempera paint and then onto the cob cutout. Continue in this manner, using different colors until the cutout is covered. When the paint is dry, complete the project by gluing construction-paper cornhusks (or real ones) to each side of the cutout.

Tootsy Turkeys

These tootsy turkeys will wiggle your little ones' toes. In advance mix brown paint with liquid soap in a shallow pan. To make a turkey, step one bare foot into the tray, then onto a 12" x 18" sheet of construction paper. Allow the paint to dry. With the toes facing down, draw or paint feathers around the foot. Then use markers to draw facial features on the footprint to resemble a turkey. Gobble, gobble!

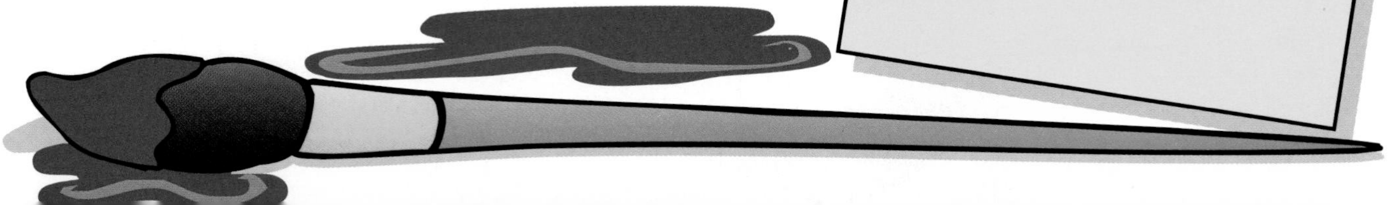

Arts & Crafts
For Little Hands

3-D Dough Decorations

These festive dough decorations stand up by themselves so they can be used as decorations, manipulatives, gifts, or even in your block area in child-created scenes. First mix up a batch of salt dough (2 cups flour, 1 cup salt, water as needed, and green food coloring). To make one tree, press out a portion of the dough until it is about 1/4-inch thick. Using a small Christmas-tree cookie cutter, cut out two tree shapes. Then cut a slit about 1/4-inch wide two-thirds of the way *down* one tree, and two-thirds of the way *up* the other. Slide one tree onto the other at 90° angles; then let the tree dry for several days. When it is dry, use craft glue to attach sequins or nonpareils.

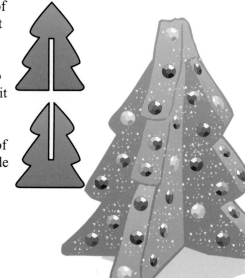

Julia Elsen, Thatcher, AZ

Window Wonders

Make your classroom shine with these seasonal decorations. In advance, cut out construction-paper outlines of holiday or seasonal shapes. Have a child choose a shape, then squeeze a line of glue around it. Next have the child select a sheet of tissue paper and place it over the glued outline. When the glue dries, have the child trim off the excess tissue paper. Display the finished projects in a sunny classroom window.

Bernice Regenstein
Bricktown, NJ

Holiday Candles

Candlelight is glowing bright on these joyous holiday nights. To make a candle, roll a piece of construction paper into a tube; then tape it together. Cut flames from construction paper or tissue paper; then glue them inside the top of the candle. Decorate a spray-can top by spray-painting it, attaching stickers, or using glitter glue. Using a thick stream of glue, center the candle on top of the decorated top. When the glue is dry, display these holiday candles around your classroom.

Dianne Joseph—Gr. K
Bayou Vista Elementary
Morgan City, LA

Refrigerator Magnets

Parents and guardians will be thrilled to receive these child-made gifts that will adorn their kitchens with style! Ask an adult volunteer to cut off a thin slice from a small log for each child in your class. Decorate one side of the wood slice with an original picture, a photo, stickers, fabric scraps, or a small ornament. Attach a strip of magnetic tape to the back; then spray the finished project with a wood sealer. (Follow the precautions on the can of wood sealer.) If desired, wrap the finished projects in the bag described below.

Wilma Droegemueller—Gr. K and Preschool
Zion Lutheran School
Mt. Pulaski, IL

Child-Made Gift Bags

Youngsters will beam with pride at their handiwork on these gift bags. For each child, cut a rectangular piece of burlap large enough to fold in half. In advance, dip the burlap edges in water-diluted glue (to prevent unraveling); then let the glue dry. Thread a blunt tapestry needle with yarn. Demonstrate a basic running stitch by showing youngsters how to move the needle through the fabric in an alternating up-and-down pattern. Then have each child sew around three edges of his folded fabric, leaving the top edge open. Help each child tie off the end of his yarn. To close each bag, use a large safety pin that has a colorful ribbon tied to it.

Wilma Droegemueller—Gr. K and Preschool

Scented Candy Canes

These candy canes look good enough to eat—but don't! They are for dazzling decoration purposes only. To make one, cut two identically sized candy-cane shapes from tagboard. Use a permanent black marker to draw section lines on opposites sides of each candy cane. Brush every other section with water-diluted glue; then shake on kosher salt—quite a bit of it. When the glue dries, shake off the excess salt. Then use red tempera paint to paint every other section of the candy canes red. While the paint is still wet, shake on more kosher salt. When the paint dries, shake off the excess salt. Then dip three cotton balls in peppermint extract. Sandwich the cotton balls between the two cutouts; then glue them in place. Use the finished projects to decorate a classroom doorway or wall and scent your room with the pleasing aroma of peppermint.

Rose Semmel
Raritan Valley Community College Child Care
Somerville, NJ

25

Cool Colors

Here's a variation of the popular crayon-melt idea that *doesn't* involve heat. First cut out an outline of a seasonal shape from a double thickness of construction paper. Then cut a piece of clear adhesive paper that is double the size of the construction-paper shape. Lay the adhesive sheet sticky-side-up on a table. (Tape the corners down if they curl up.) Cover half of the adhesive with colorful crayon shavings; then fold the other half over the shavings. Rub over the adhesive with the back of a large metal spoon. Tape the adhesive sheet to one of the cutouts. Trim the excess adhesive; then glue the remaining cutout on the back. Display these colorful creations on a sunny window or hang them from your classroom ceiling.

Mary E. Maurer
Caddo, OK

Seasonal Wreaths

Grace your hallways, windows, or classroom doors with these child-made wreaths. To make one, paint the edge of a paper plate green. When the paint is dry, fold the plate in half; then cut out the inside. Unfold the plate; then decorate it with red stickers, paint, or glitter glue. Hot-glue a fabric bow to the top. Then punch a hole near the top of the wreath and add a length of yarn for hanging. Deck the halls!

Nina Tabanian—Gr. K
St. Rita School
Dallas, TX

Frosty Friends

Recycling comes into play in making these frosty friends. In advance, collect an empty, clean plastic jar (such as the 20 oz. powdered-drink-mix containers) and an old sport sock for each child. Provide craft glue, permanent markers, and various art supplies such as sequins, pom-poms, and buttons. To make one frosty friend, stretch the sock over the top of the jar to resemble a hat (if necessary, cut the toe off the sock). Then glue on craft items and draw features to create a unique frosty friend. Display these cute fellows in a winter wonderland scene—with white packing-foam snow, and the trees from "3-D Dough Decorations." on page 24.

Debbie Amason—Gr. K, West End Elementary School
Milledgeville, GA

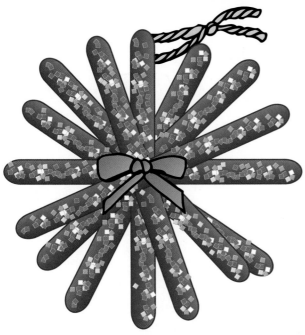

Winter Stars

Your classroom will twinkle with these stars that are reminiscent of a crisp, clear winter sky. To make a star, paint eight craft sticks the color of your choice. Sprinkle the wet paint with glitter. When the paint is dry, shake off the excess glitter. Then use hot glue to glue the craft sticks together—similar to an asterisk. When the glue is dry, hot-glue a ribbon to one of the sticks for hanging. Twinkle! Twinkle!

Linda Schwitzke—Headstart
Longview, WA

Living In Harmony

In honor of Martin Luther King, Jr.'s birthday, create these colorful crafts that convey his message of peace and unity. In advance photocopy the people patterns below. Then use that copy to reproduce the patterns on various colors of construction paper. To make one project, use a permanent marker to roughly draw land shapes on a paper plate. Color the land shapes with a green crayon, pressing down hard. Then paint over the whole plate with water-diluted blue tempera paint. When the paint is dry, cut out various colors of the people patterns and glue them to the plate. Display the finished projects on a bulletin board titled "Living In Harmony."

Peg Meehan, Mrs. M's Playcare, Narragansett, RI

Arts & Crafts
For Little Hands

Hello, Mr. Groundhog

It's time for that furry little guy to come peeking out of his hole! This February, have youngsters make these groundhog projects to do a little peeking of their own. To make one, cut the center out of a small paper plate, leaving just the rim. Color or paint the rim green or brown. Then fold down the top of a paper lunch bag and staple the plate rim to the folded-down section of the bag. Use the patterns on page 37 to make construction-paper groundhogs or have children create original groundhogs from art materials. Snuggle the groundhog in his burrow (bag). On February 2, will the groundhog see his shadow? Take a peek and see!

Rose Semmel, Stanton Learning Center, Stanton, NJ

Valentine Wonders

These sparkling creations offer an eye-catching display for any February classroom. You will need white, pink, and red construction paper; white, pink, and red tempera paint; wide paintbrushes or sponge pieces; an assortment of doilies; and glitter. To make a valentine, place a doily on a sheet of construction paper. Using a brush or sponge, dab paint over the doily. Carefully lift the doily off the paper; then sprinkle glitter in the wet paint. When the paint is dry, cut out a heart shape. If desired, glue on additional construction-paper and doily borders accents. Then display the completed projects on a board or ng them from your ceiling. Just lovely!

Gina Wachinger—Pre-K, Our Lady Of Bethlehem, Columbus, OH

Pretty Hearts

Watercolor paints and a creative eye provide the necessary ingredients for these unique projects. To make one, use a water-filled plant sprayer to dampen a white sheet of construction paper. Then use a paintbrush to drop on small puddles of paint. Allow the colors to spread and mix together. Create different effects by adding more paint, tilting the paper by hand, or spraying on more water. When the paper is dry, use a black marker to draw hearts on the paper. Then loosely cut around the black outline. Mount the heart cutouts on pieces of construction paper. Display the completed projects along a classroom wall.

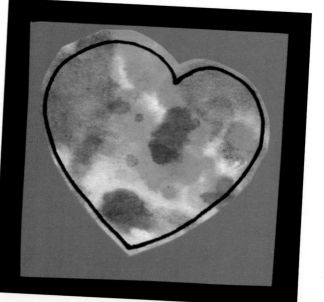

St. Pat's Weave

Over, under, over, under—a little patterning and some artwork make a fine St. Patrick's Day project. To begin, draw or use art supplies to decorate the center of a sturdy paper plate with a St. Pat's theme. Then cut slits around the rim of the plate at approximately two-inch intervals. Knot a length of yarn; then begin weaving it over and under the slits. To attach a new length or color of yarn, just tie it onto the other piece at the back of the plate. When your weaving is complete, secure the end of the yarn by tucking it in the other yarn pieces. Mount the finished projects on a St. Pat's board.

Blow Art

The spring winds are beginning to blow—and so is the paint in your classroom! To make this windy-looking picture, drop a blob of thinned paint onto a sheet of art paper. Use a straw to blow the paint around until you have achieved a desired effect. When the paint is dry, use markers or crayons to repeatedly draw around the design. Mount each page on a colorful sheet of construction paper; then display the finished projects.

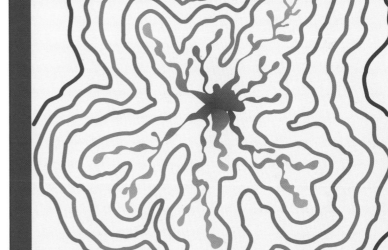

Handsome Lions

Are you studying the lion-and-lamb weather of March? If so, these child-made lions will add just the right touch to your classroom. To make a lion, draw or paint a lion's face on a paper plate. Use other art supplies (such as pom-poms, pipe cleaners, and buttons) to embellish the lion's face. Then—in several sittings, if appropriate—trace your hand a dozen or so times. Cut out the hand shapes; then glue them around the lion's face to resemble his mane. Curl the ends of the mane by wrapping the fingertips around a pencil and releasing. Glue on construction-paper ears for a "gr-r-r-r-eat" finish.

Sherry Cook—Preschool & Gr. K
Glenwood Springs, CO

29

Arts & Crafts
For Little Hands

Happy Nests

Happy thoughts of spring fly into your classroom with these beautiful projects. Provide a variety of bird-egg photos (from encyclopedias, for example) for children to examine. Next give each child a small portion of potter's clay. Encourage each child to form several small bird eggs and one nest. Using a pencil or a straightened paper clip, have each child scratch a textured look into his nest. Then rest the eggs and nests on a windowsill to dry (for several days). When the clay is dry, have each child use tempera paints to paint his eggs as he likes. When the paint is dry, arrange the eggs on top of a little Spanish moss inside the nest. (Betty Lynn Scholtz actually had a mourning dove hop into her classroom window and sit on several of their drying nests!)

Betty Lynn Scholtz—Gr. K
St. Ann's School
Charlotte, NC

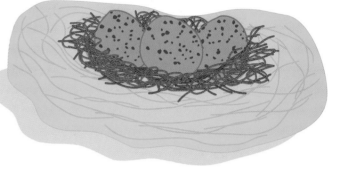

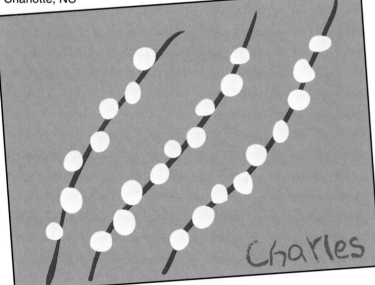

Pussy Willows All Around

In preparation for this work of art, encourage children to carefully examine a real pussy-willow branch. Then provide sheets of light brown butcher paper, brown tempera paint, and thin paintbrushes. Instruct each child to paint several long, thin branches on her paper. (Or glue pipe cleaners to the paper to resemble branches.) Then provide white tempera paint. Have each child repeatedly dip a finger into the white paint, then onto her paper around the branches. When the paint dries, display each picture on a bulletin board around real pussy-willow branches.

Catherine V. Herber, Raleigh, NC

Anne M. Cromwell-Gapp—Gr. K, Connecticut Valley Child Care Center, Claremont, NH

Feet Aflutter

Step right into this tactile experience that results in a collection of one-of-a-kind butterflies. To make one butterfly, have each student step into a shallow pan of tempera paint with one bare foot, then press that paint-covered foot onto a sheet of construction paper. Repeat the process with the other foot as shown. When the footprints dry, cut loosely around them. Then cut out a construction-paper butterfly body and glue it between the two footprints. (If your youngsters' abilities permit, this is a great time to talk about left and right—and backwards!) For a colorful spring display, mount the completed butterflies around a construction-paper tree.

Melissa Mapes—Pre-K
Little People Land Preschool
St. Petersburg, FL

Mom's Greatest Fan

These Mother's Day greetings are sure to bring smiles to your children's moms. To begin, you'll need a large sheet of sturdy construction paper programmed with "I'm your biggest fan!" and a piece of wallpaper from a wallpaper sample book. (The wallpaper sample should be rectangular—approximately 9" x 18"—so that it will fan out nicely.) Accordion-fold the wallpaper; then staple it near one end of the folded paper. Gently spread out the wallpaper to create a fan shape. Tie a ribbon around the stapled end; then glue or staple the fan to the large sheet of construction paper. Write a Mother's Day message on the background paper; then it's ready for an extraspecial delivery!

Jennifer Hart—Grs. K–3
St. Paul's Lutheran School
Prior Lake, MN

Picture-Perfect

Here's a little treasure your students can make for Mother's Day, Father's Day, or any old day! In advance, take a picture of each of your students. Also ask youngsters to bring in empty, *cube-shaped* tissue boxes. To make one frame, cut off the top and bottom panels of a tissue box. Glue three sides of the top panel to the bottom panel, being sure that the design side is showing. If necessary, trim a photo; then slide it into the opening of the frame. To make a stand for the frame, cut out a piece that is approximately two-thirds the length of the frame from a side panel of the tissue box. Fold one edge of that piece one-half inch down. Glue the folded edge to the back of the frame. And there you go—picture-perfect!

Alyson Rappaport—Substitute Teacher
Gwinnett Schools
Stone Mountain, GA

Split, Splat!

Are you stocking up on creative painting ideas? Well, try this one on for size! Cut the legs off an old pair of panty hose. Fill the toe of each leg with approximately two cups of sand. Tie each leg just above the sand to form a ball and a tail (see the illustration). Holding the tail, dip the ball into some thinned tempera paint; then hold it out at arm's length and drop it onto a sheet of butcher paper lined with newspaper. Repeat the dipping and dropping process as desired. Youngsters will be delighted to see the splatter-painted designs they create.

Lori Kent
Hood River, OR

Arts & Crafts
For Little Hands

A Gift For Dad

This colorful, child-made paperweight takes some time to create, but the end result is certainly worth it. A few weeks ahead of time, start collecting (and have children collect) envelopes that have canceled postage stamps on them. When you have a large supply of stamps for each child, have each child search his yard or your schoolyard for a rock. (You might want to give children size guidelines by comparing the size of the rock they should be looking for to a familiar object—such as a tennis ball.)

To make one paperweight, wash the rock and let it dry. Cut the stamp(s) off each envelope, leaving a border of paper around each stamp. Soak the stamps in lukewarm water for ten minutes; then gently peel off each stamp. Arrange the stamps on waxed paper and let them dry. Then use white glue to glue the stamps on the rock, overlapping them to cover the rock completely. When the glue dries, paint on a coat of Mod Podge® (or any water-based sealer). When that dries, use a permanent marker to write your name on the bottom of the rock. Dads or other male friends will be thrilled to receive their youngsters' handiwork!

Maureen Tiedemann—Gr. K, Holy Child School, Old Westbury, NY

Sand Squiggles

Decorate your classroom with these summery sand squiggles. To make one, squeeze a glue design on waxed paper, being sure that all the glue lines are thick and connected. Then sprinkle colored sand on the design. Let the project dry for approximately one week. When it is completely dry, gently peel the waxed paper from the design. Tie a loop of ribbon on the design so that it can be hung from a window, ceiling, or wall.

Anne M. Cromwell-Gapp—Gr. K
Connecticut Valley Child Care Center
Claremont, NH

Sandy Seashells

Children will love making sandy seashells to add to your beach or ocean studies. To make the shells, you will need your favorite hardening clay recipe, a rolling pin, an assortment of ocean-related cookie cutters, sandpaper, glue, paintbrushes, and play sand—regular or colored. To make one sandy seashell, roll out the dough to approximately 1/2-inch thick. Use a cookie cutter to cut out a shell shape; then let it dry for several days. When the shell is dry, gently sand it with sandpaper to make the surface rough enough for glue to stick to it. Next brush a coat of glue on the shell. Then roll the shell in the sand until it is covered. Display the dry project in your ocean-display area.

Bonnie McKenzie—Pre-K & Gr. K
Cheshire Country Day School
Cheshire, CT

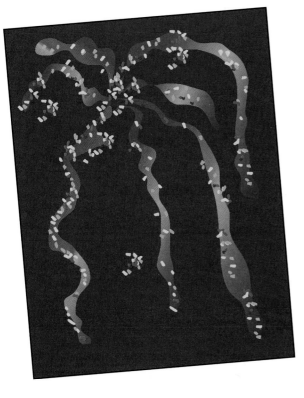

Fireworks!

Help your youngsters celebrate Independence Day with these artistic creations. To begin, give each child a sheet of black construction paper. Then have each child dip a brush into white glue and paint a firework design on his paper. While the glue is still wet, have each child shake cake-decorating sugar sprinkles onto the glue. Let it dry; then shake off the excess sprinkles. As a variation, have a child place a handful of colorful candy sprinkles on the paper first. Then have him dip the brush into the glue and brush over the candy sprinkles. Oooh! Did you see *that* one?

Adapted from an idea by Anne M. Cromwell-Gapp—Gr. K
Connecticut Valley Child Care Center
Claremont, NH

Firecracker Party Favors

Your little ones can make these party favors to decorate your classroom or to give away. For each child, you will need two small paper cups; red and blue tempera paints; scissors; red, white, and blue crepe-paper streamers; a paintbrush; and glue. To make one party favor, cut eight equally spaced slits down the side of one cup, stopping at the bottom rim. Cut the other cup in a similar fashion, but stop 1/2 inch above the bottom rim. Bend the cut pieces down, forming an open, flower-like shape. Paint the cups; then let them dry. Next glue the shallower-cut cup inside the deep-cut cup. Cut thin streamers from crepe paper; then glue them to the back of the bottom cup. When the glue dries, fill the center with candies—red, white, and blue jelly beans would be nice!

Karen Eiben and Amy Gray—Gr. K, The Kids' Place, LaSalle, IL

Bottom Cup

Top Cup

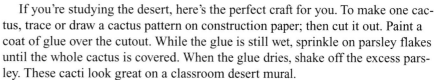

Desert Cactus

If you're studying the desert, here's the perfect craft for you. To make one cactus, trace or draw a cactus pattern on construction paper; then cut it out. Paint a coat of glue over the cutout. While the glue is still wet, sprinkle on parsley flakes until the whole cactus is covered. When the glue dries, shake off the excess parsley. These cacti look great on a classroom desert mural.

Rachelle Thompson—Gr. TK, Paxton Child Development Center, Leesburg, VA

The Rainbow Fish

Written & Illustrated by Marcus Pfister
Published by North-South Books, Inc.

In this enchanting tale, the Rainbow Fish learns about sharing, caring, and the beauty that comes from within. To extend the beauty of the story, choose from the following art techniques and have your children create a whole school of beautiful rainbow fish. Use the finished projects as journal covers, on bulletin boards, or just swimming around your classroom walls.

To make this flashy fish, duplicate the fish pattern (page 38) on colorful construction paper; then cut it out. Depending on the artist's abilities, provide a large supply of colorful, precut scales or construction-paper scraps from which scales may be torn. Starting at the tail and working toward the head, glue the scales on the body of the fish. For the shiny scale, glue on one aluminum-foil scale. Finally, add construction-paper or marker details on the head, fins, and tail.

Cheryl Martin and Leslie Wellmeyer—Gr. K, Woodlake Elementary
San Antonio, TX

Here's an impressive swimmer that can be made with a simple squeeze or two. Duplicate the fish pattern (page 38) on colorful construction paper; then cut it out. Cut a shiny scale from a piece of hologram sticker paper (available at craft stores); then attach it to the fish. Next glue on a wiggle eye. Then decorate the fish by squeezing on designs of colored glue. (Fluorescent colors look especially nice.) Allow lots of drying time for this slimy little fellow!

Chris Langemo—Gr. K, Whittier Elementary School
Long Beach, CA

This shiny critter serves as a beautiful reminder of the lessons learned from the Rainbow Fish. To make this fish, duplicate the fish pattern (page 38) on construction paper; then cut it out. Cut shades of blue, pink, and purple tissue paper into small pieces. (You can also use shades of another group of colors, such as yellow, red, and orange.) Using liquid starch, paint on the tissue-paper pieces, covering the entire fish. When that dries, glue on several shiny, aluminum-foil scales. Use a permanent marker to add other fishy details.

Jennifer Woods—Gr. K, Alma Primary School, Alma, AR

Use with "Autumn Wind Socks" on page 23.

Pattern Leaves

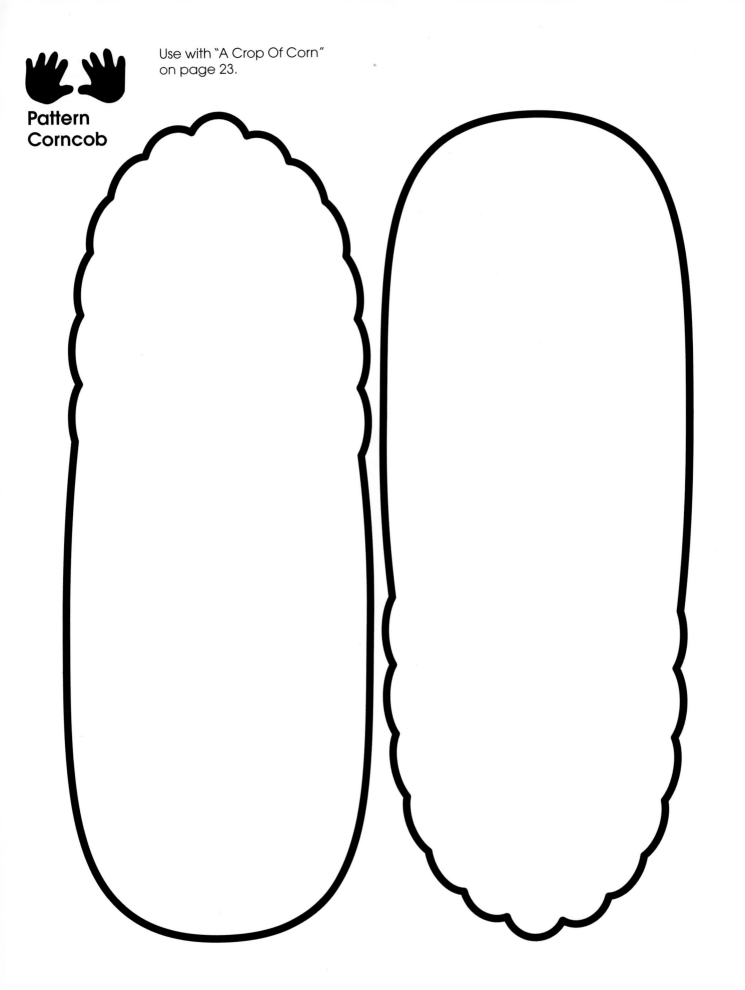

Use with "A Crop Of Corn" on page 23.

Pattern Corncob

Use with
"Hello, Mr. Groundhog"
on page 28.

Pattern
Groundhogs

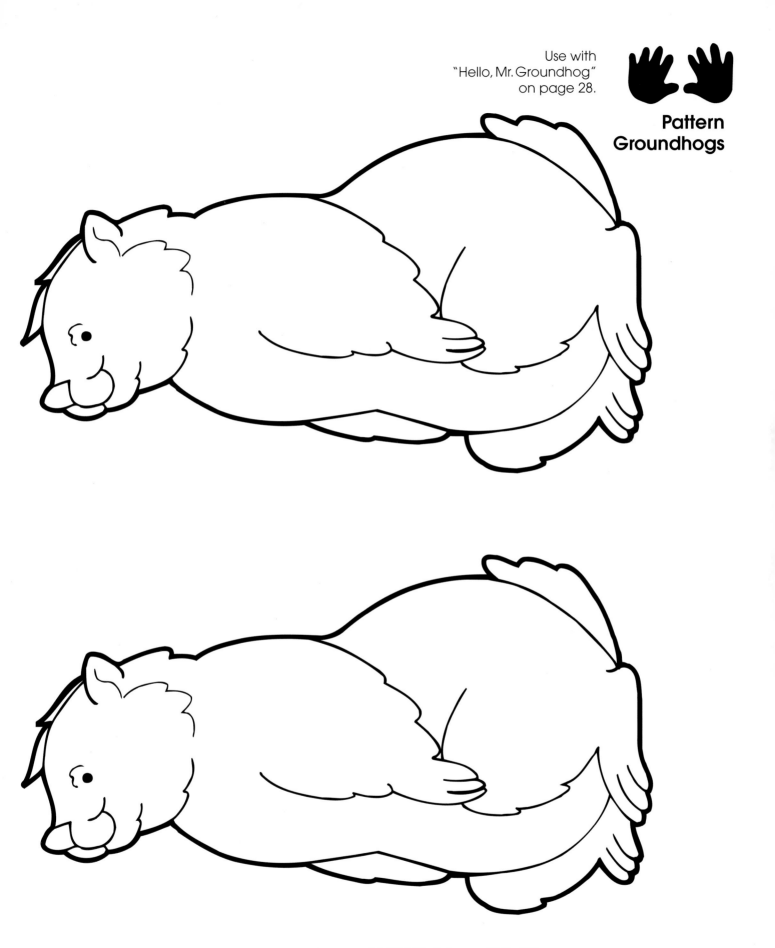

Pattern Fish

Use with the art activities on page 34.

LEARNING CENTERS

Spotlight on Centers

How Many Scoops?

Little ones will get lots of estimating practice in this center. Provide a large tub half-filled with colored, uncooked rice. Place funnels, different-sized bottles, scoops, and jars near the tub. To use this center, a student pair chooses a scoop and a container. One child places a funnel in the container; then he and his partner each estimate how many scoops of rice it will take to fill the container. Next the pair scoops rice into the funnel in the container while both students count each scoop. Each student compares his estimate to the actual number of scoops it took to fill the container.

Debbie Earley—Gr. K
Mountain View Elementary
Kingsley, PA

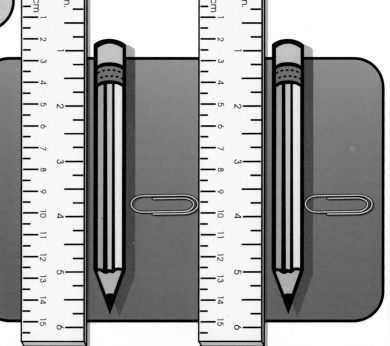

Beginning-Sound Fun

Students will be quick to visit this hands-on center that helps review beginning sounds. For each letter that you introduce, make a large, tagboard letter cutout. Stock a center with the letter cutouts, glue, and different items or pictures that start with sounds that your students are likely to know. To use this center, a child chooses a letter and glues the items that correspond with that letter on the cutout. Mount the finished letter cutouts on a wall or bulletin board for a nifty display.

Shelly Kidd-Hamlett—Gr. K
Helena Elementary
Timberlake, NC

A-Patterning We Will Go

This center provides a great activity that reinforces patterning skills. Stock the center with a supply of multiples of classroom items such as pencils, erasers, rulers, and paper clips. To use this center, a child arranges some of the items to make a pattern of his choice. Vary this activity by having one child begin a pattern and having a second child finish it.

Rochie Kogan—Gr. K
Yeshiva Ohr Yisroel
Forest Hills, NY

Feeding Sammy The Squirrel

Sammy the squirrel is a hungry critter in this counting center—so let's make sure children feed him! In advance collect a supply of acorns. Reproduce the squirrel pattern on page 52, color it, and cut it out. Tape or glue the squirrel on a bucket. Then program each of a supply of index cards with a different numeral. Place the bucket, a bowl of acorns, the numeral cards, and tongs in a center. To use this center, a child chooses a numeral card and uses the tongs to transfer the correct number of acorns from the bowl to the bucket to feed Sammy.

Jennifer Barton—Gr. K
Elizabeth Green School
Newington, CT

Story Characters

Bring your classroom books to life with this fun listening center. Place a puppet or stuffed animal that corresponds with a book and tape in a listening center. To use the center, a child holds the story character and may role-play as he listens to the story. No doubt this center will be a classroom favorite!

Diane Burshears
St. Jude The Apostle
Baton Rouge, LA

Paint Palettes

Your little artists will have a grand time learning about mixing colors at this center. Stock the center with a classroom supply of palette cutouts, paintbrushes, and red, blue, and yellow paint. To use this center, have a child use a different paintbrush to paint one dab each of red, blue, and yellow paint onto his palette. Encourage each child to use his fingers to mix different colors of paint on different spots on his palette. For example, on one spot he may mix yellow paint with red paint. What color did you get? "Color-rific!"

Daphne M. Orenshein—Gr. K
Yavneh Hebrew Academy
Los Angeles, CA

Spotlight on Centers

Whooooo Can Make A Pattern?

Patterning is the focus in this ghostly center. In advance, duplicate a classroom supply of the ghost pattern on page 53. Place the patterns, scissors, glue, and assorted construction-paper shape cutouts or assorted small objects (such as pasta) in a center. To use this center, a child cuts out the ghost pattern, then glues the shape cutouts and/or objects to the ghost, making the pattern design of his choice. Mount these ghosts on a wall or bulletin board for a "boo-tiful" display.

Sandy Lipman—Gr. K
Mercy Cares For Kids School
Albany, NY

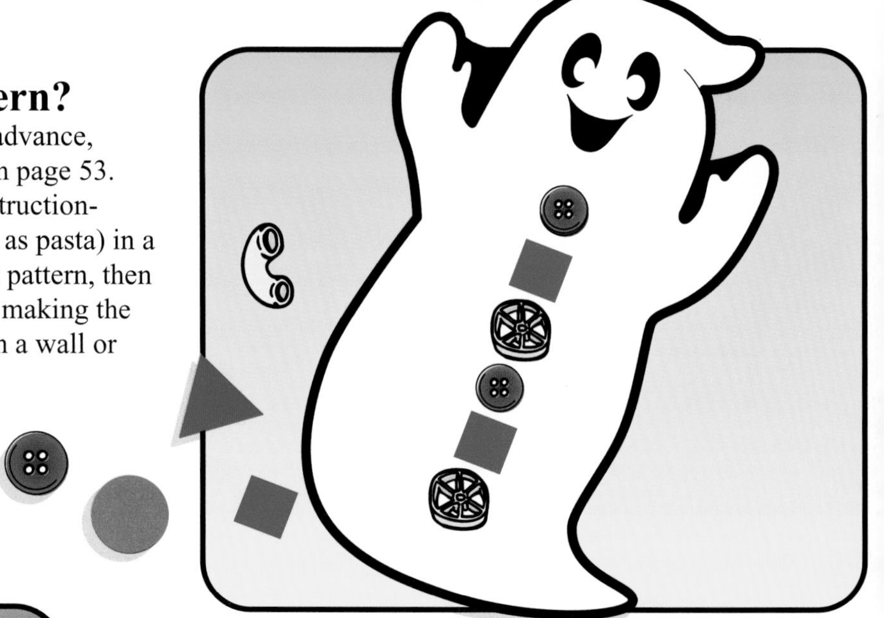

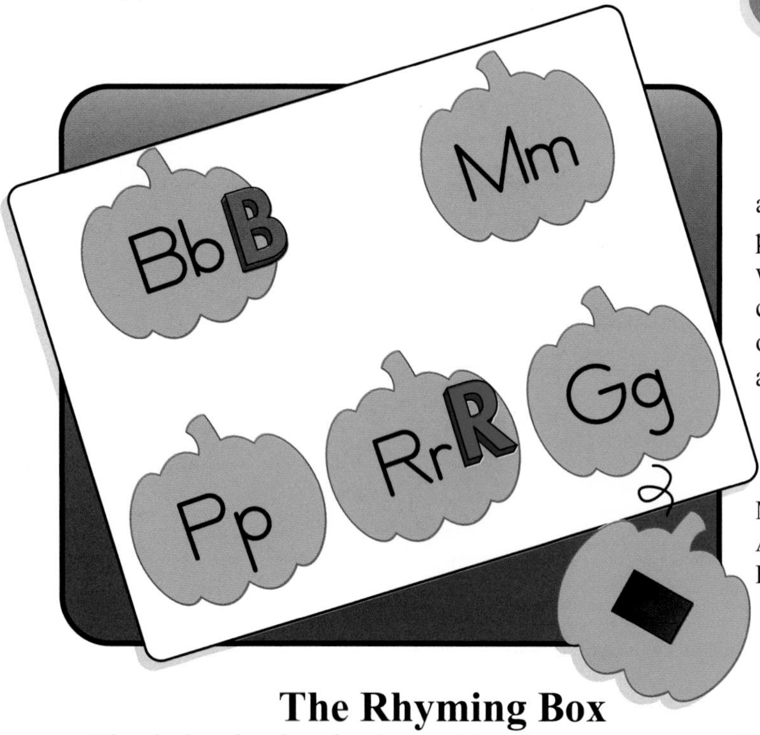

Pumpkin Patch Fun

Reinforce letter recognition with this magnetic center that will attract attention. For each letter that you wish to study, cut out a pumpkin shape from construction paper. Program each pumpkin with an uppercase and matching lowercase letter. Laminate the cutouts if desired; then attach a piece of magnetic tape to the back of each piece. Place the cutouts, an alphabet of magnetic letters, and a magnetic board in a center. To use this center, a child arranges a few pumpkin cutouts on the magnetic board. Then he matches the magnetic letters to the corresponding pumpkins.

Melissa Iverson
Academy Park Elementary
Bountiful, UT

The Rhyming Box

The timing for rhyming is now! In advance, save a small box or container such as a diaper-wipe container. Collect party trinkets, old game pieces, and small toys. Look through the collection for rhyming pairs. For example, you might have a house and a mouse. Place the rhyming pairs in the box or container. Label the front of the container with "The Rhyming Box." Place the container in a center. To use this center, a child chooses an item from the container, then tries to find an item that rhymes with the first one. It's rhyme time!

Cindy Fragosa-Johnston
Meadowbrook Elementary School
Fort Worth, TX

Turkey Feathers

Your little ones can review number recognition and counting with this math center. For each number you wish to study, duplicate and cut out the turkey pattern on page 53. Program each turkey with a different numeral. Then cut out a supply of construction-paper feathers. Place the turkeys and feathers in a center. To use the center, a child chooses a turkey, reads the numeral, and arranges the corresponding number of feathers behind it. Gobble, gobble!

Brenda Streetman—Gr. K
Briarwood Elementary
Moore, OK

Publisher's Writing House

This writing center has lots of homey appeal. In advance, purchase a house-shaped box or draw a house shape on the outside of a decorative box. Label the box with "Publisher's Writing House." Place various types of paper, stationery, crayons, chalk, stencils, markers, pencils, and envelopes in the box. To use this open-ended center, a child chooses the materials provided to write stories or letters, draw pictures, or creatively write as she likes.

Sarah Simpson—Gr. K
Pinar Elementary
Orlando, FL

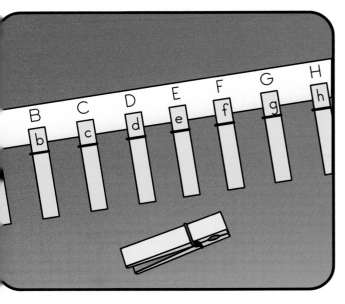

Miniblinds

Save those old miniblinds for this letter-recognition activity that also develops fine-motor skills. To prepare for this activity, remove the slats from a set of miniblinds. Use a permanent marker to program several slats with uppercase letters and several slats with lowercase letters. Then program spring-type clothespins with corresponding letters. Place the clothespins in a basket. Place the miniblind slats and the basket in a center. To use this center, a child chooses a clothespin, reads the letter, and clips it to the corresponding letter on a slat.

Ardy Nelson—Gr. K
Highland Public School
Highland, WI

Spotlight on Centers

Trim The Trees

Here's a festive center designed to reinforce numeral recognition, counting, and fine-motor skills. To make the center, cut out ten construction-paper trees. Also cut out ten construction-paper stars; then label each star with a different numeral or number word from one to ten (or the numerals of your choice). Glue a star to each tree; then laminate them. Place the tree cutouts, a hole puncher, and bright-colored construction paper in a center. When a child visits this center, have him arrange the trees in sequential order. Then have him punch out bright-colored holes onto each tree according to the number indicated on the star. When the child is done, have him pour the holes into a shoebox and save them for other crafts. (Vary this center by providing lots of unlaminated, numbered tree cutouts. Have a child choose a tree, then punch out the indicated number of holes and glue them onto the tree. Save all the trees and display them with the title "Trim The Counting Trees.")

Mary F. Philip—Gr. K
Relay Children's Center
Baltimore, MD

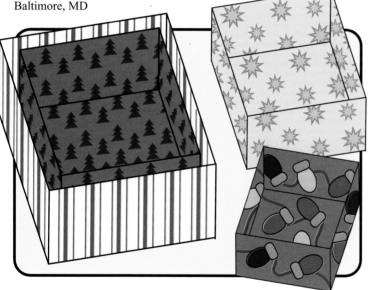

Candy-Shop Patterning

This patterning center brings sweet rewards. Draw a simple candy-shop picture on a sheet of paper. Cut it out; then glue it to a shoebox top. Stock the shoebox with a supply of assorted wrapped candies, being sure that you have multiples of each type of candy. Make sample candy patterns by gluing some of the candies to sentence strips in the patterns of your choice. Place the shoebox and pattern strips in a center. To use this center, a child chooses a pattern strip, then uses the candies from the box to repeat the given pattern. Also encourage children to make up their own unique patterns. When a child is done working at this center, he may take a candy treat with him!

Lisa Mascheri—TMD, Midway Elementary, Sanford, FL

Santa's Sizes

This center offers holiday-themed practice in size seriation. Collect an assortment of boxes that range in size such that one open box fits inside another and so on. Wrap the open boxes in colorful wrapping paper; then place all of the boxes in a center. When a child visits this center, have her arrange the boxes according to size. She can check her work by stacking the boxes one inside the other.

Karen Davidson—Gr. K
Carpenter Elementary
Deer Park, TX

44

Frosty Facts

Are your little ones getting into addition these days? If so, use these frosty figures to help reinforce addition concepts. Cut out a supply of construction-paper snowmen, hats, and snowflakes. Color, then laminate, each cutout. Use a permanent marker to program each snowman with an addition equation that is suitable for your students. Program each hat with a different numeral to correspond to the sum of each addition fact. To use this center, a child chooses a snowman and uses the snowflake manipulatives to work out the problem. When she knows the answer, she places the correspondingly labeled hat on that snowman. (If desired program the backs of the cutouts for self-checking.)

Cindy Stefanick—Gr. K
Roosevelt School
Worcester, MA

Hang It Up

If you have a pegboard in your room, this center will have you hooked. To make a letter-sound center, cut out and glue beginning-sound pictures to index cards. Tape the cards to a pegboard; then insert a hook beneath each picture. Write each initial letter on a piece of paper and cut it out. Tape the the letter to a length of yarn; then tie the yarn to any kind of ring (Chinese jacks, metal rings, the plastic rings on soft-drink bottles). When a child visits this center, have him say the name of the picture on a card and listen for the beginning sound. Then have him choose the appropriate letter to hang on the hook beneath the picture. (Vary the skills addressed at this center by matching sets to number words, colors to color words, or uppercase to lowercase letters.)

Betty Gomillion—Gr. K
South Leake Elementary
Walnut Grove, MS

Remember The Sequence Of Events

If you've gone on a field trip recently and taken photos—or will in the future—set up this center that helps children remember the good times they had and also reinforces sequencing events. Choose pictures from your collection that clearly show the sequence of events on your trip. Mount each picture on a construction-paper background. (If desired, number the backs of the pictures for self-checking.) Store the photos in a resealable plastic bag; then place them in a center that is labeled with the name of your field trip. When a child visits this center, have her arrange the photos in chronological order. What fun to reminisce!

Ann Scalley
Wellfleet Preschool
Wellfleet, MA

Our Sugar Maple Grove Trip

Spotlight on Centers

A Working Post Office

Hours of learning fun come with this classroom post office. To make one, cut apart one seam of a large appliance box. Cut out windows and doors; then paint and decorate the box to resemble a post office. Stand the post office in a section of your room; then arrange tables and bookshelves behind it to serve as the post office workspace. Position a decorated cardboard mailbox near the post office so students can mail classroom letters. On the counters arrange alphabetically labeled boxes for students to use when sorting incoming mail. Also provide a date stamp to stamp mail that is being sorted. Promotional stamps can be "bought" and "sold" as postage.

To introduce this center, read aloud Gail Gibbons's *The Post Office.* Then, when a child visits this center, encourage him to either write and mail letters, or work inside the post office as a postal worker. Lots of opportunities for reading, writing, and arithmetic!

Mimi Duffy—Gr. K
Memorial School
Paramus, NJ

Heads Or Tails?

This center relates to Presidents' Day and also reinforces math and fine-motor skills. Photocopy a classroom supply of the worksheets on page 54 (there are two per page). Cut the pages apart along the dotted lines. Place the worksheets, a few pennies, a few rows of ten Unifix® cubes, and crayons in a center. When a child visits this center, have him first write his name on a worksheet, then select a row of Unifix® cubes and one penny. Next instruct him to disassemble his row of cubes and place the cubes near his workspace. To begin the activity, tell the child that he will flip the penny ten times. Each time the child flips the penny, have him snap on a cube, then make a tally mark in the appropriate column. When all ten of the cubes are attached, have the child evaluate the results. What will it be—heads or tails?

Heidi Kazubowski and Amy Bundy—Gr. K
Norwood Primary School
Peoria, IL

Flip Boards

These flip boards can be used in a center for a wide range of skills. To make a flip board, you'll need three pieces of railroad board—all the same size. Use wide tape to tape the boards together to form a 3-D triangle. If desired, cover the board with a decorative adhesive covering. Then poke holes at the top of two sides of the triangle (see the illustration). Insert a metal clip ring into each set of holes. Program pieces of index board as desired; then punch a hole in the top of each card. Slip the cards onto the appropriate rings, and you're ready to go. (See the illustration for sample skills.)

Sewing Cards

Busy hands are happily occupied with these easy-to-make sewing cards. To make one, cut out a shape that suits your theme from poster board. Using a hole puncher, punch holes around the edge of the shape; then tie a shoelace to one of the holes. These cards are a great addition to a housekeeping or fine-motor center.

Betsy Ruggiano
Featherbed Lane School
Clark, NJ

Pog® Flip

Here's a self-checking activity that can be made in minutes. Program the backs of identical Pogs® with matching skills. For example, you could use color dots and color words, number words and numerals, or pictures and matching beginning consonants. To do this activity, have a child spread out all of the Pogs®, programmed side up. Instruct him to move the Pogs® around to match the skills. To check his work, he simply flips over the Pogs® to look for matching pictures.

Suzann Holden—Gr. K
Sacred Heart
Utica, NY

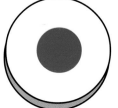

47

Spotlight on Centers

Parts Of A Plant

This hands-on listening center is blooming with solid science information. To make the center, make a tape recording describing the parts of a plant. Then cut out simple felt shapes to resemble each plant part. Store the plant parts in a resealable plastic bag. Place the tape and tape player in a center along with a flannelboard and the plant parts. When a child visits this center, instruct her to listen to the tape. As she listens, have her arrange the plant parts on the flannelboard according to the information on the tape. When the tape is over and the plant pieces are in place, encourage the child to explain the finished picture to a classmate or an adult volunteer.

Kaye Sowell—Gr. K
Pelahatchie Elementary School
Pelahatchie, MS

Jelly-Bean Graphing

Sweeten up those math skills with this appealing center idea. Duplicate the graph on page 55 for each child. Place the graphs in a center along with crayons that match the jelly beans, pencils, a few small paper cups filled with jelly beans, and a bowl of jelly beans for nibbling. To use this center, a child selects one of the cups of jelly beans to sort according to color. He then colors one jelly-bean character on the graph for each color represented in his collection. If his abilities permit, each child also writes the corresponding color word to the left of each jelly-bean character. Next he transfers his concrete information to written information by coloring the appropriate square on the graph for each jelly bean. When the graph is complete, the child returns the jelly beans to the cup and—of course—takes a few unhandled jelly beans for a job well done. During a group time, have each child bring his graph and discuss what the graphs reveal. Can your youngsters group themselves according to which cups of jelly beans they chose to use?

Leslie K. Wellmeyer—Gr. K
Woodlake Elementary
San Antonio, TX

Laundry Day

Days-of-the-week practice is featured on this clothesline, but hidden among the wash you'll also find reinforcements for directionality and fine-motor skills. To make this center, paint a scene on the inside of a file folder. When the paint is dry, laminate the folder. Punch holes where they are indicated in the illustration; then tie a length of fishing line through the holes. Attach seven small clothespins to the line. Then cut out seven clothing shapes from wallpaper samples. Label each piece of clothing with a different day of the week. Store the clothing and an answer key (as shown) in a string-tie envelope. To do this activity, a child hangs up the wash according to the days of the week. He then checks his work according to the answer key. All clean!

Marcia Kurtz—Gr. K, Acworth Elementary, Acworth, GA

Flower Power

Counting, reading, number recognition, sequencing—they're all in this "kinder-garden." To make this center, photocopy the flower, stem, and pot patterns (page 56) for each number that you'd like to include in this center. Program each flower with a number word, each stem with a dot set, and each pot with a numeral. Color the patterns; then cut them out. To do this activity, a child sequences the pots, then matches each corresponding stem and flower. The result? A lovely display of kindergarten learning.

Shelley Banzhaf—Gr. K
Maywood Public School
Maywood, NE

Take Flight!

Color-word recognition is on the rise with this visually oriented activity. For each color that you'd like to include, duplicate a hot-air balloon (from page 16) onto white construction paper. Color each basket—or glue on colored construction paper. Then color each balloon a different color. As you color, leave spaces (as shown) that correspond to each color-word's shape. Then write each corresponding color word on a separate piece of acetate. To do this activity, a child reads a color word on acetate, then places it on the appropriate balloon. If he is correct, the letters will fit inside the white space. If the letters do not fit in the space, he tries again until he is flying away with color-word recognition!

Buggy Addition

The skill is addition, but the appeal is in the bugs! In advance, gather a supply of plastic bugs. Then cut out a large construction-paper leaf for a workmat. Draw a thick center vein on the leaf to divide it into two sections; then laminate the leaf. Place blank sheets of paper, the workmat, the bugs, and some pencils in a center. To use this center, a child arranges some bugs on one half of the leaf workmat and some on the other half. Next she writes the number sentence she has just created on a sheet of paper. Then she counts the bugs to determine the answer, then writes it on her paper. She continues making and writing number sentences, as desired. Go buggy with addition!

Patricia Draper—Gr. K
Millarville E. C. S.
Millarville, Alberta, Canada

Spotlight on Centers

Go Fish!

Casting about for new math centers? Here's the bait you need. For each number that you'd like to include, cut out a fishbowl shape from blue construction paper. Laminate the fishbowls; then program each one with a different numeral. To make goldfish, paint a supply of wooden ice-cream spoons orange. When the paint dries, glue a wiggle eye on each goldfish. Place the fishbowls and the goldfish in a center. To use this center, a child chooses a fishbowl, reads the numeral, and places the corresponding number of goldfish on the bowl.

Rachel Meseke Castro, Juneau Elementary, Juneau, WI
Marsha Feffer, Salem Early Childhood Center, Salem, MA

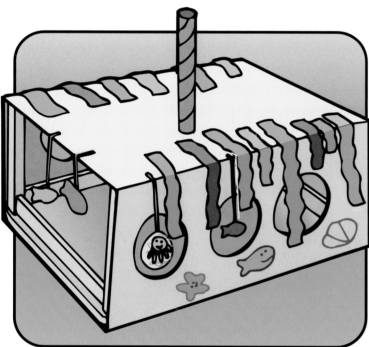

A Yellow Submarine

During your ocean studies, transform your dramatic play center or reading area into a yellow submarine! Turn a classroom table upside down. Cut an appliance box so that it fits around the table (as shown), leaving an opening at one end so children can enter and exit the craft. Remove the box; then cut out circular windows on each side. Ask volunteers to paint the box yellow. When the paint dries, position the box around the table and secure it with duct tape. Attach a cardboard tube to the top of the submarine to resemble a periscope. Then encourage your students to use art supplies to decorate the submarine with seaweed and other forms of sea life. When a child visits this center, he may choose a sea-related book to read or just explore the depths of the deep blue sea.

Trish Draper—Gr. K
Millarville Community School
Millarville, Alberta, Canada

Whale Of A Tail

You can reinforce a whole pod of different skills with this whale center. To make the center, duplicate the whale patterns (page 57) on construction paper. Program the head part of the pattern with the skill of your choice, such as a numeral, a beginning-consonant picture, or a color dot. Program the tail part of the pattern with the corresponding element. Then puzzle-cut each of the whales. To use this center, a child matches each whale with the corresponding tail.

Cindy Stefanick—Gr. K
Roosevelt School
Worcester, MA

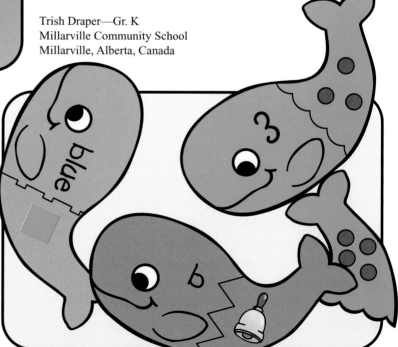

Fun Fruit Matchup

This colorful center reinforces spatial relationships, problem solving, and lots of thinking about configuration. To prepare for this center, enlarge and photocopy a large supply of the fruit patterns (page 58) on colorful construction paper; then cut them out. Make fruit cards by gluing some of the cutouts in various arrangements—and varying degrees of difficulty—on contrasting colors of construction paper. Place the remaining fruit cutouts in a basket. Put the basket in a center along with the fruit cards, blank construction-paper cards, and glue sticks. When a child visits this center, she chooses a fruit card; then she arranges some cutouts on a blank card to look just like the card she chose. When the fruit is arranged, she glues the cutouts in place.

Tammy Gronert—Gr. K
St. Joseph, Cockeysville, MD

Flowers In A Row

A little gardening at this center will go a long way to keep letter recognition and/or phonics skills in bloom in your classroom. For each letter that you'd like to include, cut out a small construction-paper card. Label each card with a different letter; then glue a craft stick to the back of each card. Form vertical rows of sand; then "plant" the letter cards in your sand table, as shown. Next cut out a large supply of construction-paper flowers. Also cut out—or have your students cut out—letters/pictures from magazines. Glue each letter or picture to a flower; then glue a craft stick to the back of each flower. Place all of the flowers in a basket near your sand table. When a child visits this center, he takes a flower from the basket, then plants it in the corresponding row. He continues in the same manner until all of the flowers have been planted.

Kaye Sowell—Gr. K
Pelahatchie Elementary School, Pelahatchie, MS

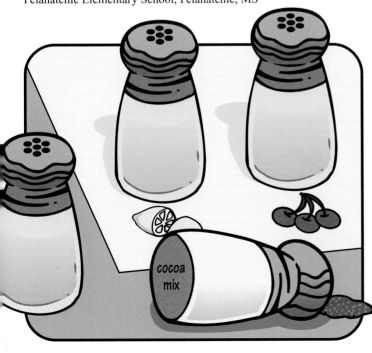

Taste Testing

This sensory center will really shake things up in your classroom. To prepare the center, collect a supply of empty saltshakers. If the shakers are clear, cover them with foil. Then fill each shaker with a different ingredient for tasting, such as salt, sugar, cinnamon, powdered hot-chocolate mix, and any flavor of a sweetened fruit-drink mix or pudding mix. Label a sheet of paper with each of the ingredients used or pictures. Laminate this answer sheet. Arrange the shakers, the answer sheet, and napkins in a center. To do this activity, have a child shake a small amount from a shaker into his hand and take a very small taste. Then have him place the shaker on the corresponding word or picture. The child continues in the same manner until all of the shakers are placed on the sheet. If you'd like to make this center self-checking, label the bottom of each shaker.

Kathy Peterson—Gr. K
C.H.I.L.D. Preschool and Kindergarten, Minneapolis, MN

Ghost Pattern Use with "Whooooo Can Make A Pattern?" on page 42.

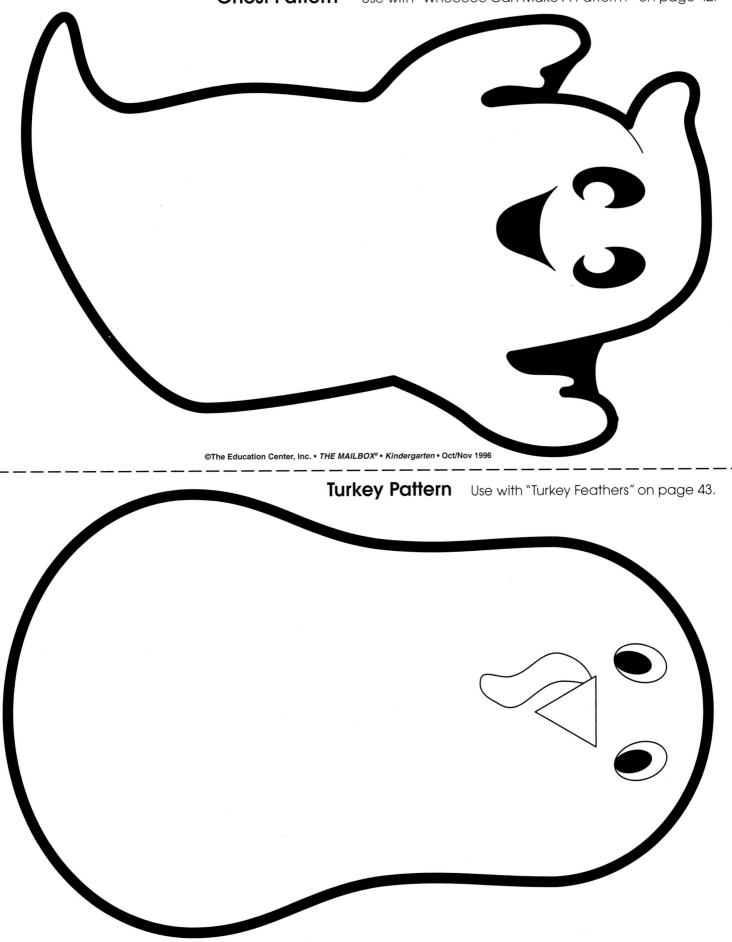

Turkey Pattern Use with "Turkey Feathers" on page 43.

Use with "Heads Or Tails?" on page 46.

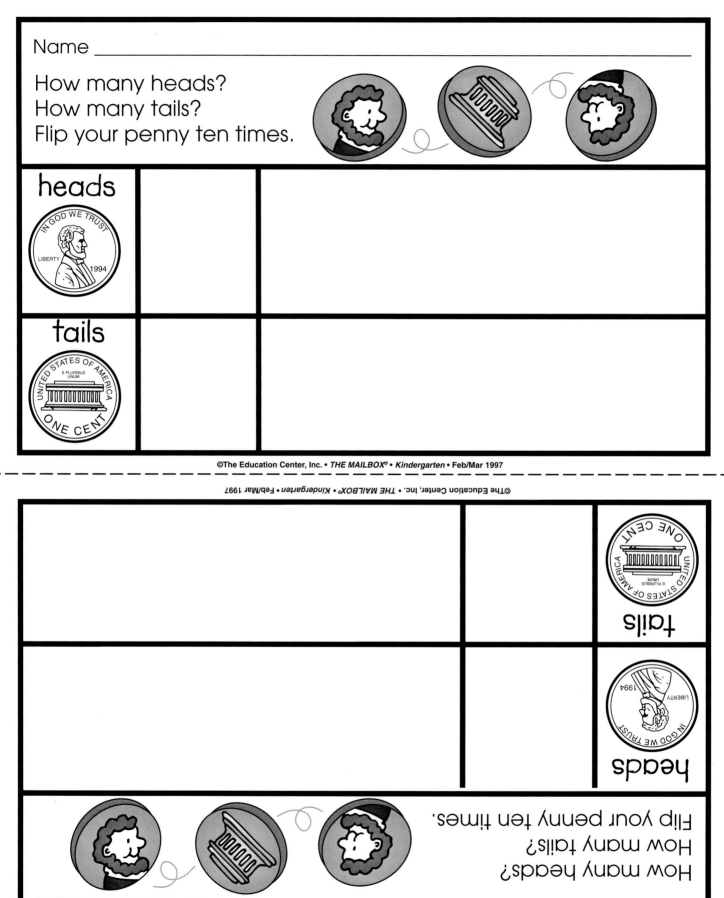

Name _____

How many heads?
How many tails?
Flip your penny ten times.

heads		
tails		

©The Education Center, Inc. • THE MAILBOX® • Kindergarten • Feb/Mar 1997

©The Education Center, Inc. • THE MAILBOX® • Kindergarten • Feb/Mar 1997

tails

heads

How many heads?
How many tails?
Flip your penny ten times.

Name _____

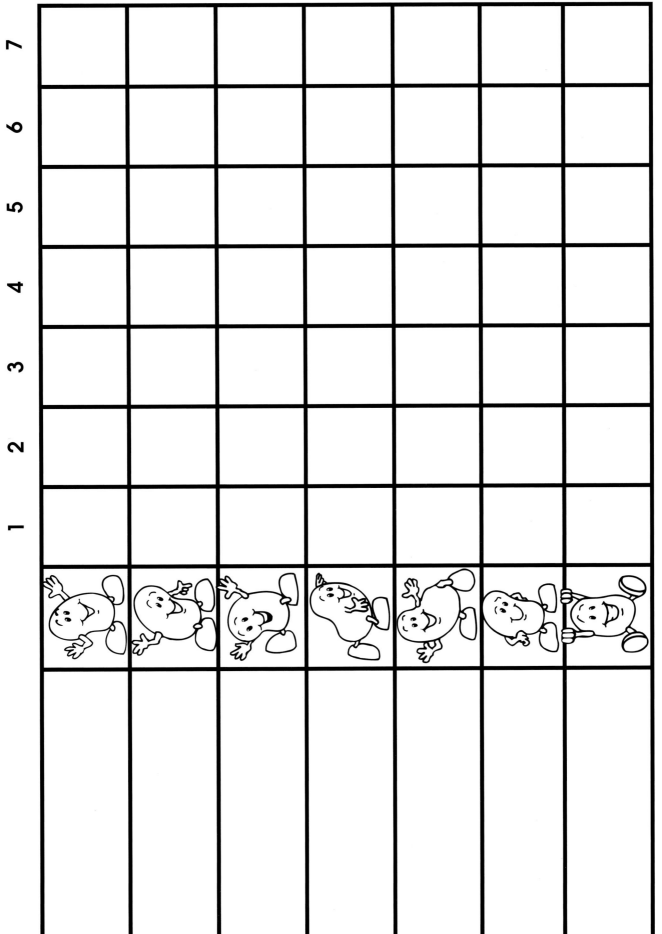

Patterns

Use with "Flower Power" on page 49.

Fruit Patterns
Use with "Fun Fruit Matchup" on page 51.

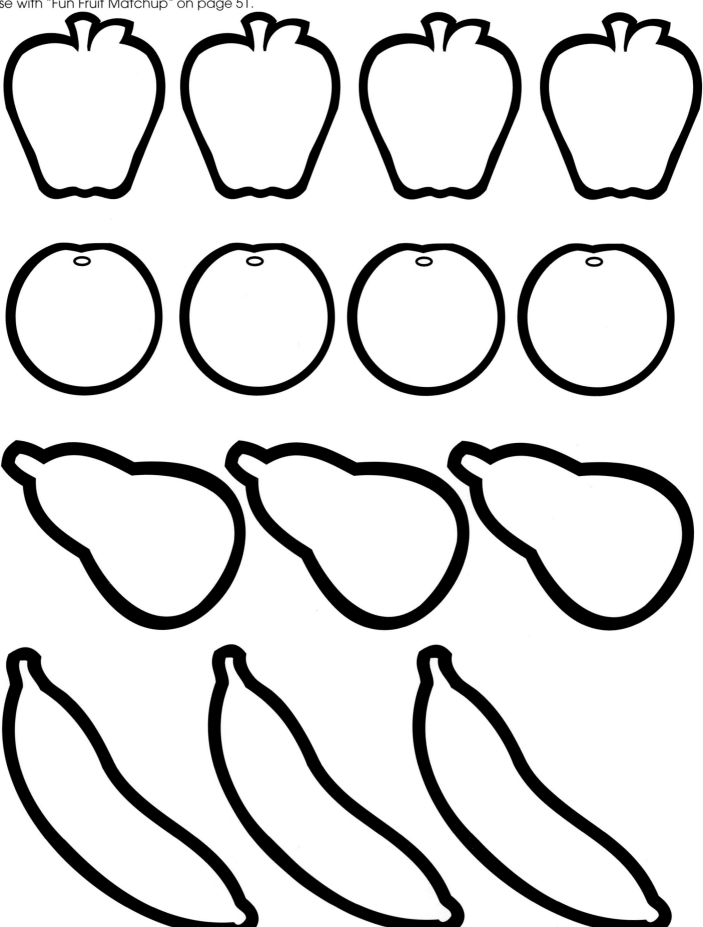

Children's Literature

Joyful Noises

A Collection Of Books That Involve Noise

Children are often the sources of joyful noises. If you stop and listen, you'll hear the enthusiastic sounds of the young on the playground, in the lunchroom, down the hall—everywhere! Although silence might sometimes be the rule in school, noise is a big part of each child's world. So here's a stash of books that celebrate the sweet and varied sounds of life—from the barn, to the pond, to the home, and beyond. These read-aloud specials call for a wide and wild array of joyful noises—and your youngsters will be only too eager to offer them!

introduction and reviews contributed by Deborah Zink Roffino

Night Noises

Written by Mem Fox
Illustrated by Terry Denton
Published by Gulliver Books

Lily Laceby is nearly 90 years old—or so people guess. Living in a cottage in the hills, her only companion is a dog named Butch Aggie. One wild winter night, as Lily dozes by the fire, the night noises begin. Butch Aggie is perfectly aware of each and every noise, while Lily remains perfectly asleep. What could those noises in the night possibly be?

This sweetly suspenseful story will engage your little ones as well as provide natural opportunities for phonics reinforcement, expanding oral language, and inspiring a little creative writing. When you share this book with your class, stop before the sources of the noises are revealed. Encourage each child to write and\or illustrate a conclusion to the story. Bind all of the pages together; then have each author share her page with the class.

After finishing the story, revisit the book to examine the noisy words. Invite children to study the words and read what they can. Then assign each of the words to a different small group of children. Have each group experiment and practice making its sound. (Encourage children to search the room for props if appropriate.) When each group has rehearsed sufficiently, reconvene for another reading of the story complete with specialized sound effects.

The Noise Lullaby

Written by Jacqueline K. Ogburn
Illustrated by John Sandford
Published by Lothrop, Lee & Shepard Books

A noise lullaby? Is that possible? If you close your eyes and listen, you'll be amazed at what you hear in the silence.

Before sharing this book, ask your children what they think they would hear if everyone in your room were to be absolutely quiet. Then read the book aloud, asking youngsters to repeat each noise after you. After discussing the book, divide a sheet of chart paper into two columns. Label one column "outside noises" and the other column "inside noises." Talk about the headings and the fact that they are opposite words. Then have each child find a quiet place to rest for a few minutes. As they rest, encourage them to listen for outside and inside noises. After a few minutes, have each child share what she heard and tell which column each of her noises should go in. Write each child's response on the chart. Did you ever think the quiet could be so noisy?

A Song For Little Toad

Written by Vivian French
Illustrated by Barbara Firth
Published by Candlewick Press

When Old Mother Toad's croaking lullaby fails to soothe Little Toad, other neighborhood moms offer their homegrown sounds to lure the little guy to sleep. The simple text offers delightful animal songs within a comfortable, appealing plot.

Youngsters will love this story—and some of them will be able to relate all too well! After sharing the book, review the lullaby of each of the animals in the story. For the nightingale's part, review its description in the book. Suggest that children whistle or hum to interpret the text as they like. Then assign each animal to a different small group of children. Read the story again, encouraging each group to chime in at the appropriate moment. Then ask youngsters to share their own favorite nighttime melodies. Oh, what sleepy noises!

Clap Your Hands
Written & Illustrated by Lorinda Bryan Cauley
Published by Scholastic Inc.

Richly detailed artwork and an interactive—and sometimes noisy—text make this book a favorite for everyone. But beware—if you read this book once, you'll be asked to read it again and again!

The noises in this book are child generated—and you won't have to do much coaxing to get your students to make the most of it! When your children are familiar with the book, read it again and ask them to make the noisy parts *very* noisy (such as "stomp your feet"), and the quiet parts *very, very* quiet (such as "pat your head"). Afterward describe *noisy* and *quiet* as *opposites*. Invite youngsters to think of other opposite words that involve noise—such as *whisper/shout, laugh/cry,* and *stomp/tip-toe*—then try them out! Write the opposite pairs on a sheet of chart paper. Keep the chart as your opposite bank and encourage children to add to the opposite list whenever they can.

"Stand Back," Said The Elephant, "I'm Going To Sneeze!"
Written by Patricia Thomas
Illustrated by Wallace Tripp
Published by Lothrop, Lee & Shepard Books

This rambunctious tale is the classic story of a powerfully noisy, impending sneeze. Its sprightly written text paves the way for radically reinforcing rhyme!

Share this story once just for the pure fun of it. After discussing the story, read it aloud once again. As you read, pause at the ends of lines that contain rhymes that you think your children might be able to supply. Encourage youngsters to try to supply the missing rhyming words by using their emergent reading strategies as well as their own feel for rhyme. This story is such a favorite that the rhyming work comes without even trying!

It's Too Noisy!
Written by Joanna Cole
Illustrated by Kate Duke
Published by Thomas Y. Crowell

We have 6 in my family.

The noisy household in this story includes yelling, singing, snoring, laughing, fighting, and crying. Noisy indeed! But the story also quietly lends itself to a discussion of family membership. So gather 'round for a listen to this retelling of a popular, old folktale.

After reading and discussing the story, ask children to talk about the number of living things in their homes and the kinds of noises that are commonly heard in their households. Then program a bulletin-board graph with a column for each numeral from 2 to 10 (or whatever numeral is appropriate for your group). Give each child a sheet of paper. Encourage him to draw and color every member of his family who lives in his home. Have him count his family members, then mount the picture in the appropriate column on the graph. When everyone's picture is displayed, discuss what the graph reveals. Did anyone have more family members than the farmer in the story? If so, how noisy is that household?

Fiona Raps It Up
Written & Illustrated by Frank Remkiewicz
Published by Lothrop, Lee & Shepard Books

Fiona and Fletcher are a pair of frenzied flamingos heading for a nesting ground. But Fiona becomes disoriented and lands on a banana boat with Rappin' Cap'n Otter. The otter's penchant for poetry gets to Fiona and a new flamingo lingo rules in this unusual, action-packed adventure.

If you've got some rappers in your classroom, this book could get very noisy! After sharing the book, read it aloud a second time. Have youngsters repeat the raps after you echo-style. Encourage children to identify the rhyming words in each set of verse. Then work together to make up original raps. Invite your students to make appropriate noises to go along with the raps. Here's one to get you started:

> It's time to clean up
> And get in line.
> Don't make loud noises;
> Whisperin' is fine.

Thump, Thump, Rat-A-Tat-Tat

Written by Gene Baer
Illustrated by Lois Ehlert
Published by Harper & Row

Bold, bright illustrations merge with a noisy, rhythmic text to make this book an interactive winner.

In advance, gather your classroom rhythm instruments. (If instruments are not available, try using upside-down plastic bowls and boxes.) Read the book aloud, carefully pointing out the noise-related words. When your youngsters are familiar with the words and the rhythm of the text, distribute the instruments. Assign some children to play the "Thump, Thump's" and some to play the "Rat-a-tat-tat's." Read the book again, encouraging each child to play his instrument at the appropriate time.

Brenda J. Hume—Gr. K, Sangaree Elementary School
Summerville, SC

Listen To The Rain

by Bill Martin, Jr., and John Archambault
Illustrated by James Endicott
Published by Henry Holt And Company

The melody and rhythm of the language in this book will lull readers into thinking that they can actually hear the rain in your very own classroom. This book is a perfect rainy-day read-aloud.

The noises of the rain seem somehow haunting, yet comforting all at once. After sharing the book, your little ones will be in the mood to experiment with this rainstick. To make a rainstick, push or hammer many small nails all around a wrapping-paper tube. Then tape a double thickness of construction paper to one end of the tube. Pour about one cup of uncooked rice into the tube; then cover the other end of the tube. Experiment with making rainy noises by alternating the position and angle of the tube. It's raining! It's pouring!

Debbie Pearce—Gr. K, Kindercare 863, Veradale, WA
Brenda J. Hume—Gr. K, Sangaree Elementary School
Summerville, SC

The Listening Walk

Written by Paul Showers
Illustrated by Aliki
Published by HarperCollins Publishers

A young girl is enticed by discovering the array of sounds she can hear in her everyday environment. This book will fine-tune your youngsters' ears for locating noises all around their world too.

In advance, cut out a large tagboard jar shape. Label the jar "Noises." Then share the story with your youngsters. After discussing the book, inform children that you are all going to go on a Listening Walk. Display the jar cutout and tell youngsters that you'd like to see if you can "fill up" the jar with noises. Explain that you will write each noise that they mention on the jar until no empty space remains. Ask them to predict whether they will be able to fill the jar or not. Then, after reviewing the description of a Listening Walk in the book, off you go! Did you fill the jar to the rim?

Oh, What A Noisy Farm!

Written by Harriet Ziefert
Illustrated by Emily Bolam
Published by Tambourine Books

A seemingly unfair chase has this entire farm in a comical uproar. Everyone abandons the barn to get in on the noisy chase. Each page calls out onomatopoetic sounds—bleat, bleat; honk, honk; bow wow. The noisy, mad dash comes to a crashing finale when the frenetic farm folk realize the truth of the matter.

Reading and language exude from this noisy book. When you share the book, ask children to raise their elbows whenever they hear words that tell a noise (such as "crash, bang" and "bleat, bleat"). When elbows go up, ask children to say the word; then write that word on chart paper. (This is a great opportunity to reinforce beginning sounds and other appropriate phonics skills.) Practice reading the words together. Then assign each noise word(s) to a different small group. According to the story's sequence, have one group begin its noise. As the first group continues, encourage the second group to begin making its noise. Continue in this manner until all the noises are in full swing. Oh, what a noisy classroom! Stop the noise by having everyone quietly shake hands to symbolize the friendship in the story.

Inside A Barn In The Country

Written by Alyssa Satin Capucilli
Illustrated by Tedd Arnold
Published by Scholastic Inc.

Look for rebus pictures, expressive-eyed characters, and a cumulative story full of country clamor in this predawn escapade.

With this book, your little ones will be reading—and squeaking, and neighing, and mooing—along with you in no time! After children are familiar with the text, display the very last picture in the book. Ask each child to think of a noisy event that might happen next. Then have one child share his thought with the class, ending with the phrase "inside a barn in the country." After that child shares, choose another child to add on to the story with his idea. Instruct the first child to repeat his line(s); then have the second child add his idea, similar to the cumulative format in the book. The last child in each sequence always ends by saying, "inside a barn in the country." Then, as a class, creatively decide what could possibly put an end to your noisy, noisy story!

After youngsters have verbally created their own story (see the paragraph at the left), have each child write/dictate and illustrate his part of the story. Ask for volunteers to illustrate the final page(s). Sequence the pages; then staple them between construction-paper covers. Make this book available for free-time reading and you're bound to hear the story—and quite a lot of noise—again and again.

Daddy Played Music For The Cows

Written by Maryann Weidt
Illustrated by Henri Sorensen
Published by Lothrop, Lee & Shepard Books

Growing up in rural America, a young girl chronicles the sounds that linger in her mind. She remembers the "kitch-ka-shoo" of her seed-corn rattle, yodeling on the radio, and the "coo-ooh, coo" of mourning doves. Fascinating for city kids and their country cousins, this sweet celebration of pastoral America emphasizes the softer noises of a young girl's childhood.

This book will inspire your children to create noisy memories of their own. After sharing the book, ask each child to pay attention to the noises he hears when it is relatively peaceful in his home—perhaps just before he falls asleep and early in the morning when he rises. Then, on separate sheets of paper, have each child illustrate a nighttime noise and a daytime noise. Encourage children to make up words to describe their noises and write them on their pages. Then bind all of the pages together. Have each child share his page and demonstrate his noise (if possible) during a group time.

The Barn Party

Written & Illustrated by Nancy Tafuri
Published by Greenwillow Books

Cristina is having a birthday party in the barn! The whole gang pets the animals, plays with a clown, dances to the music, and sings a rowdy round of "Happy Birthday." What happy, joyous noises! Suddenly one certain noise changes everything....

In advance hide an inflated balloon and a pin within arm's reach of where you'll be reading. As you share the book, stop after the text reads "Everyone was eating ice cream and cake—". Ask youngsters to describe the scene and mood on that page. When children have determined that it's a happy, carefree mood, bring out the balloon. Tell children that a certain noise changes everything. Ask them to predict what the noise might be. Then pop the balloon before their very ears. *(Please judge whether the loud burst of a balloon is appropriate for your youngsters. If not, just tell them about the pop.)* Then finish the story. Have youngsters relate how they felt when they heard the balloon pop to what happened in the rest of the story. Your readers will get a firsthand peek at what might happen when animals are startled by a sudden noise!

More Noise-Related Books

(some contributed by Rochie Kogan, Yeshiva Ohr Yisroel, Forest Hills, NY)

The Cat Who Lost His Purr
By Michele Coxon
Published by Puffin Books

The Cat Who Wore A Pot On Her Head
By Jan Slepian & Ann Seidler
Illustrated by Richard E. Martin
Published by Scholastic Inc.

Crocodile Beat
By Gail Jorgensen
Illustrated by Patricia Mullins
Published by Scholastic Inc.

Going To Sleep On The Farm
By Wendy Cheyette Lewison
Illustrated by Juan Wijngaard
Published by Dial Books For Young Readers

Good Morning, Pond
By Alyssa Satin Capucilli
Illustrated by Cynthia Jabar
Published by Hyperion Books For Children

Noisy Nora
By Rosemary Wells
Published by The Dial Press

Peace At Last
By Jill Murphy
Published by The Dial Press

Rata-Pata-Scata-Fata: A Caribbean Story
By Phillis Gershator
Illustrated by Holly Meade
Published by Little, Brown And Company

Shhh!
By Sally Grindley
Illustrated by Peter Utton
Published by Little, Brown And Company

Action-Packed Books

Harness the perpetual motion of "kinder-kids" with this selection of dynamic literature. But remember—reading, observing, and discussing the action flashing across the pages of these lively books only provides inspiration for kids who'd rather do anything than sit still! Youngsters will be mimicking the movements of creatures—sometimes winged, finned, webbed, or two-legged—that guide them to develop a sense of body awareness. Coordination skills get pulled into play as children practice sequencing, logic, and following directions. So grab a book and get moving!

introduction and reviews contributed by Deborah Zink Roffino

Hop Jump
Written & Illustrated by Ellen Stoll Walsh
Published by Harcourt Brace & Company

With speckled pizzazz and limbs akimbo, one little frog teaches the rest of the pond that movement consists of more than just hopping and jumping, hopping and jumping. The text and art swing with appealing simplicity.

Before sharing this book, ask youngsters to pretend that they are frogs and to "froggishly" move around the room. At your signal—which could be a "ribbit" or two—have each child settle in your read-aloud area. Ask children to dictate words to describe their froggy movements. As you record their responses, encourage children to use their emergent reading skills to help guide you in writing each word and in reading the list. Then share *Hop Jump* with your class. Afterwards, ask children to add froggy movement words from the book to the list. Then—at your "ribbit"—encourage children to act out the newly added frog movements as well as the traditional hop, jump!

What Shall We Do When We All Go Out?
A Traditional Song
Illustrated by Shari Halpern
Published by North-South Books

Energized with vivid illustrations of bike-riding, see-sawing, somersaulting, and more; this traditional song/book is about all of the things kids love to do!

After sharing this book with your students, try singing it. Then merge this automatically appealing topic with your youngsters' creative writing. Give each child a large sheet of construction paper. Ask each child to write about what he likes to do when he goes out to play. Then, using the book as a reference, have children cut and glue construction paper to illustrate their pages. Bind the finished pages between two construction-paper covers. Have each child share his page during a group reading time.

Bein' With You This Way
Written by W. Nikola-Lisa
Illustrated by Michael Bryant
Published by Lee & Low Books, Inc.

Packed with lively illustrations, this award-winning, rhythmical rap is a joyful celebration of diversity. The infectious, bouncy beat will have children clamoring for a reading time and time again.

Preview this book ahead of time so you will be able to read it aloud with a delightfully contagious rhythm. Then, as you share the book, encourage children to listen for the steady beat. (If necessary, guide them into the steady beat by using body language such as nodding your head or tapping your toes.) After discussing the book, share it again. This time ask youngsters to snap their fingers, tap their toes, or clap their hands to the beat. Simply irresistible!

Elephants Swim
Written by Linda Capus Riley
Illustrated by Steve Jenkins
Published by Houghton Mifflin Company

Explore the fluid movement of 17 animals in water. Richly colored paper collages display the graceful motility of ocean animals and landlubbers as they enter that water for various purposes.

Science and reading join forces in this literature-related quest. After sharing *Elephants Swim,* have each child (or small group) choose one particular animal from the book that she would like to study. Stock your science center with informational books such as children's encyclopedias or Zoobooks®, and *Elephants Swim* (refer to the notes in the back of the book). Plan to be available to help at this center when it is in use or have a volunteer sit in. Have each child draw a picture of her chosen animal, then cut it out and mount it on the top part of a large sheet of construction paper. Then encourage her to visit the center to find out additional information about her animal. Have her write/dictate what she learns on the bottom part of the page. When a child is ready to share her "report" with the group, ask her to first act out her chosen animal while the class tries to guess its identity. When the animal has been guessed, the child shares her report.

Moles Can Dance
Written by Richard Edwards
Illustrated by Caroline Anstey
Published by Candlewick Press

Naysayers and pessimists cannot dampen the irrepressible spirit of this furry little radical's desire to follow a dream. Bursting with energy, this message of self-discovery and purpose is decorated with lavish wildflowers and wondrous perspectives on nature.

They said it couldn't be done—but the young mole went ahead and did it anyway! This inspirational tale will get your youngsters primed for a new challenge. Introduce the word *perseverance* and discuss its meaning. Then arrange for an accomplished dancer to visit your classroom. After a brief demonstration, have a question-and-answer time. Then ask the visitor to teach your youngsters a few steps. As your youngsters are learning, encourage them to remember the perseverance of the little mole in the story.

Dancing Feet
Written & Illustrated by Charlotte Agell
Published by Harcourt Brace & Company

In this colorful celebration of the similarities and differences among us all, feet are walking, dancing, and skipping; hands are digging, baking, and playing. And the world is going round and round and round.

Charlotte Agell combines her talents as teacher, artist, and writer to create a joyous mood in this rare treat of a book. After sharing the book with your class, announce that your youngsters are going to author their own "Dancing-Feet" book. To begin, assign each body part in the book to a small group of children. Have each child in the group illustrate that body part and a different movement that that specific body part can do. Add each child's text to his page. For the last page, copy the text from the last four pages of the book, substituting "Children in this class" for "People young and old." Then bind the pages between two covers. Have each child share his page during a group reading time.

Feet, feet

walking in the leaves.

Dance!
Written & Illustrated by Ward Schumaker
Published by Harcourt Brace & Company

Stomp, romp, bump, and jump—energized caricatures demonstrate a score of dance steps. Confetti-covered pages suggest lots of action and simple text encourages early readers.

Dance! is a book that limbers up and stretches each reader's vocabulary—and dance repertoire! After sharing the book, encourage each child to think of a movement word that could be done in dancing. Write each child's response on a separate sentence strip; then review all of the words with your students. Next stand in front of your group holding the stack of words, and play some music. As the music plays, show the cards one at a time. Instruct students to look at each word, work together to read it, and perform the indicated movement in a dancing fashion. Change the cards as quickly or as slowly as you like.

twist wiggle clap

Rattlebone Rock
Written by Sylvia Andrews
Illustrated by Jennifer Plecas
Published by HarperCollins

Spooky sounds accompany the swing and sway of the ghoulish creatures who've come out for fun in the light of the Halloween moon.

Halloween sound effects complement the rhythmic motion of this festive story. As you share the book with your youngsters, model each sound for them; then encourage different groups of students to continue making that sound softly in the background. When you reach the second-to-the-last, two-page spread, read the text aloud; then encourage everyone to continue their appointed noise and "rock out"! As you turn to the last spread, instruct students to sit and be silent as you eerily read the text.

SWEAKA-SWEAK!
EEEEKA-EEEEK!

The Itsy Bitsy Spider
As Told & Illustrated by Iza Trapani
Published by Whispering Coyote Press, Inc.

In this richly illustrated book, readers follow that beloved little spider through a day of adventure far beyond the waterspout! This fresh retelling of a childhood favorite is sure to delight one and all.

This story offers youngsters a chance to practice fine-motor movements while they try to do the traditional itsy-bitsy-spider walk with their fingers. However, with Iza Trapani's retelling, they get to climb that imaginary spider not only up the waterspout, but also up the kitchen wall, the yellow pail, the rocking chair, and the maple tree. And for some reason, little ones never seem to tire of trying to accomplish that famous finger-walk!

I Swam With A Seal
Written & Illustrated by Charlotte Agell
Published by Harcourt Brace & Company

Imitating the unique actions of animals becomes a full-time job for two children. With enthusiasm, they copy the motions of seals, gulls, beavers, snakes, and more. Along the way, the children celebrate that which they hold in common with the animals and also appreciate their differences.

Movement words abound in this engaging story, and your youngsters are going to get a chance to try them all. After sharing and discussing the story, call one child up at a time. Secretly show that child one spread of the book that displays an animal. Point out the movement words on the page and, if necessary, whisper them to the child. Then have the child act out the part for the rest of the class to guess. When the animal is correctly identified, show those specific pictures in the book. With the child standing next to the open book, have youngsters list characteristics that are the same and different between the one child and the animal. Write their responses on chart paper; then repeat the process with another set of pictures in the book and another child.

Noah's Square Dance
Written by Rick Walton
Illustrated by Thor Wickstrom
Published by Lothrop, Lee & Shepard Books

Walk, waddle, hop, or crawl—everybody's moving and they're having a ball!

If you know some of the simplest square-dance moves—such as *bow, curtsy, circle,* and *do-si-do*—teach them to your little ones. (Or perhaps you could enlist the assistance of your school's gym teacher or a parent volunteer.) Also expose them to some traditional square-dancing music. Without even knowing it, children will be practicing directionality, sequencing, following directions, and developing gross-motor skills. After your youngsters have a feel for square dancing, share *Noah's Square Dance* with what is bound to be a captivated audience.

The Nine Days Wonder
Written by Marilyn Hollinshead
Illustrated by Pierr Morgan
Published by Philomel Books

Read aloud this based-on-a-true-story adventure of a Shakespearean dancer who crosses the English countryside in a merry spree of movement. Brilliant colors, medieval trappings, and lyrical language keep the story exciting.

Will Kemp's journey paves a perfect pathway into beginning map skills. After sharing and discussing the story, enlist the help of your youngsters in making a simple map. Begin with a sheet of chart paper. Draw a symbol to represent a familiar school landmark on the paper. Have children suggest additional destinations and add them to the map. (Nine destinations would be perfect!) When the map is complete, label it "Our [Nine] Days Wonder." Each day encourage children to start at one landmark and creatively move to the next. As your group completes each section on the map, indicate it with a dotted line. When the journey is complete, celebrate with tea and cake!

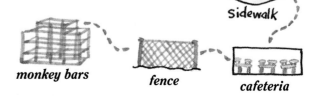

bus

flag

field

office

sidewalk

monkey bars

fence

cafeteria

Jump, Frog, Jump!
Written by Robert Kalan
Illustrated by Byron Barton
Published by Scholastic Inc.

Contagious, cumulative text punctuated by questions that require primary logic run beneath wonderful, watery pond pictures. Frog is on an action adventure that demands first-class looking and leaping!

As you read this story aloud, encourage children to look carefully at the illustrations in order to predict what's going to happen next. After youngsters are familiar with the book, put a little action into the story. Read it aloud again. Each time the text says, "Jump, Frog, Jump!", encourage your children to read the text chorally and jump into the air. Everyone will be on his toes!

After your group reading, make a reading-center activity to go along with the book. To begin, prepare simple cutouts of a fly, a frog, a fish, a snake, a turtle, a net, three boys, and a basket for flannelboard or magnet-board use. Number the backs of the cutouts from one to eight, respectively. Put the book and the cutouts in a center with a flannelboard or magnet board. Encourage children to sequence the characters in the order in which they appear in the book. (Referring to the book is encouraged.) Then have them flip the cutouts over and check their work by the numerical sequence.

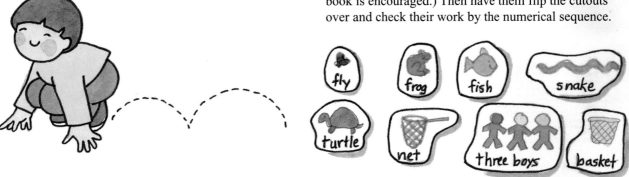

Meet The Marching Smithereens
Written by Ann Hayes
Illustrated by Karmen Thompson
Published by Harcourt Brace & Company

Here's an energetic description of a magnificent marching band. Bold, bright pictures convey the excitement as neat rows of marching musicians move across the pages. Don't let this parade pass you by!

After sharing this book, you've got the perfect opportunity to work on the steady-beat concept. Play some marching music and encourage children to march around the room to the beat. If they master the steady beat, try arranging them in rows and have them continue to march to the beat while maintaining the rows. Who knows—reading this book just might inspire the premiere musicians for the next generation of your town's high-school band!

Caps For Sale
Written & Illustrated by Esphyr Slobodkina
Published by Scholastic Inc.

One of the most popular books ever written, this award-winning classic continues to hold appeal for children of all ages.

A reading of this book naturally lends itself to a game of "Monkey See, Monkey Do." Try this version: Have students stand in a circle. Choose one child to be the lead monkey. Ask him to think of an action and do it. Have all of the other children perform the same action. Without stopping the action, call out, "Next!" Then have the child to the left of the leader change to another action. (Children should move directly from one action to the next, without any downtime.) Continue in this manner until you reach the original lead monkey. By then, your little monkeys will be tuckered out and ready for a rest...perhaps under a tree?

More Action-Packed Literature

Clap Your Hands
Written & Illustrated by Lorinda Bryan Cauley
Published by Scholastic Inc.

With adorable art that lures to be studied over and over, this book is a winner! For anyone who'd rather be moving, give this book a try.

A Gaggle Of Geese
Written & Illustrated by Philippa-Alys Browne
Published by Atheneum Books For Young Readers

Bold and brilliant pages match animals with the names given to them when they are in groups. Poetic language in limited text offers a rare opportunity for youngsters (and their teachers) to learn about animal actions in a gam, a troop, a charm, a parliament, an army, and more.

My Cat Jack
Written & Illustrated by Patricia Casey
Published by Candlewick Press

Jack the cat is into movement alright! He stretches up, then stretches down, licks his paws, pounces, and purrs. He bends and twists—and sometimes, he gets a bit tangled up.

Slither, Swoop, Swing
Written & Illustrated by Alex Ayliffe
Published by Puffin Books

Vibrant collage illustrations provide an irresistible invitation for little ones to explore an array of movement vocabulary. Swing, waddle, pounce, swoop—come join the move-along fun!

Toddlerobics
Written & Illustrated by Zita Newcome
Published by Candlewick Press

Mature, sophisticated kindergarten kids might enjoy a look back at the frenzied activity over at the toddler gym. Nodding, shaking, dancing, stomping, bumping, turning, and twirling—plus precious multicultural images of these little guys in action—will delight from head to toe.

All Kinds Of Christmases

Woven in among the traditional trimmings of the holiday season, here's an offering of literature selections that spotlight all kinds of Christmases. You'll find everything from a Mexican posada, to a candlelighting on a frozen Alaskan island, to a group of merry bovines that drop in for a Christmas-Eve game of baseball!

reviews contributed by Deborah Zink Roffino

Pancho's Piñata

Written by Stefan Czernecki and Timothy Rhodes
Illustrated by Stefan Czernecki
Published by Hyperion Paperbacks For Children

Stylized folk art sparkles across these pages, providing details of a Mexican village and its Christmas customs. Applying fancy to fact, this lively fable offers a heartwarming explanation of the traditional Christmas piñata.

After sharing the story, have each child contribute to the making of a class piñata. Several days (or weeks) before you'll be using the piñata, inflate and tie a round balloon. Brush a mixture of 3 parts white glue and 1 part water on a section of the balloon; then apply torn pieces of newspaper. Continue covering the balloon in this manner. For strength, apply extra layers of newspaper—allowing drying time between each layer. Next snip the rim of a paper cone, fold the rim pieces outward, and glue them to the balloon opposite the knot. Also glue on 4 other paper cones (not on the knot). Let it dry. Brush on the glue mixture and apply tissue-paper pieces to cover the entire area. When dry, tape yarn to the top of the balloon for suspending the piñata. (If you wish to fill your piñata, cut a slit near the top, and poke nuts and candies inside.)

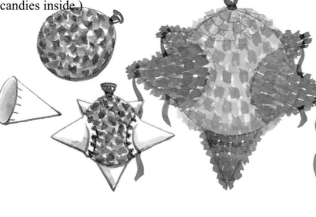

An Island Christmas

Written by Lynn Joseph
Illustrated by Catherine Stock
Published by Clarion Books

A Caribbean dialect bubbles merriment on the pages of this joyful account of Christmas on a tropical island.

Enlighten your youngsters' world view with this story that enhances diversities found in languages, climates, foods—and even Christmas trees. After sharing the book, make a tropical Christmas tree for your classroom. Use white paint (or shoe polish) to paint a tree branch. Secure the dry branch in a pot of dirt. Then invite each child to bring in an ornament from home. After a child has shared about his ornament, have him hang it on your tropical Christmas tree. Oh Christmas tree!

A Christmas Surprise For Chabelita

Written by Argentina Palacios
Illustrated by Lori Lohstoeter
Published by BridgeWater Books

Young Chabelita's mother must leave their home in Panama to teach in another city. As Christmas approaches, Chabelita prepares her recitation for the school play—wishing all the while that her mother would be there. Can wishing make it so? Resonant paintings offer glimpses into Latin American life.

Chabelita's Christmas surprise inspires the thought that gifts don't always come wrapped in packages. Encourage your youngsters to think of gifts that they could give or receive that wouldn't be wrapped in packages, such as a hug, a kind word, or a favor. Invite each child to write about and illustrate her thoughts, then share them with the class.

O Christmas Tree

Written by Vashanti Rahaman
Illustrated by Frané Lessac
Published by Boyds Mills Press, Inc.

Festive Caribbean colors flavor this touching tale inspired by the author's childhood in the West Indies. Written as the author speaks—with a West Indian flair—the text slips from dialect to standard English and back. This story offers beauty in Christmas everywhere—for true!

After sharing this story, decorate your classroom with a scene straight from the window of Anslem's home in the Caribbean. Mount royal blue bulletin-board paper along a wall in your classroom. Then have each child make a poinsettia by cutting out eight red construction-paper leaves and three or four green ones. Instruct him to arrange and then glue the cutouts to a small paper plate. Provide small yellow pom-poms to glue in the center of each flower. Then have each child mount his poinsettia on the blue paper. Beautiful—for true!

Amy Pierce—Pre-K
Pierce Private Day School
Irving, TX

Hold Christmas In Your Heart
African-American Songs, Poems, And
Stories For The Holidays
Compiled by Cheryl Willis Hudson
Published by Scholastic Inc.

Some have a driving, rhythmic beat; while others are as soft as a snowflake whispering through a gentle winter sky. Choose your favorites from among this collection to share with your youngsters.

The poem, "California Christmas" on page 25 of the book, lends itself to an eye-opening same-and-different lesson. After sharing this poem with your students, label one column of a chart "California Christmas" and the other column "[Your state] Christmas." (If you happen to live in California, label your second column "Alaska Christmas" or something similar.) Reread the poem aloud, stopping after each typically Christmas element is mentioned. Ask your students which side of the chart that particular element should go on; then write it in the appropriate column. Afterwards summarize the similarities and differences between each area of the country.

La Nochebuena South Of The Border
Written & Illustrated by James Rice
Published by Pelican Publishing Company, Inc.

All the trappings of a Mexican celebration are described in this humorous bilingual account of Papá Noel's visit on Christmas Eve.

Before sharing this story with your class, read aloud your favorite version of *'Twas The Night Before Christmas.* Then shake up the traditional stereotypes a bit by offering *La Nochebuena South Of The Border.* Discuss the similarities and differences between the two stories. Then reread the story, asking youngsters to stop you when you read a Spanish word. Write each Spanish word along with its English definition on a sheet of chart paper. As a class practice saying the Spanish words and memorizing their meanings. As you go through the holiday season, encourage youngsters to use these words...Feliz Navidad!

King Island Christmas
Written by Jean Rogers
Illustrated by Rie Muñoz
Published by Greenwillow Books

Just off the coast of a frozen Alaskan island lies a stranded ship that holds the island's new priest. The villagers have been anticipating the new arrival for months, but now the angry Bering Sea prohibits safe passage to or from the ship. Without the priest, there would be no one to help them celebrate Christmas.

This story introduces bits and pieces of the Inuit culture along with a problem-solving opportunity. As you share the story, stop after reading the fourth block of text. At that point, encourage your students to think of solutions to the villagers' problem. After each child shares his thoughts, finish reading the story. Guide students to conclude that cooperation and hard work brought Christmas to King Island.

Too Many Tamales
Written by Gary Soto
Illustrated by Ed Martinez
Published by G. P. Putnam's Sons

Have you ever tried to fix a problem only to make the entire situation worse? This is the story of a little girl, a treasure that is thought to be lost, and a desperate attempt to reclaim the perfect Christmas Eve.

There will be lots of discussion when you share this book with your students—just ask your youngsters for their opinions regarding Maria's actions! After your discussion, find out if any of your students' families have tamales for the holidays. Also ask children to tell about other holiday family favorite foods. Then send home a copy of page 79 with each child, asking the child to return it to school. Trim and photocopy a classroom supply of each returned recipe for each child. Staple each child's set of pages together to make a compilation of everyone's favorite holiday recipes. You might also ask parents to send in their traditional dishes for your youngsters to try. Then you can have a smorgasbord of holiday samplings!

A Dozen Silk Diapers: A Christmas Story

Written by Melissa Kajpust
Illustrated by Veselina Tomova
Published by Hyperion Books For Children

From high on a rough-hewn beam, a large family of spiders witnesses the birth of a baby in a stable. This sweet Christmas story, based on a German legend, tenderly tells the age-old story from a different perspective—kind of an overview, you might say.

This charming story has a math lesson tucked away in the cobwebs. After reading and discussing the story, ask if anyone knows what the word *dozen* means. Encourage youngsters to count the diapers in the illustration on page 27 of the book, and guide them to determine that a dozen equals 12. Then have your students practice the concept by gathering groups of a dozen items from your classroom. Have each child show his dozen and manipulate the items as the class counts chorally.

The Baker's Dozen: A Saint Nicholas Tale

Retold by Aaron Shepard
Illustrated by Wendy Edelson
Published by Atheneum

From the Dutch colonists in New York State comes this moving legend of the baker who needed to learn generosity from the great saint. Magnificently detailed paintings, thick with texture and color, augment a tender story.

If your little ones studied the concept of a dozen (in *A Dozen Silk Diapers*), this story is a great follow-up to expand their thinking. In advance, cut out several tan construction-paper cookies for each child. Set up cookie-decorating stations including elements such as sponge painting, nonpareils, and construction-paper scraps. After reading and discussing the story, encourage each child to decorate several cookies. When the projects are dry, combine all of the cookies. Then separate the cookies into batches of a dozen each. Will your youngsters elect to count out a *baker's dozen?*

Country Angel Christmas

Written & Illustrated by Tomie dePaola
Published by G. P. Putnam's Sons

Dusty pastels with bursts of teal blue sky adorn the pretty pages in this fantasy about three little angels who long to have a part in the Christmas celebration in heaven. DePaola's love of classic Christmas shines through to create a new story for the holidays.

You'll want to savor every charming detail on the pages of this sure-to-be Christmas favorite. After you've shared the story with your youngsters, discuss how the littlest angels played a very important part in the Christmas celebration. Then encourage children to discuss with their families what they might take part in during this holiday season. As you go through the days ahead, pay close attention to those children who fulfill important—but perhaps unsung—roles in your classroom. Recognize these children by writing a comment on and signing a copy of an award for each child. Then send the awards home for special recognition.

What A Little Angel!
Tara shared today.

What A Little Angel!
Derik helped clean our classroom.

The Gift Of Christmas

Written by Philemon Sturges
Illustrated by Holly Berry
Published by North-South Books Inc.

Christmas is a sensory experience full of magical sights, sounds, tastes, and feelings. This elementary rhyming verse reminds children to treasure these memories in the making. Rich, buoyant pictures dance on pages full of mirth and joy.

After reading and discussing this book, invite each child to participate in making a classroom version of *The Gift Of Christmas*. Remind youngsters to think of things that aren't necessarily *presents* that make their holiday special. Then have each child write and illustrate her ideas on a large sheet of art paper. Bind all of the pages together between two construction-paper covers; then have each child share her page during a group reading time.

My Christmas is special because my Grandma makes rouschki.

Santa Cows

Written by Cooper Edens
Illustrated by Daniel Lane
Published by Green Tiger Press

Set to the cadence of " 'Twas The Night Before Christmas," this bovine parody tickles with nineties' touches and ageless humor. A Holstein, a Guernsey, and four more breeds replace Rudolph and friends to provide a truly "mooo-ving" holiday eve.

This whimsical tale is just the thing to get those imaginations rolling! After sharing the book, encourage youngsters to imagine their own twists on the traditional Christmas Eve plot. Then have each child write about and illustrate her idea. Bind all of the pages together; then have each child share her page during a group reading time. Although your little ones will be using their emergent reading and writing skills, developing language, designing strategies, reinforcing fine-motor skills, and more—they'll think they're just having fun!

Christmas Always…

Written & Illustrated by Peter Catalanotto
Published by Orchard Books

Santa's not the only enchanted visitor for wide-eyed Katie this Christmas Eve. Luminous swirls whisper the appearance of each new guest—until jingling bells announce the arrival of the evening's final visitor.

Childhood dreams and imaginings will be spun into motion by a reading of this fanciful tale. After discussing the book, ask each child to write and illustrate a story about a friendly nighttime visitor. Invite each child to share his story with the class; then mount the stories on a bulletin board titled "In My Dreams."

Mother Hubbard's Christmas

Written & Illustrated by John O'Brien
Published by Boyds Mills Press

With a wink of his eye toward Mother Goose, John O'Brien reshapes this traditional nursery rhyme into a comical Christmas tale. Your youngsters will love every new word!

Before you share this book with your class, review the traditional "Old Mother Hubbard." Then out with the old and in with the new! Read aloud John O'Brien's holiday rendition and enjoy all the giggles and grins. After sharing the story once, talk about the rhyming words in the book. Then reread the story aloud, pausing at the end of every other phrase and encouraging your students to fill in the rhyming words. Oh, what fun!

The Worst Person's Christmas

Written & Illustrated by James Stevenson
Published by Greenwillow Books

With just a simple little twist in perspective, all the "merrys" and "happys" turn into a constant round of "bah, humbugs!" This amusing curmudgeon provides a humorous story and lots of opportunities for thinking.

As you discuss this story, guide children to notice how the kindness of others rubbed off on the worst person. Then encourage each child to spread a little holiday cheer of his own by making a greeting card. If you don't already have a class picture, take a picture of the class and have it developed before you begin this activity. Then give each child a large construction-paper tree and a color copy of the class. Encourage each child to cut out each child's face and glue it to his tree. Then have him write or dictate a holiday message before delivering his card to a special someone.

Patricia Harrell—Gr. K
Gulf Gate
Sarasota, FL

More Kinds Of Christmases

The Christmas Blizzard
Written by Helen Ketteman
Illustrated by James Warhola
Scholastic Inc.

Silly fun when Santa decides to move from the North Pole to Indiana. Even though Indiana is the coldest place Santa could find, there doesn't seem to be any snow on the way for Christmas.

The Christmas Teddy Bear
Written & Illustrated by Ivan Gantschev
North-South Books Inc.

This warm story grows out of the author's memories of very cold Christmases in eastern Europe. When a blizzard blows in on Christmas Eve, Grandpa is lost in the watercolor woods. The bright red cap on the teddy bear he clutches for his granddaughter helps to save his life.

Christmas Trolls
Written & Illustrated by Jan Brett
G. P. Putnam's Sons

The traditional trimmings of a northern European holiday border each vibrant page as young Treva finds their holiday decorations mysteriously disappearing.

The Small One
Written by Alex Walsh
Illustrated by Jesse Clay
Disney Press

Classic Disney watercolors transport readers to a town of long ago. There a child desperately seeks a good home for his beloved donkey, Small One.

A Southern Time Christmas
Written by Robert Bernardini
Illustrated by James Rice
Pelican Publishing Company, Inc.

In this loose parody of the most famous Christmas poem, Santa sheds his coat and feasts on chicken and grits to get through that long night down south.

Dear Parent,

We are learning about all different kinds of holiday traditions. We'd like to know about your family's favorite—or unusual—holiday foods. Please write below one of your favorite holiday recipes so we can include it in our Family Favorites cookbook.

Thank you!

A _____ Family Favorite!
(family name)

Strummin' Hummin' Dancin' Along

A Collection Of Books About Music

Through the sky, along the wind, over the waves of the ocean, music echoes across the world. Children hear the strains in schoolyards, in churches, pouring forth from every shop they enter. Their feet tap rhythms, their hands clap beats, their bodies sway and can't be still for the refrains that run through their minds. Here's a collection of children's literature that celebrates music, from near and far, in harmony with any curriculum.

introduction and reviews contributed by Deborah Zink Roffino

Crocodile Smile
10 Songs Of The Earth As The Animals See It
Written & Sung by Sarah Weeks
Illustrated by Lois Ehlert
Published by HarperCollins Publishers

Ease your way into a musical theme with this book/cassette set. These original songs about endangered animals will give you an instant understanding of some of the reasons why Sarah Weeks has been called "enchanting." As always, Lois Ehlert's illustrations are spellbinding.

This book/cassette set is great for a listening center, but you'll also want to get your students *actively* involved with the music. To prepare for the next activity, play the tape as students create tambourines from paper plates. Have each child paint the backs of two paper plates—one of which has six evenly spaced holes punched just inside the rim area. When the plates have dried, help each child tie (or loop) yarn in each of the six holes. After having him drop pieces of uncooked pasta on one plate, assist the child in stapling the rims of the plates together, allowing the yarn to hang out as streamers. Then it's time for the music making to begin!

Adriana Garcia Chalela—Gr. K
American School Foundation of
*   Guadalajara*
Guadalajara—Jalisco, Mexico

Now that your students have their own tambourines, gather some rhythm sticks too. From *Crocodile Smile,* focus on "Take It Slow" and "Crocodile Smile" to give students an awareness of differences in tempos. Begin by giving each student a rhythm stick and encouraging him to tap it on the floor to the rhythm of "Take It Slow" as you play the tape. Talk with students about the slow speed of the tapping. Encourage them to explain how this slow speed relates to tortoises. Put the rhythm sticks aside and have each youngster tap his tambourine against his palm as you play "Crocodile Smile." Encourage students to think about the rhythm in "Crocodile Smile" and ask them to talk about the beat. How is it different from the rhythm in "Take It Slow"? What words would they use to describe this beat?

Ben's Trumpet
By Rachel Isadora
Published by Mulberry Books

If inspiration could make a trumpet appear in thin air, Ben would have wished one into existence. Thankfully his desire for a real trumpet and his dream to belt out some brassy jazz of his own do not go unnoticed.

A few minutes before you read this book, play a recording of some jazz music that features the trumpet. Keep the music playing softly in the background as you begin to read *Ben's Trumpet.* After sharing the story, continue to play the jazz music and encourage your students to indicate when a trumpet is playing. Remind your students that Ben heard other instruments, and have them name some of these others. Then have your students listen carefully as the jazz music continues to play. Help them identify the piano, sax, trombone, and drum parts as you show the related pictures from the book.

Five Live Bongos
By George Ella Lyon
Illustrated by Jacqueline Rogers
Published by Scholastic Inc.

The comically spirited illustrations in this book are a perfect counterpoint for this tale of homespun music frenzy. Flashbacks are likely since surely—at one time or another—each of us has tapped out a tune on a pot, a pan, or an old tin can.

The thought of a Found Sound Band is just too good to resist. After reading *Five Live Bongos* to your students, explain that your class is going to create a Found Sound Band too. Ask that each child bring from home one or more soon-to-be-trashed (nonbreakable) items that happen to make ding-dandy sounds. As the items are brought in, collect them in boxes or baskets. After moving your aspiring musicians out of earshot of other classes, provide them with their unusual collection of "musical instruments" and let the music making begin!

Pete Seeger's Storysong Abiyoyo
By Pete Seeger
Illustrated by Michael Hays
Published by Scholastic Inc.

One thing is for sure. If this tune can mesmerize a terrible giant, it can surely transfix your wee ones. Get the book/cassette set so that your students can take in the full effect of Pete Seeger's animated storytelling and ukulele playing.

Share the book with your students as you play the recording. If your students completed the tempo activities (page 81) associated with *Crocodile Smile,* ask them if they noticed anything about the rhythm of the "Abiyoyo" song. It was played both slowly and quickly, and also several speeds in between. Sing "Abiyoyo" with your students, having them vary their speed. Repeat this singing exercise, but this time have students move to the beats they are singing. Youngsters will giggle and undoubtedly fall down—who wouldn't?—as they vary the speed of their singing. Bring this activity to a satisfying close by bringing both the tempo and the volume all the way down—just as Seeger does on the audiocassette.

Barn Dance!
By Bill Martin, Jr., & John Archambault
Illustrated by Ted Rand
Published by Henry Holt & Company, Inc.

These days it gets easier and easier to forget the simple music making of days gone by. This book helps us remember you don't actually need to plug in an instrument to feel the electricity of music. Turn back the clock as you turn the pages in this foot-stompin' tale of a musical full-moon night.

Before you read *Barn Dance!* to your students, get a recording of square-dance music. Read the story—starting your square-dance recording when the crow begins to call the dance in the story. Pause for a few minutes to tap your toes, clap your hands, and dance to the beat of the music. As youngsters join in, show them a few square dance-related moves. Then continue to play the music softly as students settle back down to hear the rest of the story. Then provide some old-timey instruments and encourage some students to play along. Perhaps you can find an old jug, a washboard, and some spoons for starters. Yee-haa! When the music finally stops, find out what your youngsters think of this kind of music.

The Maestro Plays
By Bill Martin, Jr.
Illustrated by Vladimir Radunsky
Published by Harcourt Brace & Company

This maestro really gets dramatic with his music! The language in this short tale is so vivid, you can practically hear the music that may have been described with a single word.

Collect a wide range of musical tapes. Ask students if they know what a *maestro* is. After explaining that a maestro is "a conductor or teacher of music," share the book. Then encourage students to pretend to conduct music as you play tapes. Play just a brief sample from a tape, then ask that students describe what they heard with just a word or two. Continue playing snippets from a variety of musical pieces—pausing each time to have students describe the music with either real or made-up words and contrast it with other music they have conducted. Was it faster, slower, louder, softer? Was it played glowingly, marchingly, or swingingly?

Meet The Marching Smithereens
By Ann Hayes
Illustrated by Karmen Thompson
Published by Harcourt Brace & Company

"Budder-ump, budder-ump, boom, boom, boom!" Drums in the distance tell us the marching band is on its way. Lively animal characters parade past as each musical instrument is introduced in turn.

Read the story aloud. Then ask each child to choose a musical instrument mentioned in the story that he would most like to play. Have students group themselves according to the instruments that they have selected. Play some marching-band music and have youngsters parade around the room pretending to play their imaginary instruments. Continue marching and playing for several songs. Before your band gets too worn-out, bring them to a halt and encourage them to discuss marching bands that they have seen.

I Know An Old Lady
Illustrated by G. Brian Karas
Published by Scholastic Inc.

"Kinder-kids" love this cumulative ballad and get a kick out of the comical drawings as the aged gentlewoman grows larger with each snack. Both reluctant and accomplished readers will sing through this one.

This story/song never loses its appeal to children. Sing the story several times—encouraging your youngsters to join in as they are able. When the children have learned most of the words, record them singing the song. Put this recording in your listening area along with headphones, this book, and other books by the same title. Encourage youngsters to compare the different versions of the story to decide which they like best.

On Top Of Spaghetti
By Tom Glazer
Illustrated by Rob Barber
Published by Good Year Books

Once you've survived childhood, the words of this song are indelibly etched in your memory. This simply depicted rendition of the song makes it accessible to emergent readers.

Sing and read your way through *On Top Of Spaghetti* with your students. Then ask students to think of a way to give this old song some new personality by singing and acting it out in different ways. For this activity, provide a variety of rhythm instruments and several different props to represent musicians of different backgrounds. Then have students suggest and demonstrate ways to perform a rock-and-roll, calypso, jazz, or rap version of the song using the props and the musical instruments.

The Itsy Bitsy Spider
As Told & Illustrated by Iza Trapani
Published by Whispering Coyote Press, Inc.

The ups and downs of a spider's life are depicted in this soft and easy story song. Gentle hues assure the calm, quiet, business-as-usual temperament that this song has always had.

Read and sing aloud *The Itsy Bitsy Spider*. Ask students what the spider did over and over again. After students have decided that the spider went up and down repeatedly in the story, ask them to listen to some musical sounds that go up and down in pitch. Use either a set of bells or a xylophone to play several ascending notes in a series. Can your students tell that the notes are getting higher and higher? Repeat this exercise with a descending series of tones. Sing the song several more times—each time having a student play an ascending series of notes as the spider goes up and a descending series as the spider goes down.

The Teddy Bears' Picnic
Arranged & Performed by Jerry Garcia & David Grisman
Illustrated by Bruce Whatley
Published by HarperCollins Publishers, Inc.

An old-fashioned picnic, a few cuddly bears, and a loping tune are just the right elements to accompany a teddy bears' picnic.

Play the recording of *The Teddy Bears' Picnic* as you show the pages of this book. When the story is done, play it again. This time ask youngsters to listen carefully to the music. Can they guess which instruments are playing the song? Show students a guitar and a banjo. Let children pluck the strings. Do the two instruments make similar sounds? What could make them sound different? If possible have someone lead a sing-along with the guitar or banjo. There's nothing quite like a sing-along!

It's Raining, It's Pouring
By Kin Eagle
Illustrated by Rob Gilbert
Published by Whispering Coyote Press, Inc.

Most of us remember only the main verse of this traditional song. But this lively book presents several weather-related verses that will put the old man through a whole host of episodes.

Prepare for this activity by borrowing (or making) some maracas and a rain stick like the ones found in nature stores. Have students join in as you sing your way through the storysong. Then provide several students with either maracas or shaker instruments to shake to the beat of the song as everyone sings the main verse together. As the verse ends, have a student turn the rain stick over so that everyone can enjoy the sound of falling rain.

Berlioz The Bear
By Jan Brett
Published by G. P. Putnam's Sons

Jan Brett's husband, who was the model for Berlioz, is a bassist in the Boston Symphony Orchestra. Students may be fascinated to know that a group of human musicians posed as models for the scenes in the book.

If you're planning a musical outing, use *Berlioz The Bear* to pique students' interest, or use it as an amusing follow-up to a music-related field trip. At the conclusion of the book, show students the musical piece Berlioz played as an encore. Play a recording of Rimsky-Korsakov's "Flight Of The Bumblebee," and have youngsters discuss why the piece may have been named after a bumblebee.

America The Beautiful
By Katharine Lee Bates
Illustrated by Neil Waldman
Published by Atheneum

This picture book brings each phrase in "America The Beautiful" to life. Waldman's sparkling acrylic renderings give us example after example of the splendor within our own country.

It can be especially difficult for young children to learn the words to patriotic songs. After all, the words are easily confused and sometimes *seem* completely meaningless. Read this book aloud—pausing to talk about the connections between the words and the pictures on each two-page spread. Ask if any of your youngsters have ever seen sights like the ones in the book. After having done this, restart the story—but this time sing your way through it together.

The Wheels On The Bus:
An Adaptation Of The
Traditional Song
By Maryann Kovalski
Published by Little, Brown and Company

In this rollicking version of the old song, there are tons of fun to be had. After only one time through, children will be begging to sing and play their way through the song time and time again.

Read and sing the story from start to finish, encouraging your students to join in. Then show students some instruments. Have them discuss which instruments would be best suited to depict each of the bus-related sounds in the story. Then encourage each child to take an instrument and chime in with it at the appointed moment. "Toot, toot, toot! Clink, clink, clink! Ssh, ssh, ssh!"

More Music-Related Books

References To Use When Making Simple Musical Instruments

Music Crafts For Kids:
The How-To Book Of Music Discovery
By Noel Fiarotta & Phyllis Fiarotta
Published by Sterling Publishing Company, Inc.

This book offers lots of ways for kids to enjoy music in all its forms—including singing, dancing, playing instruments, and enjoying the sounds of nature.

Making Music:
Six Instruments You Can Create
By Eddie Herschel Oates
Illustrated by Michael Koelsch
Published by HarperCollins Publishers, Inc.

Detailed and well-illustrated instructions show how to construct six simple musical instruments with readily available materials.

Songbooks & Anthologies

Raffi's Top Ten Songs To Read
By Raffi & others
Published by Crown Publishers, Inc.

Raffi says that once children know a song, it's fun and easy for them to follow it in pictures and in words—which is exactly what you can do with this book.

How Sweet The Sound:
African-American Songs For Children
Selected by Wade & Cheryl Hudson
Illustrated by Floyd Cooper
Published by Scholastic Inc.

Work songs, spirituals, and gospel sounds are collected between these covers. Dreamy pictures fill the background with joy.

De Colores And Other Latin-American Folk Songs For Children
Selected, Arranged, & Translated by José-Luis Orozco
Illustrated by Elisa Kleven
Published by Dutton Children's Books

Combining childhood recollections and adult research, this musician/author includes notes and music for Latin-American folk songs in Spanish and English. Look for examples of architectural style, native instruments, and festival attire in the bright, whimsical collage artwork.

Los Pollitos Dicen:
The Baby Chicks Sing
Collected & Adapted by Nancy Abraham Hall &
    Jill Syverson-Stork
Illustrated by Kay Chorao
Published by Little, Brown and Company

Bilingual text and music lie within lighthearted watercolors in this collection of traditional games and nursery rhymes from Spanish-speaking cultures. This book offers universal themes in singsong verse.

Something Funny Is Going On Around Here!

Around the magical age of five or six, most children develop a keen awareness that something very funny is going on around them. And what kindergartner doesn't love to *attempt* the delivery of a punch line—again, and again, and again? Tap into the delightful wave of giggles sweeping over your youngsters with these stories that remind us all that—something funny really *is* going on around here!

introduction and reviews contributed by Deborah Zink Roffino

Why A Disguise?

By Laura Numeroff
Illustrated by David McPhail
Published by Simon & Schuster

A master of children's humor, Laura Numeroff offers this manual—of sorts—containing some of the top reasons for a kid to go incognito.

Begin by asking children to offer definitions for the word *disguise.* As a class, agree on a definition and write it on the board. Then read the book aloud, encouraging children to notice David McPhail's humorous illustrations. Afterward reassess your class-written definition. Having agreed upon a final definition, ask each child to create a disguise at home. When all disguises are in, have small groups of students, in turn, hide behind a partition and don their disguises. Then have them come into view so the rest of the class can guess their identities. Next ask each child to illustrate himself in a disguise, then write about/dictate when he would most like to wear it. Bind all the pages together into a class book and have each child share his page with the group.

Billy's Beetle

By Mick Inkpen
Published by Harcourt Brace Jovanovich

Sometimes the things we are looking for are right under our very noses. Such is the case with Billy's beetle….

Your youngsters will get a kick out of being on the *inside* of the humor that plays out in this lively story. And it might be satisfying when they find out that it's the *smallest* member of the search party who actually saves the day! After reading and discussing this story, collect books containing search-and-find–type art such as *Animalia* by Graeme Base or any of the Where's Waldo series by Martin Handford. Make these books available in your reading center, and encourage your youngsters to search and find on their own.

Dogs Don't Wear Sneakers
and
Chimps Don't Wear Glasses

By Laura Numeroff
Illustrated by Joe Mathieu
Published by Simon & Schuster

Tapping the funny bone once again, Laura Numeroff uses lively rhythm and rhyme to provide a pack of preposterous animal situations for little ones to ponder.

After sharing these books—and when the giggles calm down—you've got a prime opportunity to reinforce rhyme. Reread the books aloud, pausing at the end of every third phrase—or where the rhythm naturally breaks. When you pause, encourage students to provide the missing rhyming word. Write all the pairs of rhyming words on a sheet of chart paper. When you've rhymed your way through both books, read your list of rhymes together. Encourage children to use their emerging reading skills to also try reading the list independently during center time.

Never Ride Your
Elephant To School

By Doug Johnson
Illustrated by Abby Carter
Published by Henry Holt And Company

Moms might have forgotten to impart this particular rule about elephants, so be sure to share this animated winner with your students.

After sharing this story, dip into science by giving your students just a taste of the *actual* size of an elephant! Tape sheets of butcher paper to a wall at least 11 feet high. Draw a simple outline of an elephant on a transparency. Using an overhead projector, back it away from the wall until the image is approximately 11 feet tall at the shoulder—the height of an African elephant. Trace the elephant on the paper; then cut it out. Mount the cutout on the wall; then have children stand by the elephant, comparing their sizes. Ask children to write about/dictate and illustrate additional drawbacks or advantages to having an elephant in school. After each child shares his page, display the pages on the elephant.

Dogzilla

By Dav Pilkey
Published by Harcourt Brace & Company

Dogzilla—four paws and a cold, wet nose—invades the city of Mousopolis! Led by their brave commanding officer, the Big Cheese, the soldier mice gather resources to rid their burg of the beast. Absolute magic for the kindergarten set!

This thoroughly entertaining story presents a prime plot for problem solving. When you read the story aloud, stop after the text reads, " 'I've got an idea,' squeaked the Big Cheese...." Encourage children to write about/dictate and illustrate their own solutions to the town's problem. After each child shares his idea, start reading again from the beginning of the book right up to the surprise ending!

I think they should get a giant leash.

Officer Buckle And Gloria

By Peggy Rathmann
Published by G. P. Putnam's Sons

It gets plenty boring listening to Officer Buckle read safety tip after safety tip. In fact, nobody listens. That is, until Officer Buckle is given a crowd-pleasing canine partner—Gloria. But when Gloria steals the show, will Officer Buckle give up safety tips forever?

There'll be lots of giggles and grins when you share this book with your class. After discussing the book, assign each child a different safety tip. Give each child a large star cutout; then ask her to illustrate Gloria demonstrating that tip. When the illustration is complete, write the tip on the cutout or on a sheet of attached paper. Post all of the tips around your classroom for handy reminders.

Do not ride with strangers. Malinda

Carl Caught A Flying Fish

By Kevin O'Malley
Published by Simon & Schuster

The nimble meter of this text is a takeoff on "Mary Had A Little Lamb," and the ludicrous lines tell the improbable tale of a fish who turns Carl's life upside down.

Read this book aloud as you encourage children to look carefully at the witty illustrations. After discussing this tumultuous tale, try *singing* the book together, adapting the text to the tune of "Mary Had A Little Lamb." Then write the words *flying* and *fish* on the board. Guide children to determine that both words start with the same letter. Then challenge your students to think of additional animals and describing words that start with the same letter, such as *dancing dog, bouncing bear,* and *racing rabbit.* How many can you think of?

The Old Woman And Her Pig

Retold & Illustrated by Rosanne Litzinger
Published by Harcourt Brace Jovanovich, Inc.

Take a delightful ride on this lyrical, cumulative tale as a spry old gal tries to get home with her porky new pet. Repetitive phrases and whimsical illustrations add to the retelling of this old English tale.

After sharing this story with your class, prepare a manipulative story. Assign each child (or group of children) a different character from the story—the old woman, the pig, the dog, the stick, the fire, the water, the ox, the farmer, the rope, the rat, the cat, or the cow. Ask each child to draw and color his character on construction paper; then cut it out. Back each character with tagboard; then laminate it. Attach a craft stick to the back of each character. Read the story and tape it; then place the book, the tape, and the stick puppets in a listening center. Invite students to listen to the story and manipulate the puppets accordingly.

Green Wilma

By Tedd Arnold
Published by Dial Books For Young Readers

Poor Wilma wakes up one day to find that she is—green! And it isn't easy being green. Expressive watercolor illustrations and charming text make this an endearing selection for little ones.

When you discuss this book, guide students to realize that Wilma was actually a frog *dreaming* that she was a human. Then invite your students to do some colorful dreaming of their own. Ask each child to choose a color. Then encourage her to illustrate and write/dictate an imaginary story that begins "One day I woke up...." Have each child share her page with the group; then display the pages along with the title "Colorful Kids."

One day I woke up purple.

Moira's Birthday

By Robert Munsch
Illustrated by Michael Martchenko
Published by Annick Press Ltd.

When asked by a young girl for a new birthday story, Robert Munsch wrote this book in response! Engaging text coupled with rambunctious illustrations make this a read-aloud favorite.

This story lends itself to many manipulative math matters. In advance, cut out a supply of construction-paper pizza slices and pieces of cake—14 of each or a number to suit your needs. Then share the story with your youngsters. After discussing the story, ask students how many kids Moira's parents agreed to have. Using your students and the cutouts as manipulatives, ask questions such as the following: "Including Moira, how many kids were her parents expecting?"; "How many slices of pizza will be needed for each child to have one slice? Two slices?"; and "If all of the children except one wanted cake, how many pieces of cake would be needed?" Continue making up related story problems, encouraging your children to create some of their own.

What's So Terrible About Swallowing An Apple Seed?

By Harriet Lerner & Susan Goldhor
Illustrated by Catharine O'Neill
Published by HarperCollins Publishers

I would like David

Lots of little lessons are laced within this delightful story about a little girl, an apple seed, and a very imaginative big sister!

Share this book once just for the sheer delight of it. Then invite some critical thinking. Reread the story, asking students to think about what the problems were and what caused them. Then have children share how they think the problems were resolved. After determining that Katie apologized and Rosie forgave her, translate this lesson to your classroom. If a child realizes—after the fact—that he'd like to offer someone an apology, it's sometimes hard to bring things up again. Help out by providing several wide craft sticks programmed with "I would like to say, 'I'm sorry.' " Store them in a small basket on your desk along with some sticky notes. When a child would like to apologize to someone, have him write his name on a sticky note, attach it to an apology stick, and replace the stick in the basket—with the sticky note up. At an appropriate time, talk with that child and encourage him to offer his apology. This clears a lot of consciences and helps maintain a positive classroom environment.

Mortimer

By Robert Munsch
Illustrated by Michael Martchenko
Published by Annick Press Ltd.

Merry-making Mortimer has muddled the minds of his mother, his father, his 17 brothers and sisters, and 2 police officers. Little ones will love the mischievousness of this little guy—and some might be able to relate all too well!

Robert Munsch has provided ample opportunities for choral reading—with lots of expression! As you read aloud, encourage students to read the repeated ascending/descending "thumps" along with you, using an ascending/descending tone of voice. Also invite youngsters to sing along each time Mortimer sings in the story. Afterward extend the story with this twist on traditional musical chairs. Arrange all of your children's rest mats or carpet squares—minus two—in a large circle. Choose one child to be It and hide her eyes. Instruct the remaining children to walk around the circle singing/chanting Mortimer's song. Then have It ring a bell and say, "Mortimer, be quiet." At that point, each child must try to find a mat. The outstanding child sits in the middle of the circle as play continues until only one child remains.

Riddle-icious
By J. Patrick Lewis
Illustrated by Debbie Tilley
Published by Alfred A. Knopf, Inc.

If you like a good rhyme and a good riddle, this book's for you! Twenty-eight poems offer clever clues to challenge young readers, and the infectiously funny illustrations add to the book's appeal. You'll want to savor every page of this thought-provoking work.

Prepare your students for this book by telling them that they will need to listen to every word and look very carefully at the pictures in order to solve the riddles in this book. As you read aloud, encourage children who think they know the answer to silently give the thumbs-up signal (thereby giving everyone a chance to think at his own pace). When all or most thumbs are up, discuss the riddle's answer. Afterward encourage each child to ask his family members to tell him any riddles they might know. Have the child and his family members write and illustrate a riddle. Each day, set aside a time for any new riddles that come along. What fun!

What has 4 wheels and flies?

a garbage truck. Kevin

Those Can-Do Pigs
By David McPhail
Published by Dutton Children's Books

These perky porkers provide the stuff a good book is made of. With compelling rhyme and enchanting illustrations, this latest McPhail offering is sure to tickle your fancy.

It's clear that the author's imagination is in full swing in this book—so enjoy it to the fullest! Then take the opportunity to discuss the concepts of *real* and *imaginary*. Discuss which of the book's events are real and which are imaginary. For example, a pig really does eat and drink, but does it eat and drink toast and tea? Make a chart with the headings "real" and "imaginary"; then list each child's comments under the appropriate headings.

Real
• Pigs eat.

Imaginary
• Pigs don't drink tea.

The Day Jimmy's Boa Ate The Wash
By Trinka Hakes Noble
Illustrated by Steven Kellogg
Published by Dial Books For Young Readers

Quickly becoming a comic classic, this cumulative tale relates the not-so-humdrum events of what started out to be an ordinary class trip to the farm. Be on the lookout for lots of innuendo in Steven Kellogg's zany art.

After sharing this story, snake activities will be on the rise! Inform students that a boa constrictor can be from 10–14 feet long. Providing rulers and a large supply of Unifix® cubes, challenge your youngsters to construct a cube line to represent the length of a boa constrictor. Then, using the cube line, help them cut a similar-sized piece of rope so they can bend, coil, and otherwise manipulate the rope to imagine how a boa constrictor might move. Also lay out a long sheet of butcher paper. Draw a snake shape on the paper; then arrange it near your art center. Encourage children to cooperatively color the snake. In your reading center, provide old magazines and workbooks, and have children cut out pictures that begin with *S*. During a group time, glue the pictures onto the paper snake.

The Topsy-Turvies
By Francesca Simon
Illustrated by Keren Ludlow
Published by Dial Books For Young Readers

Here's a family who have got life all figured out—backwards, sideways, and inside out! The oblivious Topsy-Turvies will engage even the most reluctant of readers.

This story provides a humorous springboard to reinforce the concept of *opposites*. As you read the story aloud, encourage students to point out the opposite concepts that they notice. After discussing the story, ask each child to imagine that he is part of the Topsy-Turvy family. Have him illustrate a situation the *opposite* of how it would normally be done in his real family. As they're learning more about opposites, your youngsters will have lots of laughs sharing their pictures.

Beware Of Boys

By Tony Blundell
Published by Greenwillow Books

Clever twists on our favorite fairy tales have a small boy outwitting the Big Bad Wolf.

The Glerp

By David McPhail
Published by Silver Burdett Press

The Glerp eats anything in sight. And since he has just decided to go for a walk, this means trouble for anything that crosses his path!

If Dogs Had Wings

By Larry Dane Brimner
Illustrated by Chris L. Demarest
Published by Boyds Mills Press, Inc.

Packed with color and action, these giddy musings suggest what the planet might be like—if dogs had wings.

Strudwick: A Sheep In Wolf's Clothing

By Robert Kraus
Published by Viking

This "fairy-tale-ish" comedy will tickle readers since few characters are really whom they seem to be. Bold collage illustrations give the pages energy.

Rachel Fister's Blister

By Amy MacDonald
Illustrated by Marjorie Priceman
Published by Houghton Mifflin Company

Rachel Fister's little blister evolves into a saga of grand proportions. Spirited rhyme and lively pictures propel the story to its sweet conclusion.

Turtle Pattern

Use with *Turtle's Day* on page 95.

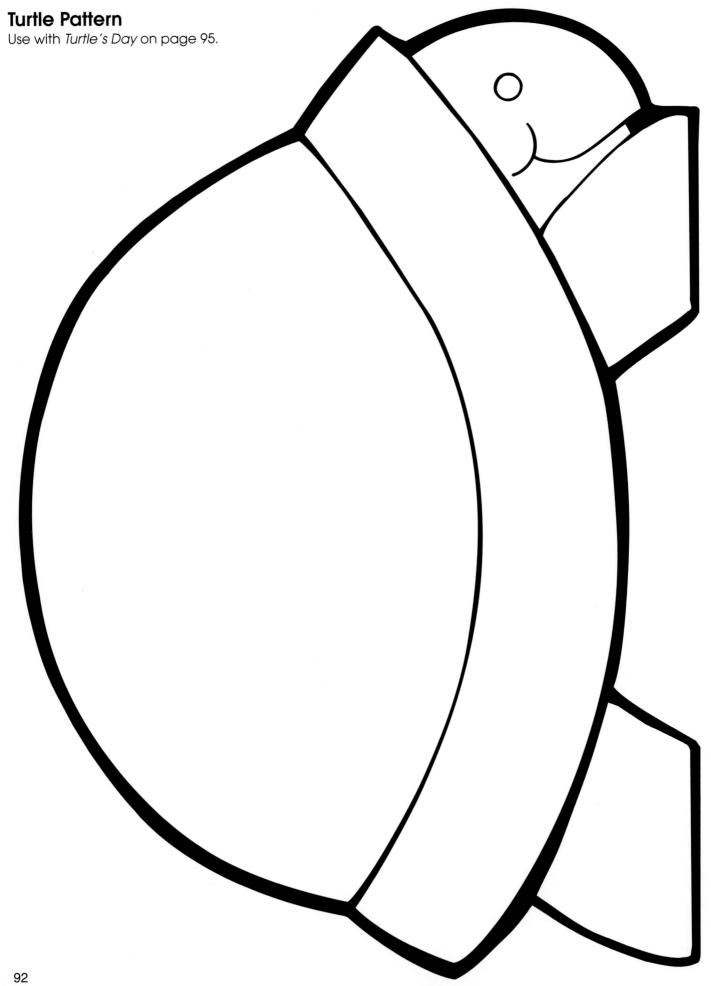

Reptiles All Around

It doesn't seem to matter to youngsters that reptiles are scaly creatures that often have rather creepy-looking features. In fact, that just might make these slinky vertebrates all the more fun! This collection of books provides opportunities for kids to get a closer look at and learn more about reptiles.

ideas and introduction contributed by Deborah Zink Roffino

What Is A Reptile?

By Susan Kuchalla
Illustrated by Paul Harvey
Published by Troll Associates

A simple text accompanied by clear, watercolor illustrations makes this title a good selection to help introduce your students to reptiles.

There will be lots of brainstorming incited by this book, so be sure to have a marker and a sheet of chart paper readily available. As you begin, show students the cover of the book. Read the title aloud; then ask children to share what they think a *reptile* is. As you read the book aloud, continue to ask, "What is a reptile?" When children—prompted by the text—offer responses, record them on the chart paper. (If desired, have child volunteers add illustrations during center times.) As you continue your reptile study, save this chart—it's a great way to practice reading and to look back and see how much everybody is learning!

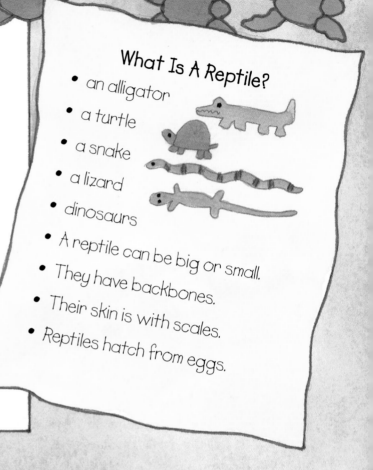

What Is A Reptile?

- an alligator
- a turtle
- a snake
- a lizard
- dinosaurs
- A reptile can be big or small.
- They have backbones.
- Their skin is with scales.
- Reptiles hatch from eggs.

Four Types Of Reptiles

Turtles and Tortoises

Snakes and Lizards

Crocodiles and Alligators

Tuataras

What Is A Reptile?

By Robert Snedden
Photographed by Oxford Scientific Films
Published by Sierra Club Books For Children

This selection uses up close photography to edge your students one step closer to the real thing...but not too close!

After you've gotten your youngsters talking about reptiles (see *What Is A Reptile* by Susan Kuchalla above), use this book to aid in further exploration and scientific classification. By way of review—and to plant some some thought-provoking seeds—read aloud pages 4–5. After discussing those two pages, have children examine the photos on pages 6–7. Paraphrasing if necessary, read the text aloud. Then ask children to name the four different types of reptiles. Write each type of reptile on a different sentence strip. Mount the sentence strips on a board titled "Reptiles." Then encourage children to look through the rest of this book and the other books listed in the nonfiction list on page 98. Invite each child to use art supplies to create any reptile that he finds interesting. Then have each child mount his reptile in the correct category on the board.

Turtle's Day

By Ron Hirschi
Photographed by Dwight Kuhn
Published by Cobblehill Books

Take a slow crawl with turtle—close to the earth, among the flora and fauna. Large, simple text explains each vivid photo to teach children about this likeable, hard-shelled reptile.

First prepare child-made books by duplicating the turtle-book cover pattern (page 92) for each child, plus one extra. To make the book pages, cut out the extra pattern; then trace it on white paper. Reproduce the plain pattern four times. Program one page with "Turtle sees…," another page with "Turtle eats…," another page with "Turtle is frightened by…," and the last page with "Turtle protects herself by...." Duplicate a class supply of each page. After sharing *Turtle's Day,* give each child a cover page. Encourage him to study the pictures in the book and color his cover to resemble a box turtle. Next read the text on the programmed pages together. Ask each child to illustrate a completion to each sentence starter. Then have him cut out his cover and book pages, stack them together, and staple them along the edge. Encourage children to share their turtle books with their family members.

Look Out For Turtles!

By Melvin Berger
Illustrated by Megan Lloyd
Published by HarperCollins Publishers

A variety of turtles crawl and swim across these pages—accompanied by facts that will fascinate kindergarten kids.

After sharing this book, invite your children to explore measurement with one of the interesting facts presented in the book—the great range of turtle sizes! First review pages 23–25. Then divide your class into small groups, giving each group a supply of Unifix® cubes. Assign each group a measurement for a turtle, such as 3 cubes, 10 cubes, 25 cubes, or even 72 cubes! Have each group construct a stack of the indicated number of cubes, then use art supplies to create a turtle of that approximate size. (For reference, provide additional resources from the literature list on page 98.) When all turtles are finished, encourage students to work together to arrange the turtles from smallest to largest. Afterward display these turtles, in order by size, on a wall.

They Thought They Saw Him
By Craig Kee Strete
Illustrated by Jose Aruego & Ariane Dewey
Published by Greenwillow Books

In a vibrant game of hide-and-seek, a comely little chameleon darts among leaves, branches, and rocks. Each time, his color changes—protecting him from a barrage of predators. This is a top-notch combination of science, adventure, and fun.

In advance, trace the chameleon pattern (right) several times on a sheet of paper. Then duplicate and cut out one pattern per child. After sharing the story, introduce and discuss the term *camouflage.* Encourage students to discuss the different environments the chameleon was in during the course of the story and how he protected himself in each environment. Then explain that chameleons can change their colors—ranging from green, yellow, white, brown, or black to spotted or blotched. Next divide your class into small groups and give each child a chameleon cutout. Walk around your school grounds, assigning each small group a different environment. Back in the classroom, have each child use art supplies to decorate his chameleon so that it will blend in with his group's assigned environment. In turn, have each group secretly situate its chameleons in its given place. Then have the other groups observe each of the chosen spots, trying to find the total number of chameleons.

All About Alligators
By Jim Arnosky
Published by Scholastic Inc.

With dusky watercolors that showcase the natural world, Jim Arnosky offers an overview of alligators and other reptiles. The simple text addresses questions about the fearsome gator, in and out of the water.

This book is an excellent tool to help your youngsters author an "All-About-Alligators" big book for your classroom library. Before you share the book with your class, assign each small group of students a question (such as those mentioned on the first page of the book's text and "What type of animals are alligators?", "How are alligators and crocodiles different?", "How are baby alligators born?", and "How are alligators good for other wildlife?"). Give each small group a large sheet of art paper and help them write a sentence starter to answer its assigned question. Then read aloud Jim Arnosky's *All About Alligators,* encouraging each group to listen and watch for the information that addresses its assigned question. Afterward have each group illustrate and dictate to complete the page. Bind the finished pages between two covers; then have each group share its page with the class.

Hide And Snake

By Keith Baker
Published by Harcourt Brace & Company

Twisting, turning, whirling, twirling—a sassy snake goes curling through every scene. A riot of color provides 14 terrific places for a snake to hide. Large text and lots of fun finding the snake.

After reading this book aloud with your youngsters, extend the story by having them make some fancy snakes of their own. Have each child cut out a long snake from butcher paper. Then invite children to study the pictures in *Hide And Snake* or some of the nonfiction books in the literature list on page 98. Guide children to note the interesting patterns in the real and imaginary snakes. Then encourage each child to use art supplies to decorate his snake as he likes. Invite each child to share his finished snake with the class, asking his classmates to identify the pattern in his snake. Then mount all of the snakes around your classroom walls.

The Yucky Reptile Alphabet Book

By Jerry Pallotta
Illustrated by Ralph Masiello
Published by Charlesbridge Publishing

With wonderfully detailed illustrations, the artist and author offer readers a yucky reptile for each letter of the alphabet. But are they really yucky? It's for you to decide!

Before sharing this book, label one side of a two-columned graph "Yucky" and the other side "Not Yucky." Label each side of the graph (vertically) from *A* to *Z*. As you share the book, take a vote on each reptile. Ask your students to do one action (such as *patting their heads*) if they think that particular reptile is yucky, and another action (such as *touching their toes*) if they don't think that reptile is yucky. Record the votes with tally marks. When you finish the book, go back and count the marks together; then write a numeral next to each set of marks. Prompt students to practice greater/less than skills by determining which reptile was voted the all-time yuckiest!

Nonfiction

*I Wonder Why Snakes Shed Their Skin
  And Other Questions About Reptiles*
By Amanda O'Neill
Published by Kingfisher

Reptiles (A New True Book)
By Lois Ballard
Published by Childrens Press®

Reptile (Eyewitness Books)
By Colin McCarthy
Published by Alfred A. Knopf, Inc.

Roaring Reptiles
By D. M. Souza
Published by Carolrhoda Books, Inc.

Scaly Babies: Reptiles Growing Up
By Ginny Johnston & Judy Cutchins
Published by Morrow Junior Books

Amazing Crocodiles & Reptiles
By Mary Ling
Photographed by Jerry Young
Published by Alfred A. Knopf, Inc.

Turtle And Tortoise
By Vincent Serventy
Published by Scholastic Inc.

What's Under That Shell?
By D. M. Souza
Published by Carolrhoda Books, Inc.

Fiction

Claire And The Friendly Snakes
By Lindsey Tate
Illustrated by Jonathan Franklin
Published by Farrar • Straus • Giroux

Follow The Moon
By Sarah Weeks
Illustrated by Suzanne Duranceau
Published by HarperCollins

The Iguana Brothers
By Tony Johnston
Illustrated by Mark Teague
Published by Scholastic Inc.

Kancil And The Crocodiles: A Tale From Malaysia
By Noreha Yussof Day
Illustrated by Britta Teckentrup
Published by Simon & Schuster Books For
  Young Readers

Komodo!
By Peter Sis
Published by Greenwillow Books

Slither McCreep And His Brother, Joe
By Tony Johnston
Illustrated by Victoria Chess
Published by Harcourt Brace & Company

Small Green Snake
By Libba Moore Gray
Illustrated by Holly Meade
Published by Orchard Books

A Snake In The House
By Faith McNulty
Illustrated by Ted Rand
Published by Scholastic Inc.

Snap!
By Marcia Vaughan
Illustrated by Sascha Hutchinson
Published by Scholastic Inc.

Getting Kids Into Books

Getting Kids Into Books

Elmer

Elmer by David McKee (Lothrop, Lee & Shepard Books) is a story about a patchwork elephant that really stands out in a crowd. After reading the story aloud, extend the story and reinforce colors by having your little ones create a patchwork-elephant stick puppet. To make one, reproduce the elephant pattern (page 101) on gray construction paper; then cut it out. Using a variety of crayons or markers, color each block on the pattern. Glue a wiggle eye to each side of the elephant. Then label both sides of a tongue depressor with *Elmer* and the author's name. Glue the tongue depressor on the elephant. Reread the story and have your youngsters hold up the corresponding side of the puppet as the elephant changes colors in the story.

Janet S. Witmer—PreK–K Home Daycare, Harrisburg, PA

"With A Gulp, And A Gurgle..."

Ten Sly Piranhas by William Wise (Dial Books For Young Readers) invites your youngsters to actively participate as you read this counting story. Read the story and encourage your youngsters to clap each time the text reads "And with a gulp," and to make a swallowing sound where the text reads "and a gurgle." Then provide each child with a paper plate and ten goldfish crackers. Reread the story and encourage each child to eat one of his crackers each time a piranha is eaten in the story. And then there were none!

Robin McDonald—Gr. K, Westside Elementary School, Clewiston, FL

Johnny Appleseed

After reading Steven Kellogg's big-book version of *Johnny Appleseed* (First Mulberry Big Books), your students will be eager to make their own apple trees. Supply each child with one sheet each of white and brown construction paper, some green and red tempera paint, and a small sponge. Have each student tear the brown paper to create a paper tree trunk; then glue the trunk in the center of the white sheet of paper. Next have him dip the sponge into the green paint and sponge-paint leaves around the top of the tree trunk and grass around the bottom. When the green paint is dry, complete the project by having the child dip his finger in the red paint and repeatedly press it onto the page to resemble apples.

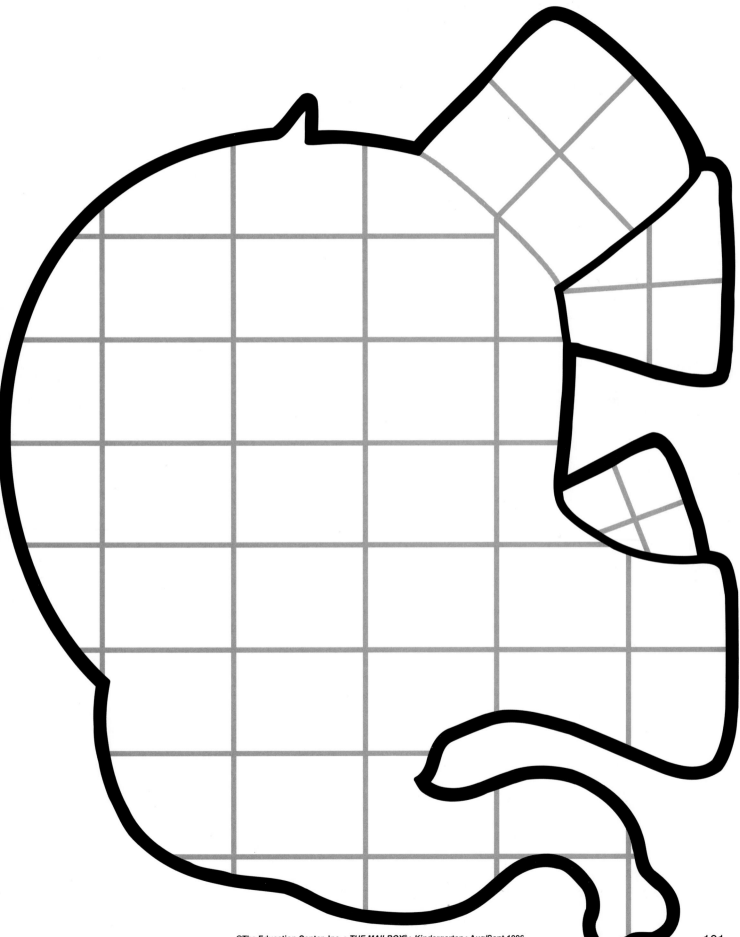

Getting Kids Into Books

Our Nighttime Dreams

As the days are becoming noticeably shorter, children may wonder where the sun goes at night. In *Where Does The Sun Go At Night?* by Mirra Ginsburg (Greenwillow Books), the imaginations of youngsters are led through a magical night with the sun. Following a reading of this story, ask students to recall the sun's and other pictured characters' dreams. Ask youngsters to tell about some of their own dreams; then invite them to create a big book of dreams. Give each child three white paper cloud cutouts. Have him illustrate a dream on one cutout, write about the dream on another, and glue his photo on the third. Then have each child glue all of his cutouts onto a 12" x 18" sheet of construction paper. Stack the completed pages between two construction-paper covers and staple them together along the left edge. Title the book "What We Dream At Night." Place the big book in the reading center for students to enjoy.

Johanna Jansen—Gr. K, St. Agatha School, Portland, OR

Being The Best

The Very Worst Monster by Pat Hutchins (Greenwillow Books) is a monstrously delightful story depicting an older sibling's quest for attention when a new baby is brought into the home. Prior to reading the story, duplicate a copy of the certificate on page 103 for each student. After reading the story aloud, ask students to name some things they think they are exceptionally good at doing. Guide them to consider all sorts of things, such as telling stories, skating, cleaning up, and even snuggling. Then encourage each child to write her name on a certificate, then color it. Write each child's dictated skill or attribute to complete the statement. Invite each child to take her certificate home to share with her family.

Lori J. Brown—Pre-K, LVBH Day Care Center, Palmyra, PA

My Good Night Book

Margaret Wise Brown captures the true spirit of a child's need to wish all a good night in *Goodnight Moon* (Scholastic Inc.). Share the story; then invite each child to make his own good night book. For the cover, have the child glue orange paper strips on a sheet of blue construction paper so that the page resembles a window. Then ask him to press foil star stickers in the resulting boxes to create a nighttime view from his window. Print the title "My Good Night Book" on the cover. Stack several sheets of white paper programmed with "Good night, _____," between the front cover and a construction-paper back cover. Staple the book along the left edge. Encourage each student to illustrate each page with a picture of something that he would like to wish a good night. Then have him write/dictate his completion to the sentence. Ask the children to share their books with a partner.

Helaine Rooney—Gr. K, Georgian Forest Elementary, Silver Spring, MD

I'm The VERY BEST That I Can Be When I

You're #1

Name _____

Getting Kids Into Books

Pretty Poinsettias

In this beautiful retelling of a Mexican legend, Tomie dePaola writes and illustrates how the exquisite red poinsettia came to be through the unselfish giving of a little girl. After reading and discussing *The Legend Of The Poinsettia* (G. P. Putman's Sons), make these poinsettia projects to adorn your classroom. To make one, cut two coffee filters with six petals each. Dip the flower shapes into water-diluted, red food coloring; then let them dry. Glue construction-paper green leaves to a sheet of black construction paper. Then arrange and glue the two flower shapes atop each other on the paper. To the center of the flower, glue on three small, yellow pom-poms. To make the stem, run a thick stream of glue down from the flower. Sprinkle red and green glitter on the glue, let it dry, and shake off the excess glitter. Lastly, glue a yellow construction-paper pot to the bottom of the page.

Peggy A. Wiles, Kellom Primary Center, Omaha, NE

Goldilocks has been in my classroom and ...
she broke my crayons.

Goldilocks And Who?

After sharing a version of *Goldilocks And The Three Bears,* your little ones will be inspired to make this class book. Program a page with "Goldilocks has been in my classroom and…." Duplicate the page for each child. Then encourage each child to dictate and illustrate to complete the sentence. Bind all the pages between two construction-paper covers; then have each child share his page with the class during a group reading time.

Missy Haussler—Gr. K, Pleasant Run Elementary, Cincinnati, OH

A Present For Santa

John Burningham has created a truly entertaining story that encourages children to think of Santa in a slightly unfamiliar light. After reading and discussing *Harvey Slumfenburger's Christmas Present* (Candlewick Press), invite each child to think about giving a gift to *Santa.* Then have each child decorate a separate sheet of paper to resemble a wrapped gift. On another sheet of paper, have him illustrate and write about the gift that he would like to give to Santa. Then staple the top edge of the gift-wrap page to the illustrated page. Have each child show his decorated page, then lift the flap to share about his gift to Santa.

I would give Santa a new pair of socks.

Thematic Units

Zippity Zappity Zoo!

"Zoo-y" Tips
For Setting Up Your Classroom
And Beginning A New School Year

At the beginning of a new school year, a teacher's time seems to disappear with the wind—or faster! So take advantage of the ideas and reproducibles in this unit to create a fresh, new, zoo-themed look for your classroom. The zoo theme blends nicely with the animal unit (beginning on page 112) and is just right to visually lure hesitant first-timers into your classroom.

ideas contributed by Elizabeth Trautman

ZOO

Maggie Sam Beth Alex

Caroline Devin Bobby Drew Cody

Morgan Allie Rusty Kelsey Pete Brandon

Welcome! Welcome!

Your new kindergartners will eagerly anticipate the first day of school when they receive a personalized welcome packet from their very own teacher. Write a note (such as the one shown in the illustration) on the notecard pattern on page 109. Then, for each child, duplicate all of the patterns (page 109) on construction paper. Personalize each child's note and add your signature. Also write each child's name on a ticket and a nametag. Then cut out the patterns and laminate the ticket and the nametag. A week or so before school begins, send each child's packet to his home. This little gesture goes a long way toward creating a sense of security and belonging for each of your new arrivals.

Who's At The Zoo Today?

You'll save precious moments using this "teacher-free" attendance-taking method, and your students will practice name recognition and responsibility at the same time. Enlarge and trace the zoo pattern (on page 119) onto craft paper. Color the picture; then glue it to a sheet of tagboard. For each child in your class, glue a personalized library pocket onto the picture. Laminate the tagboard with laminating film (available from The Education Center, Inc.). Use a razor blade to cut a slit in each child's library pocket. Display the finished picture for child accessibility. On the first day of school, have each child match his name on his ticket to his name on the attendance board. When he has found his name, have him slide his ticket in the correct pocket. Just a glance will let you know who's at school today.

As each child leaves for the day, have him remove his ticket and deposit it in a plastic pail. The next morning, each child gets more name-recognition practice as he sorts through the tickets to find his name. In no time at all, youngsters catch on to the routine and roll call can be taken with just a glance.

Dear **Jackson**

I am so glad that you will be in my class this year. We will have lots of fun and learn many new things.

Look at the pictures on this note. Can you guess what we will be studying when you come to school?

On the first day of school, please bring your ticket and wear your nametag.

See you soon!

Ms. Crane

Classroom Ticket

Jackson

Admit One

Jackson

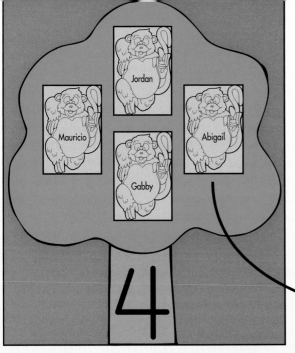

Hanging Around Centers

The monkeys from "So Glad You're Hanging With Us" can help eliminate the center-time chaos that sometimes occurs at the beginning of the year. For each center in your room, glue a construction-paper tree to a separate sheet of tagboard; then display each tree near a different center. To each tree canopy, attach the loop sides of Velcro® dots corresponding to the number of children permitted in that particular center. Also program the corresponding numeral on the tree trunk. When center time begins, have each child remove her monkey from the big tree and attach it to an available place on a center tree. When she leaves that center, she removes her monkey. She may attach it to another center tree, or—if center time is over—return it to the big tree.

So Glad You're Hanging With Us

Draw youngsters into your classroom and the zoo theme with this mischievous-looking display. For each child, duplicate one monkey (page 110) on construction paper. Laminate and cut out the monkeys. Use a permanent marker to write a different child's name on each monkey. Mount a large, construction-paper tree on a small bulletin board or a wall. For each child, attach the hook side of a Velcro® dot to the canopy of the tree. Attach the loop side of the dot to the back of a monkey. Then attach each monkey to the tree and add a welcoming title.

That Decorative Touch

Here's a tip that lends a creative flair to plain classroom carpets and/or individual student mats. (If you don't already have plain carpets or mats, check out carpet-store remnants or discount-store specials.) Gather a supply of zoo-related stencils. Then use fabric paints to stencil around your carpet and mats.

And if you're into stenciling, invest a few more minutes in creating a special Share Chair that helps promote self-esteem, oral language, and vocabulary—not to mention a rhyme! Stencil the back and seat of a canvas director's chair. Invite children to sit in the chair for special times of sharing.

Ronda Caster, Supply Elementary, Supply, NC

Jammin' Bear's Jingle Time

Since music works a magic that nothing else can, create a special music place and music cue for your classroom. Enlarge and trace the Jammin' Bear pattern (page 111) on sturdy paper. Color, laminate, and cut out the picture. If desired back the picture with a sheet of tagboard for durability. Display Jammin' Bear in your music area along with a set of jingle bells. When you introduce Jammin' Bear to your students, encourage them to listen to the sound of Jammin' Bear's jingle bells. From that time on, whenever your youngsters hear the bells, they'll know to gather in the music area. Works like a charm!

Zoo Staff

Manager
All-purpose helper (messenger)

Maggie

Grounds Supervisor
Check for classroom cleanliness.

Vanetta

Equipment Supervisor
Take out and bring in playground equipment. Pass out classroom supplies.

Ryan

Gatekeeper
Line leader, door holder

Tyler

Zoo Doctor
Care for classroom plants and animals.

Sidney

Zoo Lines

These paw prints will help you eliminate that beginning-of-the-year, lining-up bunching and crunching. Cut out construction-paper paw prints and laminate them. (You might like to consider using different colors of prints to distinguish each set or for patterning purposes.) Position each set of prints where you'd like your students to line up. As children line up, have them place their feet on the paw prints. Just perfect!

"Paws" For The Weekly News

Prance your zoo theme right into the daily news. At the beginning of each week of your zoo theme, choose five children (or groups) to each border a separate sheet of titled chart paper with paw prints. To do this, you might provide sponges and paint, stamps and stamp pads, or colorful markers. As you gather together at the end of each day, invite your class to dictate any newsworthy events from that day. Write their responses on one of the decorated sheets of chart paper. At the end of the week, save the chart-paper pages to create meaningful "read-the-room" activities. First add a cover page with that week's date; then staple the pages together. Hang each week's pages on a rack so children can practice reading—and read to classroom visitors.

Zoo Staff

Your kids will take pride in their official titles when it's their turn to be on the zoo staff—and classroom maintenance will go on without a hitch! Post the titles and corresponding job descriptions on your helpers bulletin board. Discuss the importance and responsibilities of each job with your youngsters. Then pin on nametags (from page 109) to indicate who is responsible for which job. Rotate names or add other children's names as often as you like.

Hungry Hippo

While this hungry hippo takes care of the lunch count, your youngsters will be working on a variety of skills. First enlarge and trace the nametag pattern (page 109) onto sturdy paper. Color it; then mount it on a board. Add the title "What's For Lunch?" Then program a different large index card with each of the lunch choices that are available at your school. Mount each day's choices on a bulletin board or large graph. In the morning, encourage each child to pin his hippo nametag (from page 109) in the appropriate column. Then you've got your lunch count in a glance and the perfect opportunity for counting; discussing *more, less,* and *equal;* letter and name recognition; beginning sounds; and more!

Pam Crane

Use with "Welcome! Welcome!" and "Who's At The Zoo Today?" on page 106 and "Hungry Hippo" on page 108.

ticket **nametag**

notecard

Monkey Patterns

Use with "So Glad You're Hanging With Us" and "Hanging Around Centers" on page 107.

Animals All Around

Gallop into math, pounce into science, hop into reading and language, and waddle into positive socialization. No matter how you get there, all kinds of learning opportunities are nestled in this thematic unit revolving around all kinds of animals.

ideas contributed by Lucia Kemp Henry

Animal Reading Corner

Immerse your youngsters in a wide variety of animals—some familiar and some not so familiar—by stocking your reading center with a collection of nonfiction animal books (see the list on page 116 for recommended titles). Encourage children to visit the center and carefully examine the animals in the books. Have paper and drawing supplies available for those children who would like to practice writing some of the animal names or who become artistically inspired as they look through the books. During your group times, encourage children to discuss the animals they have been noticing as they read. For continued reference, keep an ongoing record of your youngsters' comments on chart paper.

All Kinds Of Animals

Use this poem to reinforce emergent reading skills and oral language, as well as introduce some basic differences and similarities among animals. Copy the poem onto chart paper; then read it aloud to your class. After discussing the poem, read it several times together, having youngsters join in as they are able. When your students are familiar with the poem, set it up in your art center and encourage youngsters to decorate the border around the poem. Then display the finished work in your classroom.

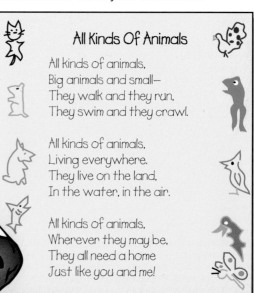

All Kinds Of Animals

All kinds of animals,
Big animals and small—
They walk and they run,
They swim and they crawl.

All kinds of animals,
Living everywhere.
They live on the land,
In the water, in the air.

All kinds of animals,
Wherever they may be,
They all need a home
Just like you and me!

Classification Station

This classification station can be tailor-made to fit the needs and abilities of your youngsters. In advance, duplicate a supply of the animal patterns (pages 117–118) on construction paper. Color, laminate, and cut out the animals. Stimulate your youngsters to think in terms of various attributes by setting up your choices of the classification stations that follow:

Natural Environment

To classify the animals by environment, prepare a sorting board by taping three sheets of construction paper together, leaving a small space between each sheet (for folding purposes). Label one sheet "land," another "water," and the last "land and water." Add picture cues if desired. To do this activity, have a child sort the animals according to the environments in which they live. Have spare sheets available for those youngsters who determine that some animals live in an environment that is not represented on the board. (For example, some children might suggest that birds live in the air.) Encourage youngsters to name the new categories for these animals. (If desired, color-code the animals and the environments for self-checking.)

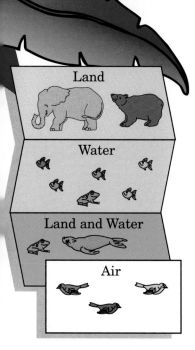

Farm Or Zoo For You

To classify by farm or zoo animal, duplicate the farm and zoo patterns (page 119) on construction paper. Color and cut out the patterns. Then glue each pattern to a different large sheet of construction paper and laminate the pages. Encourage each child to sort the animals in the appropriate places.

Size

Cut a small, medium, and large circle from construction paper; then write the size word on each circle. Encourage children to sort the animals according to the size of the pictures. Also create a size seriation activity by having youngsters arrange an appropriate selection of the animals from smallest to largest.

Can I Keep Him?

Your little ones might get some humorous discussions going about whether or not some of these animals would be suitable for home living. For this activity, provide each child with his own set of animal patterns, a sheet of construction paper, and crayons. Have each child draw and color a picture of his home. Then encourage him to decide which of the animals might make good pets, and glue them to the scene. Some of the animal choices might be up for debate!

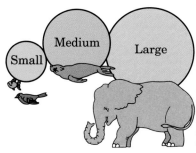

Travelin' Along

To classify animals according to how they travel, prepare a sorting board similar to the one described in "Natural Environment," but use four sheets of construction paper. Label the sections "walk/run," "swim," "hop/jump," and "fly." Have each child sort the animals accordingly.

I Spy

An enjoyable exposure to classical art is a natural by-product of sharing Lucy Micklethwait's *I Spy A Lion* (Greenwillow Books). On each spread of the book, the reader is coaxed to find an animal that is shown in a magnificent work of art. Some are easy to spot, and some will take a little extra focus of that spying eye. Children will love the search!

Life-Size, Yikes Size!

Astonish your little ones with some life-size scientific facts about the larger members of the animal kingdom. Choose one (or more) of the animals below; then use an opaque projector to project that animal pattern (from pages 117–118) onto a large sheet(s) of craft paper. Back up the projector until the image reaches approximate life size. Trace around the outline; then cut it out. Tape the life-size animal to a wall so that its feet are touching the floor. Invite youngsters to compare themselves with these magnificent beasts.

whale (Orca)—up to 30 feet long
elephant (African)—about 11 feet tall at the shoulder
bear (brown)—about 8 feet long
lion (male)—about 9 feet long and 3 1/2 feet tall at the shoulder

Animal Patterns And Colors

This multidisciplinary activity requires that all thinking caps be securely fastened. First title a bulletin board "Animal Patterns And Colors"; then add the labels "Stripes," "Spots," and "Colors." (Leave an open space at the bottom for those animals that need a category of their own.) Using ideas from your reading-corner books or their own imaginations, have children use various art supplies to create animals to display on the board. Assist each child in mounting his animal on the board. Then have him use those emerging reading and writing skills to write/dictate a label for his animal. Some of the trickier animals will require extra thinking. For example, is that butterfly spotted? No, it's striped! Wait—it's colored! What will your label be?

All In An Animal

If you made life-size animals in "Life-Size, Yikes Size!", you've got the perfect opportunity to cross into other areas of the curriculum with these creatures:

Measurement
Your large classroom animals are ideal for measuring activities. Provide measuring tools such as Unifix® cubes, rulers, yardsticks, and construction-paper paw prints. Encourage children to use the tools to explore measuring the animal(s) in different ways. For example, one child might measure the animal from nose to tail, while another measures from foot to ear. Have each child record his results on a chart.

Artistic Interpretation
During center time, invite youngsters to visit the reading corner to study the colorings and markings of the life-size animals that you made. Encourage students to look for colors as well as stripes, spots, or other interesting patterns/markings. Then line the floor below the animal cutout with newspaper and provide paints, sponges, and paintbrushes. As children rotate through centers, invite them to take turns painting your life-size animal. (If your youngsters get really inspired, you might like to have an easel-painting option available too!)

Action! Action!

Read aloud *Pretend You're A Cat* by Jean Marzollo (Dial Books For Young Readers). Before the first few words are out of your mouth, your little ones will just have to get up and get moving! For each page, choose a group of students to pantomime the text as you read aloud. Before you read the last line of each page, have the pantomiming group sit down. Then read the last line aloud and ask for volunteers to act out responses to the last line of text on each page. (If possible, videotape the readings and performances. When your youngsters watch the video, serve animal crackers.)

Action Words

Build on the vocabulary of action words introduced to your youngsters in *Pretend You're A Cat.* Select one (or more) action word(s) from each animal's description. Write these words on separate sheets of chart paper. Then ask youngsters to brainstorm a list of additional animals that can move in the same way. During center time, encourage child volunteers to cut out pictures from magazines or draw to illustrate your new vocabulary charts.

Animal Activity

Here's a game with a variety of benefits—your youngsters will be using reading skills, visually decoding pictures, counting, dramatizing, taking turns, building socialization skills, and moving, moving, moving! To make the gameboard, simply program a sheet of tagboard with three rows of colorful circles as shown. Write "Start" at one end of the rows, and "Finish" at the other end. Duplicate and color two sets of the activity cards on page 121; then cut out the cards. Laminate the cards and the gameboard. One to three players may play.

To play, give each child a marker such as a bean, button, or pom-pom to place at the start end of a row. Stack the activity cards facedown. Have one child draw a card, read it, perform the action, and move his marker the appropriate number of spaces. Proceed in turn until each child has reached "Finish." (If you run out of cards, shuffle the used ones and make a new stack.)

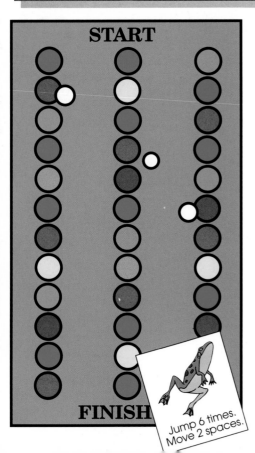

115

Animal Big Book

After all this animal activity, your youngsters will be ready to author this big book. For each child, reproduce the big-book text (page 120) on construction paper. Have each child cut out the text, then glue it to the bottom of a large sheet of construction paper. Then encourage each child to draw the animal of his choice in the space above the text. Have each child write/dictate the animal's name in the first blank. Then ask him to suggest a *sound* word to write in the next blank, and write the animal name again in the third blank. Complete the text by having the child write an *action* word in the last blank. Bind all of the pages together. Share the book during a group reading time, and encourage your class to read the text and act it out together.

I pretend I'm a ___lion___.
It's so fun to do!
I can ___roar___
    like a ___lion___
And I can ___jump___
    like one, too.

Animal Books

ABC Books

An Alphabet Of Dinosaurs by Peter Dodson
Illustrated by Wayne D. Barlowe
Published by Scholastic Inc.

Critter Crackers: The ABC Book Of Limericks by Kathryn Barron
Published by Landmark Editions, Inc.

The Ocean Alphabet Book by Jerry Pallotta
Illustrated by Frank Mazzola, Jr.
Published by Charlesbridge Publishing

My First Book Of Animals From A To Z
Illustrated by Turi MacCombie
Published by Scholastic Inc.

Robert Crowther's Incredible Animal Alphabet
Published by Candlewick Press

V For Vanishing: An Alphabet Of Endangered Animals by Patricia Mullins
Published by HarperCollins

Nonfiction

Dance With Me by Ron Hirschi
Photographed by Thomas D. Mangelsen
Published by Cobblehill Books

The Lifesize Animal Counting Book
Published by Dorling Kindersley, Inc.

Zoos Without Cages by Judith E. Rinard
Published by National Geographic Society

Fiction

Counting Cows by Woody Jackson
Published by Harcourt Brace & Company

A Dog's Best Friend by Massimo Mostacchi
Illustrated by Monica Miceli
Published by North-South Books

How Many Bears? by Cooper Edens
Illustrated by Marjett Schille
Published by Atheneum

The Moonglow Roll-O-Rama by Dav Pilkey
Published by Orchard Books

Quick As A Cricket by Audrey Wood
Illustrated by Don Wood
Published by Child's Play

What A Wonderful Day To Be A Cow by Carolyn Lesser
Illustrated by Melissa Bay Mathis
Published by Alfred A. Knopf, Inc.

Animal Patterns
Use with "Classification Station" on page 113
and "Life-Size, Yikes Size!" on page 114.

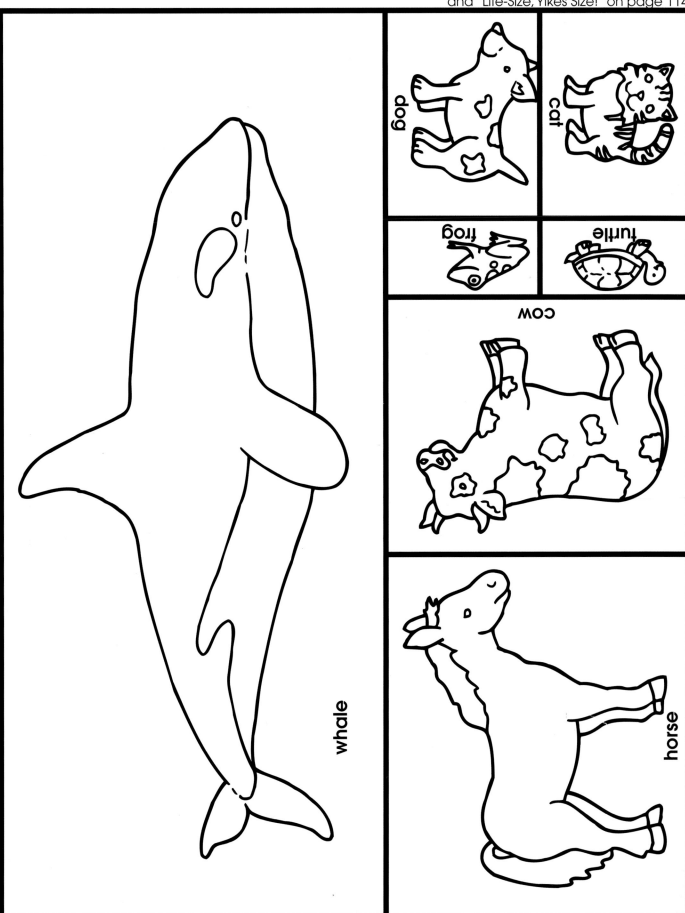

dog

cat

frog

turtle

cow

whale

horse

Animal Patterns

Use with "Classification Station" on page 113
and "Life-Size, Yikes Size!" on page 114.

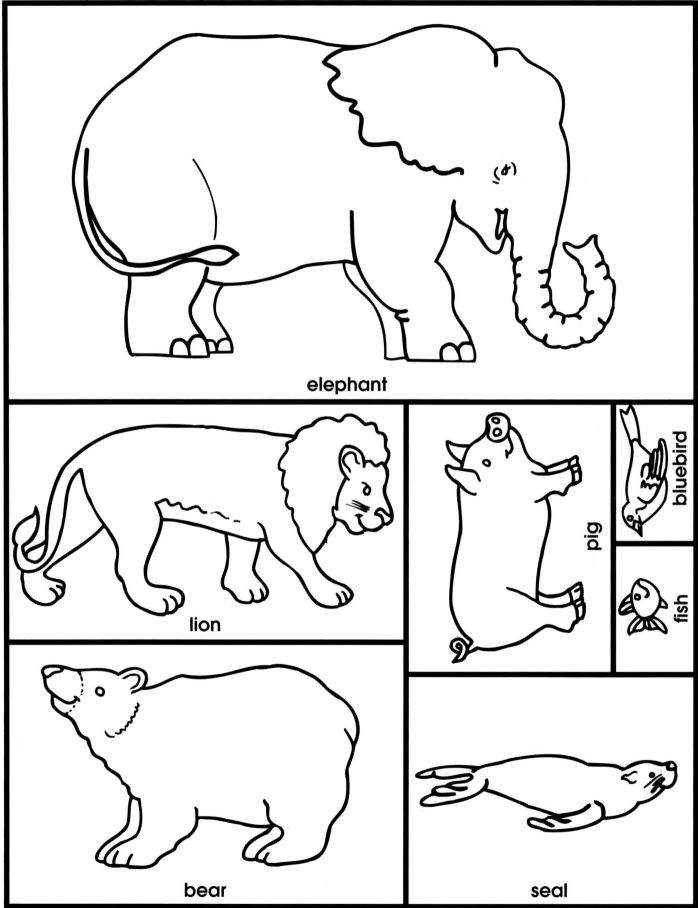

elephant

lion

pig

bluebird

fish

bear

seal

farm

zoo

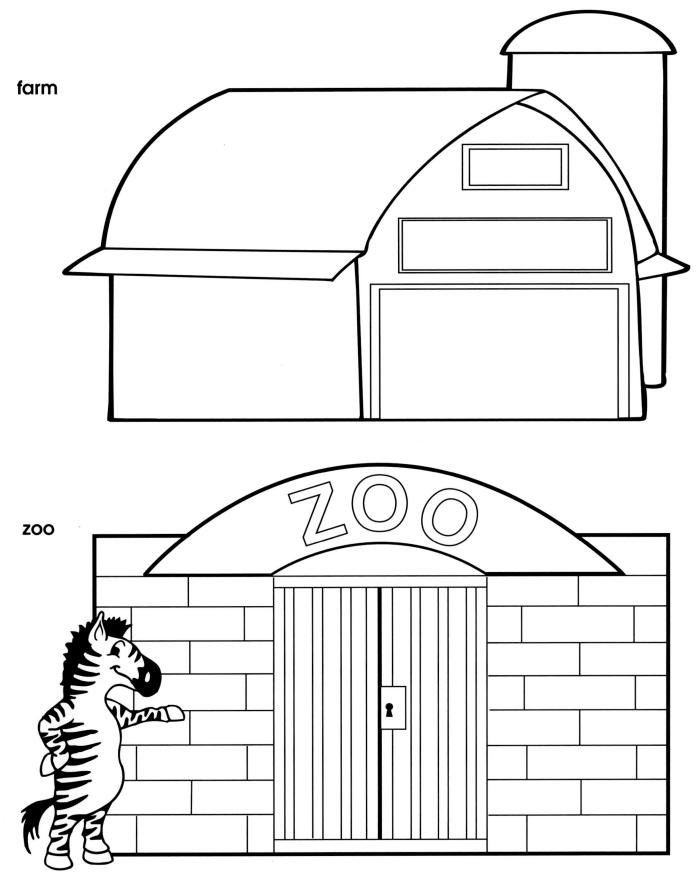

Use with "Who's At The Zoo Today?" on page 106 and "Classification Station" on page 113.

I pretend I'm a _____.

It's so fun to do!

I can _____

like a _____.

And I can _____

like one, too.

Award

I've been studying animals—
ask me to tell you about it!

Note: Photocopy the award for each child. Send an award home with each participating child at the end of your unit.

Jump 6 times.
Move 2 spaces.

Moo 4 times.
Move 2 spaces.

Gallop 10 times.
Move 2 spaces.

Roll 5 times.
Move 2 spaces.

Flap 8 times.
Move 2 spaces.

Clap 9 times.
Move 2 spaces.

Hop 7 times.
Move 2 spaces.

Jump 4 times.
Move 2 spaces.

Stand on 1 leg.
Count to 10.
Move 3 spaces.

Ducks, Geese, And Swans
The Wonderful World Of Waterfowl

The coming of fall brings changes for many feathered friends in our world—and ducks, geese, and swans are particularly interesting creatures at this time of year. Introduce your youngsters to the wonders of waterfowl with the science-oriented activities in this unit.

by Lucia Kemp Henry

Meet The Family

Ducks, geese, and swans are some of the most watchable birds in the world. They are often brightly colored and can be seen in many of the same places as the human population. Use the waterfowl patterns on pages 128–129 and the information below to help introduce your youngsters to the three branches of the waterfowl family tree.

To create an educational flannelboard or magnet board, duplicate the patterns; then color, laminate, and cut out each picture. Attach the hook side of a piece of Velcro® or a strip of magnetic tape to the back of each one. Then display the cutouts, identifying each bird by name and noting its particular characteristics. For a center activity, have youngsters group the pictures into the three main groups of waterfowl. For a variation, ask students to arrange the birds in size order.

- **Ducks** are generally the smallest of the waterfowl and the most brightly colored. Compared to geese and swans, ducks have shorter necks and legs. The vocal sound made by a duck is called *quacking*.

- **Geese** are usually medium-sized waterfowl—smaller than swans, but larger than ducks. A goose's neck is a little longer than that of a duck, but not as long as a swan's. The vocal sound made by a goose is called *honking*.

- **Swans** are the largest members of the waterfowl family. The impressive *trumpeter swan* can weigh more than 40 pounds and have a wingspan of more than eight feet! Swans can be easily recognized by their long, graceful necks. The vocal sounds made by swans range from whistles to trumpetlike calls.

Family Names

Each of the three main waterfowl families has special names for the male, female, and baby birds. Your youngsters will enjoy learning these special names as they explore language in this rhythmic chant. Of course, they'll just *have* to make the appropriate waterfowl sounds at the end of each verse!

Quack, little duck family, quack all together!
Daddy is a **drake** and he loves autumn weather.
Mommy is a pretty **duck** with a pretty feather.
Baby is a **duckling.** Now quack all together!

Honk, little goose family, honk all together!
Daddy is a **gander** and he loves autumn weather.
Mommy is a pretty **goose** with a pretty feather.
Baby is a **gosling.** Now honk all together!

Call, little swan family, call all together!
Daddy is a **cob** and he loves autumn weather.
Mommy is a pretty **pen** with a pretty feather.
Baby is a **cygnet.** Now call all together!

The Telltale Signs

Each group of waterfowl has unique physical features that make them identifiable—especially to the discerning kindergarten eye. *A First Look At Ducks, Geese, And Swans* by Millicent E. Selsam and Joyce Hunt (Walker And Company) offers an excellent introduction to developing that discerning eye. After sharing the book, display photos of ducks, geese, and swans from colorful sources such as *Zoobooks 2®: Ducks, Geese, And Swans,* written by John Bonnett Wexo (Wildlife Education, Ltd.). Encourage children to look at the pictures and share their observations, emphasizing the presence of webbed feet and bills on all waterfowl. Then have youngsters examine pictures of other common birds such as robins, owls, eagles, chickens, and hummingbirds. After they've studied the feet and beaks of these birds, ask youngsters whether they think these birds belong to the waterfowl family. Encourage them to explain their reasoning.

After this lesson, create a sorting center using photocopies of all of the bird pictures. Mount the copies on individual squares of tagboard; then laminate the squares. Have students sort the picture cards into two piles—one for "waterfowl" and one for "not waterfowl." 123

Waterproof Waterfowl

Begin a discussion by asking children if they've ever stepped into a cold swimming pool or a cool bathtub. How did they feel? How long could they stay in the water? Then ask children how they think waterfowl can stay in cold water for long periods of time. After your discussion, explain that ducks, geese, and swans have a special way to keep warm. They use their bills to tidy up each feather and spread oil from a gland near their tails all over their feathers. This is called *preening*. The oil prevents water from soaking into the feathers. By remaining dry, the waterfowl stay warmer, too.

Your youngsters can do a simple experiment to show how oiled feathers repel water. For each child, provide two large, dry bird feathers or two feather shapes cut from brown or white bulletin-board paper. Fill one small container with plain salad oil and another with water. Also provide an eyedropper and a paintbrush. Then ask each youngster to follow the procedure below.

1. Using the eyedropper, squeeze a few drops of water on one of your feathers. What happens?
2. Brush salad oil on the other feather. Let it soak in.
3. Squeeze a few drops of water on the oiled feather. What happens?

Now that students can see how waterfowl keep warm and dry, extend the activity by asking youngsters how humans keep from getting wet and cold. Provide several samples of fabrics—such as cotton, vinyl, denim, and rubber—for students to test. Have them place a few drops of water on each square of fabric. Which ones absorb water? Which ones repel water? Make a class chart to show the results. Encourage children to draw conclusions from your chart.

On The Move

Even the most well-oiled waterfowl can't survive without food to eat. That's why ducks, geese, and swans head toward warmer regions for the winter months. Copy the poem below onto chart paper. Ask if any of your youngsters have observed flocks of birds making their trek southward. Then introduce the term *migration,* explaining that to migrate, waterfowl travel from one area to another in search of more abundant food and better weather conditions. Then read the poem together, encouraging youngsters to join in as they are able.

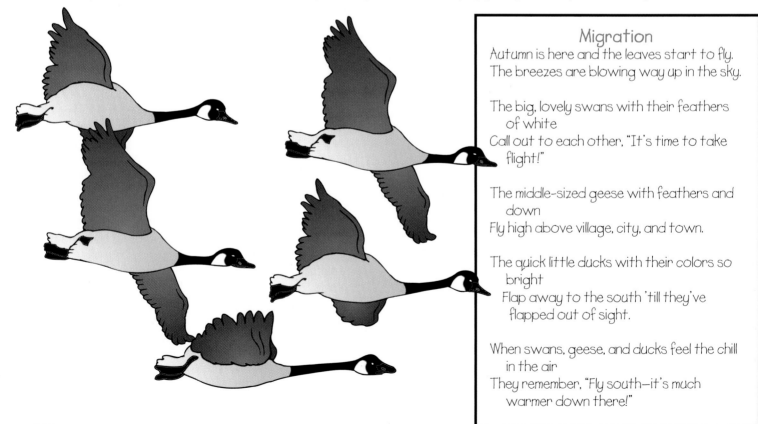

Migration

Autumn is here and the leaves start to fly.
The breezes are blowing way up in the sky.

The big, lovely swans with their feathers
    of white
Call out to each other, "It's time to take
    flight!"

The middle-sized geese with feathers and
    down
Fly high above village, city, and town.

The quick little ducks with their colors so
    bright
    Flap away to the south 'till they've
    flapped out of sight.

When swans, geese, and ducks feel the chill
    in the air
They remember, "Fly south—it's much
    warmer down there!"

Frozen Food

This experiment will help illustrate why waterfowl might have difficulty finding food when temperatures drop. Place a small section of turf (grass and soil) and some scattered birdseed in a disposable pan. Show the pan to your students and explain that the grass and seed represent the types of food eaten by waterfowl. Then, to represent winter's rain and snow, pour water into the pan to cover the turf and the birdseed. Place the pan in the freezer to replicate winter's freezing temperatures.

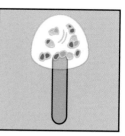

When the water is frozen, have youngsters examine the grass and seed. Discuss how they have changed. Guide students to the conclusion that winter weather diminishes the availability of food for waterfowl.

Further demonstrate this frozen-food phenomenon when you make a snack of Frozen-Bird-Food-On-A-Stick. Pour fruit juice into an ice-cube tray. Sprinkle some granola into each cup of the tray. Cover the tray with aluminum foil; then poke a craft stick through the foil into each cup. Freeze. When the cubes are frozen, pop them out and give one to each child. See how long it takes for youngsters to reach the granola in their treats. Then encourage youngsters to imagine what would happen if they had bills instead of mouths!

Migration Chant

Re-create the sounds of a glorious symphony of migrating waterfowl! Divide your class into three groups and assign each group a part of this lively chant. (If desired, have a group leader hold up one of the figures from "Meet The Family" on page122 to designate his group's identity.) As each group recites its verse, encourage children to act out the second half of the verse. Ask the other two groups to make the appropriate waterfowl sounds softly in the background. As a variation, use this chant to call youngsters as they line up. Recite each stanza of the poem to encourage your little ducks, geese, and swans to "fly" into their places and "migrate" to other areas of your school building.

Ducks say, "quack!"
It's time to go.
Migrate now!
Here comes the snow!
Ducks fly high.
Ducks fly low.
Ducks fly south.
Away they go!

Geese say, "honk!"
It's time to go.
Migrate now!
Here comes the snow!
Geese fly high.
Geese fly low.
Geese fly south.
Away they go!

Swans trumpet out,
It's time to go.
Migrate now!
Here comes the snow!
Swans fly high.
Swans fly low.
Swans fly south.
Away they go!

A Lesson From Geese

When geese migrate, they travel in a *V* formation. Ask your students if they know why. After discussing their ideas, tell youngsters that geese fly in a *V* so that each goose can get a little help from the draft that is created by the goose in front of it. To prompt thinking, divide your class in half and have each group arrange itself in a *V* formation. Encourage them to discuss who is helping whom in each *V*. Eventually they'll figure out that no one helps the lead bird! At that point, explain that when the lead bird tires, it drops back into the *V* and another bird takes over.

Why not take this goosey lead into your classroom? Survey youngsters to find out which classroom job they think is the hardest. Is it putting all the blocks away? Cleaning up the floor? When you have determined the hardest job, ask youngsters to remember the geese and give suggestions for how this classroom task might best be accomplished. Guide youngsters to determine that just as the geese work together to make the load lighter, so can children!

Where Did YOU Come From?

Hans Christian Andersen's beloved tale, *The Ugly Duckling,* offers solid science information, strong moral lessons, and a timeless classic to be treasured by one and all. Share a version of *The Ugly Duckling* with your youngsters. (The version told by Marianna Mayer is a good choice, as is the one illustrated by Monika Laimgruber.) After discussing the story, engage each child's imagination by asking him how he thinks the swan egg got in the duck's nest in the first place. Have each child write about and illustrate his idea. Then bind all of the pages together. Encourage each child to share his page during a group reading time.

Act It Out

After you've read *The Ugly Duckling* with your class, they're sure to enjoy singing the song of the same title by Greg & Steve. When youngsters are familiar with the song, assign a child to role-play the ugly duckling and the rest of the children to role-play the other ducks and the swans. Then play the song and let the action begin!

The Wonderful World Of Waterfowl

Making this display will give each of your students a chance to recall what he has learned in your waterfowl unit. Display a variety of waterfowl books in your art area. Provide a supply of different sizes of paper plates, construction paper, markers, and crayons. Before you begin, remind youngsters to think of the differences between ducks, geese, and swans. Also let them know that the books are available for their reference. Then have each child cut a paper plate in half to resemble the body of a duck, a goose, or a swan. Encourage each child to use the rest of the supplies to create the waterfowl of his choice. Mount the finished projects on a board titled "The Wonderful World Of Waterfowl."

A Flock Of Good Books

Fiction

Catching The Wind
Written by Joanne Ryder
Illustrated by Michael Rothman
Published by Morrow Junior Books

The Day The Goose Got Loose
Written by Reeve Lindbergh
Illustrated by Steven Kellogg
Published by Scholastic Inc.

Five Little Ducks
Songbook by Raffi
Illustrated by Jose Aruego & Ariane Dewey
Published by Crown Publishers, Inc.

Make Way For Ducklings
by Robert McCloskey
Published by Puffin Books

Nine Ducks Nine
by Sarah Hayes
Published by Candlewick Press

Petunia
by Roger Duvoisin
Published by Alfred A. Knopf Books
   For Young Readers

Quacky Duck
Written by Paul & Emma Rogers
Illustrated by Barbara Mullarney Wright
Published by Little, Brown And Company

The Snow Goose
by Pirkko Vainio
Published by North-South Books

Nonfiction

A First Look At Ducks, Swans, And Geese
Written by Millicent E. Selsam & Joyce Hunt
Illustrated by Harriett Springer
Published by Walker And Company

The Goose Family Book
Written by Sybille Kalas
Published by Simon & Schuster Children's Books

All Night Near The Water
by Jim Arnosky
Published by Putnam Publishing Group

Waterfowl Patterns

Use with "Meet The Family"
on page 122 and "Migration Chant" on page 125.

ruddy duck

tundra swan

trumpeter swan

Waterfowl Patterns

Use with "Meet The Family" on page 122 and "Migration Chant" on page 125.

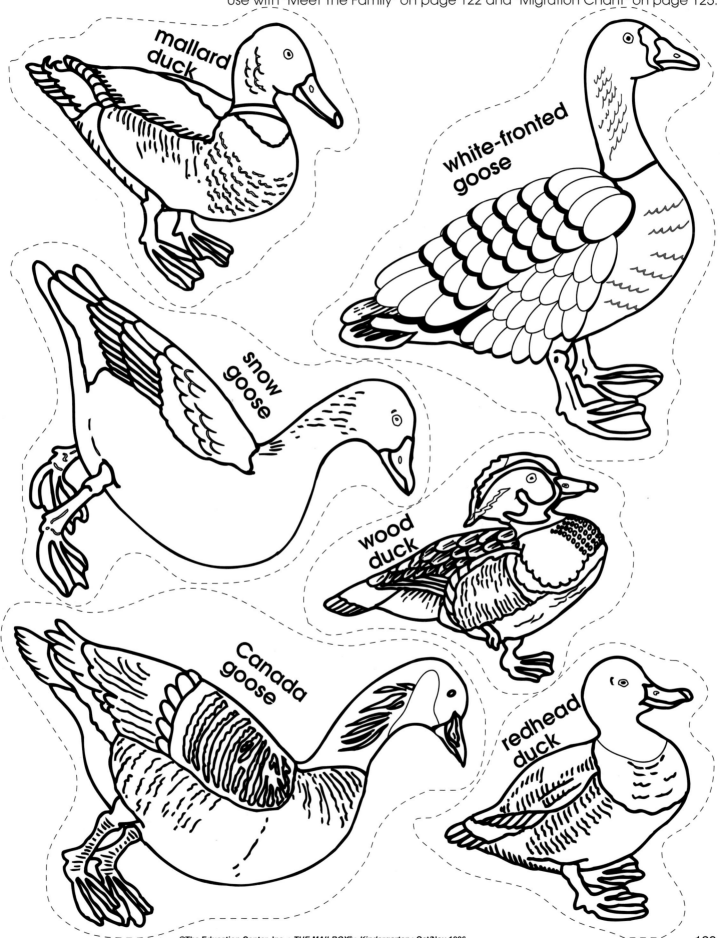

mallard duck

white-fronted goose

snow goose

wood duck

Canada goose

redhead duck

SOUP'S ON!

Stir up a batch of these soup-based learning activities to make your busy winter classroom a warm learning environment. Activities that include language arts, math, and literature will nourish your youngsters' minds and help satisfy their hunger for fun.

ideas by Lucia Kemp Henry

SOUP COLLECTION

Enlist the help of your youngsters in gathering together a wide assortment of soups. Label a large basket or crate "soup." Then encourage youngsters to donate soups that come in a variety of containers such as cans, boxes, packets, and cups. Use the resulting soup collection throughout your soup unit.

ALL SORTS OF SOUP

Your youngsters' sorting skills will heat right up with this activity. In advance, label an index card for each different type of soup container in your collection. Arrange the cards on the floor or a table in an area large enough for youngsters to make a graph of the soups. In turn, have each child select a soup from the collection and place it appropriately on the graph. Continue in this manner until all the soups have been placed. As a class, discuss what your graph reveals.

RECORDING INFORMATION

This graphing activity reinforces each child's understanding of how concrete information can be recorded. In advance, place a classroom supply of the soup graph (page 134) near your class's concrete graph. (If needed, program the blank column on the graph before duplicating.) As each child visits this area, have her color the boxes on the graph to represent what is shown on the concrete graph. When each child has a completed graph, position your students so that they cannot see the concrete graph. Then ask youngsters to look at their own graphs as you ask questions such as "How many *cans* of soup are on our real graph?" As each answer is given, send a child to check the given response against the real graph.

WHAT'S MISSING?

Visual memory is the name of the game in this fun activity. Begin by displaying an arrangement or pattern of soups. (You can be as simple or as complex as your youngsters' abilities permit.) Ask your children to look carefully at the array of soups. Then instruct them to close their eyes while you remove one of the soups from the display. Have youngsters open their eyes and guess which soup is missing. Continue to play in the same manner, having child volunteers set up and remove the soups.

SOUP CHANT

There's rhythm and rhyme and lots of new vocabulary in this soup chant that's just right for expanding oral language skills. Copy the chant on a sheet of chart paper and add visual cues to the page if desired. When your youngsters are familiar with the chorus, assign different verses to individual children (or small groups) and have everyone join in on the chorus.

Chorus: Soup is super on a wintry day. It warms me up in a yummy, yummy way.

Verse 1: Chicken soup, bean soup, chowder too. Alphabet, matzo ball—I love you!

Chorus: Soup is super on a wintry day. It warms me up in a yummy, yummy way.

Verse 2: Vegetable, tomato, egg-drop soup. Onion or potato—slurp a scoop!

Chorus: Soup is super on a wintry day. It warms me up in a yummy, yummy way.

Verse 3: Crumble up crackers—put 'em on the top. When I sip soup, I just can't stop!

Chorus: Soup is super on a wintry day. It warms me up in a yummy, yummy way.

A STORYTIME EXPERIENCE

This unique storytime idea just might incite a new understanding and interest in reading and even spelling! Before you share the book, provide each child with a scoop of alphabet pasta and a workspace (such as a vinyl placemat or tabletop). As you share *Alphabet Soup* by Kate Banks (Alfred A. Knopf, Inc.), encourage each child to manipulate his pasta letters along with the story.

CLASSROOM PUBLISHING

ALPHABET SOUP

Each youngster will be proud to contribute a personalized page to this class-made book. To begin, give each child a copy of the soup-bowl pattern on page 135. Have each child use paints or crayons to decorate her soup bowl and to color the soup inside the bowl. Then have each child sort through alphabet pasta to find the letters in her name. Instruct her to glue the letters on the soup portion of her page. When the pages are dry, bind them together between two construction-paper covers. Be sure that this soon-to-be-favorite read-aloud is available for free-time reading.

SOUP DU JOUR

Oui! Oui! With this weeklong project, your youngsters will learn a French saying, author a soup book, and enjoy a sampling of soup each day. (Hopefully, you will have each type of soup in your classroom soup collection.) In advance, photocopy five soup bowls (page 135) on art paper for each child. Write the name of each day's soup on a separate sentence strip. If desired, have each child copy the name of the soup du jour (soup of the day) onto his soup bowl. When all of the pages are done, have each child compile his pages. Bind each child's pages between two decorated construction-paper covers. Encourage each child to share his soup book with his family.

On Monday: Serve tomato soup with pizza-flavored fish crackers. Then have each child use red finger paint to paint tomato soup in his bowl. Have each child glue fish crackers to the soup.

On Tuesday: Serve chicken noodle-o soup. Have each child use yellow tempera paint to paint chicken soup in his bowl. When the paint is dry, encourage children to attach gummed paper reinforcers.

On Wednesday: Serve vegetable soup. Have each child color his soup brown. Then use cuts of vegetables and tempera paints to make vegetable prints in the soup.

On Thursday: Serve potato soup. Have each child combine white tempera paint with yellow tempera paint until he has achieved a desired color. Then have him paint the soup in his bowl. When that paint is dry, have him dab the tip of a sponge into white paint and lightly sponge-print potato chunks in the soup.

On Friday: Serve minestrone. Have each child color his soup with a combination of red and brown. Then have him glue pasta and dried beans onto the soup base.

UNCLE WILLIE AND THE SOUP KITCHEN
Written & Illustrated by DyAnne DiSalvo-Ryan
Published by Morrow Junior Books

When a young boy encounters the sights of homeless people in the city, he feels sad and a little scared. "Sometimes people need help," his Uncle Willie tells him. So the boy accompanies Uncle Willie to the city's soup kitchen. There he begins to see his neighbors in a different light.

After sharing *Uncle Willie And The Soup Kitchen* with your youngsters, perhaps they'll be motivated to make a difference in your city or town. After discussing the story, brainstorm ways in which your students think the class could spread a little kindness to the people who need help in your community. For example, you might agree to save extra pennies for a certain amount of time, and then donate them to your town's soup kitchen. Or you might even decide to donate your entire soup collection!

SOUP-RELATED LITERATURE

Mean Soup
Written & Illustrated
by Betsy Everitt
Published by
Harcourt Brace & Company

One mean-feeling boy and a wise and caring mother provide the seasoning in this tasty tale about a frustrated youngster who needs to blow off a little steam.

GRRR...

Growing Vegetable Soup
Written & Illustrated by Lois Ehlert
Published by Harcourt Brace
Jovanovich, Publishers

In illustrations as big and as bright as life, a father and child go about the business of growing—and then making—vegetable soup. And when all is said and done, of course somebody's got to eat it!

Soup Graph

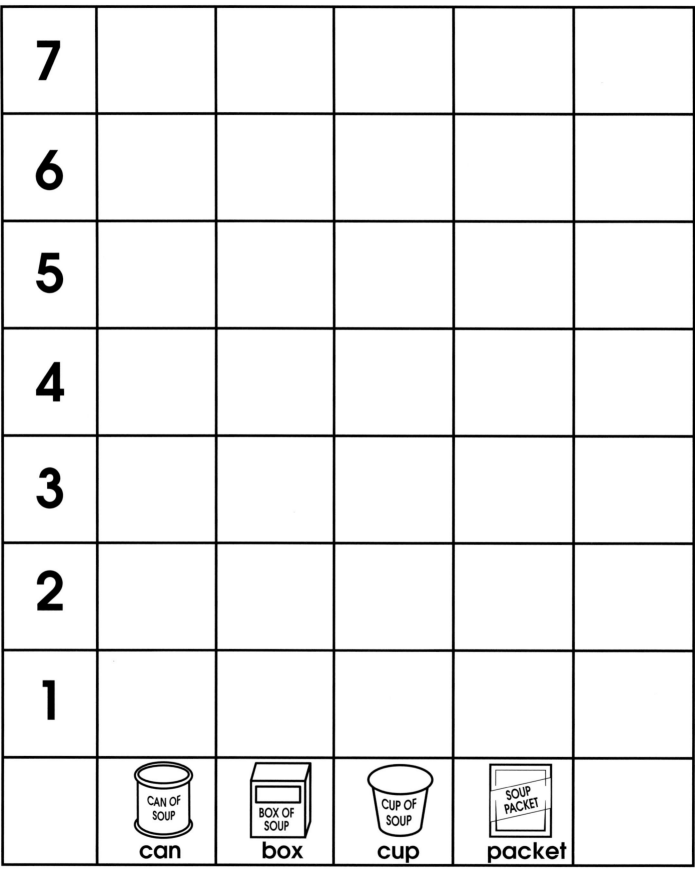

	7					
	6					
	5					
	4					
	3					
	2					
	1					
		can	box	cup	packet	

Note To The Teacher: Use with "Recording Information" on page 130.

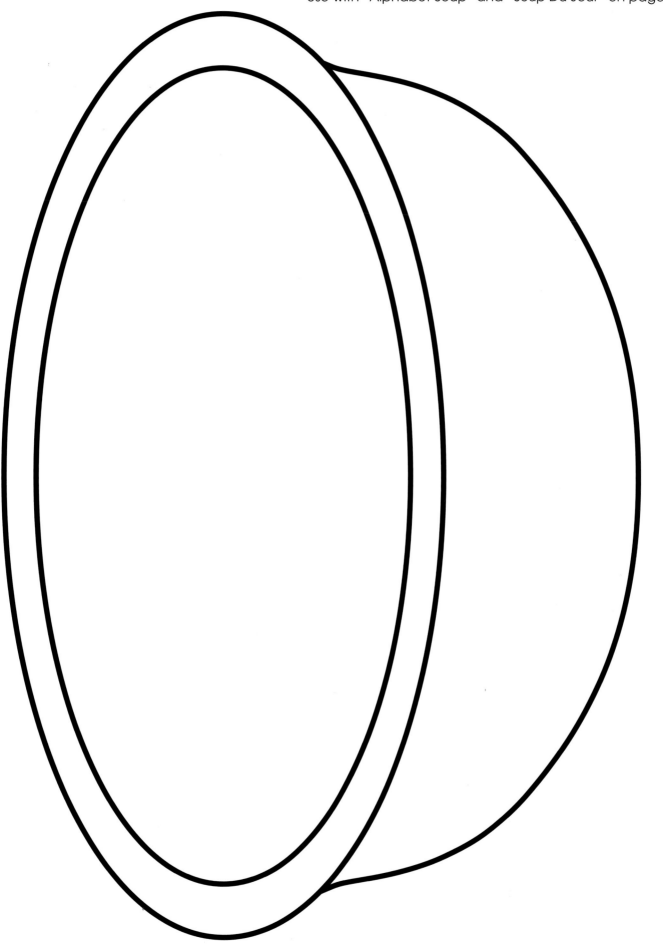

©The Education Center, Inc. • *THE MAILBOX®* • *Kindergarten* • Dec/Jan 1996–97

Cruisin' Across The Curriculum

Get moving with these activities that hook up transportation
with loads of cross-curricular learning.

ideas contributed by Kristine Puls

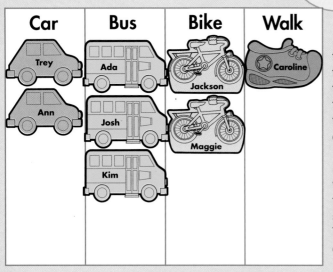

Car	Bus	Bike	Walk
Trey	Ada	Jackson	Caroline
Ann	Josh	Maggie	
	Kim		

Traveling To School

Get your transportation study on the road by inviting youngsters to share how they travel from home to school. To prepare duplicate the pattern from page 140 that best depicts each child's mode of transportation. Cut out the patterns. Also make extra patterns for those students who travel to school using several different means of transportation. Then program a sheet of chart paper labeled to correspond to each mode of transportation used.

Read aloud *This Is The Way We Go To School* by Edith Baer (Scholastic Inc.). Encourage students to discuss the many different ways children around the world get to school. Then have each child tell how he travels to school. Ask him to select a pattern that corresponds with his mode of transportation and write his name on it. Then have him tape his pattern in the appropriate column on the chart. Discuss what the completed chart reveals.

Going Places

Invite youngsters to travel through a storm—a brainstorm, that is—on their way to creating a transportation big book. In advance, duplicate the bus pattern (page 140). Enlarge and trace the pattern on two large sheets of construction paper; then cut out each vehicle (these will be the book covers). For the book pages, trace around the cutouts on large sheets of white construction paper and cut along the resulting outlines. Then collect magazines containing an assortment of vehicle pictures.

Prompt your students to brainstorm a variety of modes of transportation. Write student responses on the backs of the book covers. Then have each child glue magazine cutouts of different types of transportation onto her page. Or invite her to illustrate her choice of transportation. Stack the completed pages between the two book covers, with the brainstormed lists on each cover facing inside the book. Bind the book along the edge; then write the title "Going Places" on the front cover. Place the book in your reading center for students to cruise through during their reading time.

jet boat
yacht wagon
plane canoe
helicopter skates
car

Movin' Along

Give your students a *real* ride to observe the world of transportation around your community. In advance, make arrangements for some form of transportation for your class—vans, a bus, a commuter train, or any travel combination. Plan a route that will give students the opportunity to witness a variety of travel forms. For instance, your route might take the class past a lake, across a railroad track, near an airport, and into the streets of town. As you travel, encourage youngsters to be on the lookout for forms of transportation. Ask them to point out vehicles and identify where they travel—on land, in water, or in air. Take along an instant camera to take snapshots of the many different forms of transportation observed. After returning to the class, have youngsters use the photos (or their own drawings) to create a display depicting where each form of transportation travels. Title the display "Movin' Along."

Pam Crane

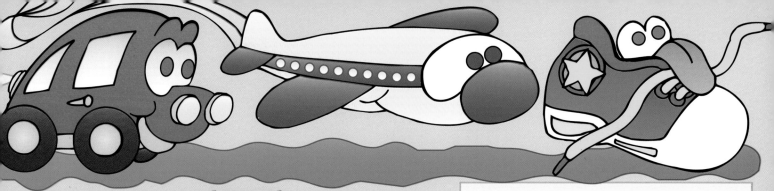

Land Travel

Show off different kinds of land transportation with a special exhibit. In advance, arrange to have parents, co-workers, car dealers, or other resource persons provide different types of land transportation for your exhibit. Some show-entry suggestions might include cars, trucks, bikes, wagons, skates, sleds, strollers, motorcycles, and recreational vehicles. (If your school's space or resources prevent having an exhibit of real vehicles, you might ask students to bring in toy models.) On the day of the show, pair each student with a volunteer—perhaps an older student or an adult helper. Give each pair a sheet of paper and a pencil. Ask the volunteer to record comments and observations made by the student while they visit the exhibit. Encourage students to note the features of each vehicle such as its wheels, the seats, its size and shape, and whether or not it uses an engine.

After returning to class, give each child several sheets of construction paper. Have the child and his partner refer to his page of comments as he illustrates a different type of land vehicle on each page. Ask his partner to write the child's dictation on the corresponding page. Bind each child's pages between two sheets of construction paper. Write his dictated title on the front cover; then exhibit the books in the media center or other prominent places for other students, teachers, and parents to read.

Carol A. Parent—Pre-K, Washington Christian School, Silver Spring, MD

It has one seat, but someone can sit on the back.   Tanner

Traffic Patterns

Without rules and patterns, transportation vehicles would certainly be in a jam! Make this patterning center; then invite your little ones to establish some traffic patterns of their own. Duplicate six or more copies of each pattern on pages 140–141. Color and cut out each pattern; then laminate the cutouts. Paint a long straight line on a length of bulletin-board paper to resemble a road. When a child (or group of children) visits this center, invite him to arrange the cutouts in a pattern on the road. Encourage other students to repeat the pattern with more cutouts. Then remove the cutouts and have a different student begin a new pattern.

Wanda R. Reding—Gr. K, Greenbrier Elementary
Greenbrier, TN

A Convoy Of Sounds

Round up the trucks—we're gonna have a convoy! Youngsters will be riding in high gear when they make initial-letter-to-sound hookups with this truck convoy. Enlarge the truck pattern on page 43; then duplicate the pattern on construction paper as many times as the desired number of letter-sound association pairs. Cut out each truck; then cut apart each cab from each trailer. Glue a picture on the trailer side of the truck. Write the corresponding first letter on the cab section. (If desired, program the backs for self-checking.) Then laminate the truck sets. To use, have a child match each trailer to a cab by pairing the picture's initial sound with its corresponding letter. Now that's a big ten-four, good buddy!

The Wild Blue Yonder

Youngsters' imaginations will soar when they create their own flying machines. Provide a cardboard box for every two or three students. Prepare each box by turning and taping the top and bottom flaps inside the box. Then gather scraps of poster board and a variety of items that can be used to create instrument panel gadgets—such as spools, an assortment of plastic lids, and clock stamps and stamp pads.

Encourage students to discuss the many different types of vehicles that fly. For inspiration, provide illustrations from a book such as *Airplanes And Flying Machines* (First Discovery Books by Scholastic Inc.) and read aloud *Flying* by Donald Crews (Scholastic Inc.). Then invite each group of students to use the provided materials to make any kind of flying machine. Help the groups as necessary to cut and attach materials. Afterward invite students, in turn, to pilot their machines on imaginary flights—over cities, mountains, the sea, the jungle, or even the North Pole. After each flight, ask the pilot to share something about his trip.

Coming In For A Landing

Of the many forms of air travel, students are probably most familiar with the airplane. With this activity, youngsters can land a new vocabulary word while reinforcing letter-recognition skills. To prepare, enlarge and duplicate 26 copies of the airplane pattern on page 141. Cut out each pattern; then print a different lowercase letter on each cutout. On each of 26 construction-paper squares, print a different uppercase letter. Then cut off the tops and the sides with the handles of 26 plastic gallon jugs. These will be the airplane hangars. Tape an uppercase letter card to the top of each hangar. Then create a learning center by arranging the jugs side by side on the floor and placing the airplane cutouts nearby.

To introduce this center, read aloud *Let's Fly From A To Z* by Doug Magee and Robert Newman (Cobblehill Books). After sharing the book, remind the class that a *hangar* is the name of the place where planes are repaired or stored. When a child visits this center, instruct him to park each airplane in the hangar with the corresponding uppercase letter. After the child parks all the planes, offer him a complimentary handful of peanuts for a job well done!

The Airplane Song

Teach this song to youngsters to heighten their enthusiasm for learning about airplanes.

(sung to the tune of "Take Me Out To The Ball Game")

Take me out to the airport.
Take me up to the gate.
Buy me a ticket to fly so high.
I want to fly through the big, open sky!
Let me zoom, zoom, zoom! See, I'm soaring
Above cars and buses and trains.
For it's great to fly through the sky on a big airplane!

Water Travel

Give your youngsters some numerical nautical experience right in your own classroom. To make ten sailboats, collect ten foam meat trays. For each boat, cut a triangle sail from a sheet of craft foam. Cut two one-inch horizontal slits approximately one inch apart—one above the other—on the sail. Slip the end of a wide craft stick through one slit, then the other. Using a permanent marker, print a different number word on each sail. Press a ball of school clay onto the center of a tray, then push the craft stick into the clay. Before filling your water table, use a tub crayon to write each numeral from one to ten around the inside top edge of the table to indicate docks in a harbor.

Introduce students to water travel by reading *Harbor* by Donald Crews (Greenwillow Books). Then invite each child, in turn, to navigate a sailboat through your water-table harbor to its own dock. Put a boat in the water. Have a child read the number word on the sail, then blow through a straw to sail the boat to its dock. When the boat reaches its dock, have the child remove it from the water; then put a different boat in the water for the next child to dock.

Magnetic Tugboat

While students learn about the mighty power of a tugboat, they can also be introduced to the power of a magnet. Enlarge the tugboat and ship patterns on page 141; then duplicate one tugboat pattern and a supply of ship patterns on construction paper. Color, cut out, and laminate each pattern. Punch a hole near the back of the tugboat; then thread a length of yarn through the hole and tie it securely. Tie the other end of the yarn around a magnet. Gather a variety of objects—include some objects that will and some that will not be attracted to a magnet. Glue or tape a different object to the end of each of the ship cutouts. Then have youngsters sponge-paint a harbor scene on a length of bulletin-board paper. Guide them to paint the docks, piers, and warehouses on the right half of the paper. Then explain to students that a tugboat is used to move ships—many of which are much larger than the tugboat. Place several ships along the left half of the harbor scene. Invite a child to move the tugboat past the ships one at a time, passing the magnet over the item attached to the ship. If the item is attracted to the magnet, ask the child to "tow" the ship to a dock on the right side of the harbor. Afterward, discuss the results of your youngsters' towing efforts.

Literature Link

The Big Book Of Things That Go
Published by Dorling Kindersley Publishing, Inc.

The Wheels On The Bus And Other Transportation Songs
Illustrated by Dick Witt
Published by Scholastic Inc.

Sail Away
Written and Illustrated by Donald Crews
Published by Greenwillow Books

Freight Train
Written and Illustrated by Donald Crews
Published by Greenwillow Books

Truck Song
Written by Diane Siebert
Illustrated by Byron Barton
Published by Thomas Y. Crowell

Little Toot
Written and Illustrated by Hardie Gramatky
Published by G. P. Putnam's Sons

Transportation Patterns

Use with "Traveling To School" and "Going Places" on page 136, and "Traffic Patterns" on page 137.

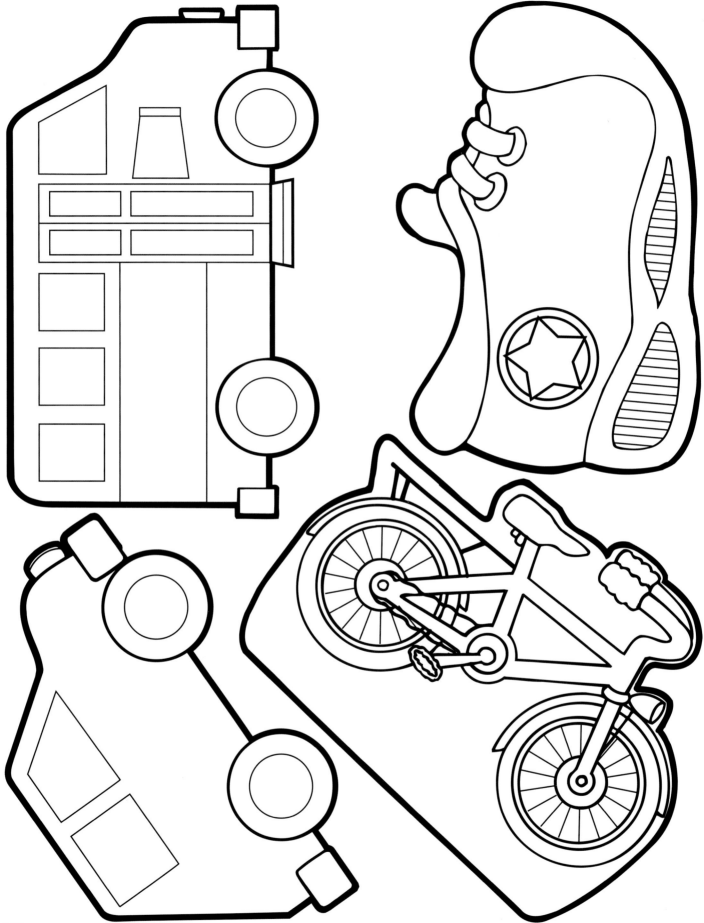

©The Education Center, Inc. • *THE MAILBOX®* • *Kindergarten* • Dec/Jan 1996–97

Use with "Traffic Patterns" and "A Convoy Of Sounds" on page 137,
"Coming In For A Landing" on page 138, and "Magnetic Tugboat" on page 139.

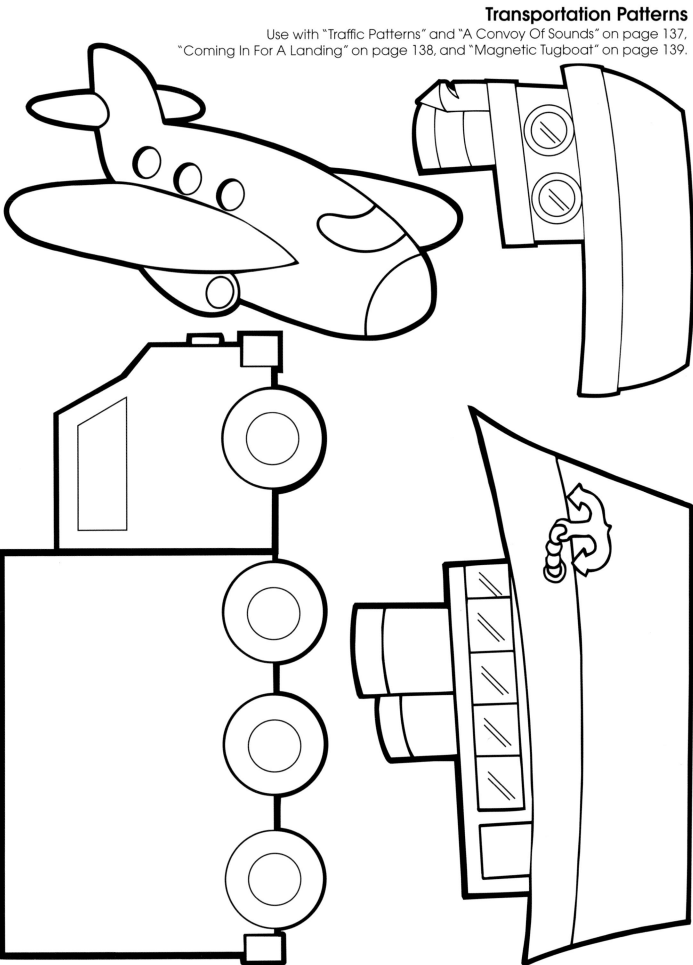

Pancakes!

Hotcakes, griddle cakes, flapjacks, pancakes—whatever you call 'em, they all stack up to lots of cross-curricular learning fun.

ideas contributed by Mary Rice

Pancakes, Pancakes!
Written & Illustrated by Eric Carle
Published by Scholastic Inc.

Introduce your pancake unit with Eric Carle's tale of Jack, a young boy who awakens one morning with a giant hankering for a big pancake. However, unlike children of the 1990s, Jack soon learns that he's got quite a list of chores cut out for him before he can actually sink his teeth into his delectable breakfast treat. With a feast of colorful artwork, Eric Carle tells a story of an old-fashioned breakfast that will prime your students for pancakes, pancakes!

Now And Then
After reading and discussing *Pancakes, Pancakes!* with your youngsters, the stage is set for social studies. Ask each child to think about and share what she would need to do at her house if she wanted a pancake for breakfast one morning. Record the responses on a chart. Then prompt children to recall what Jack needed to do before he was able to eat his pancake. Also record those responses. Compare and contrast the responses; then guide children to think about when (in history) this story probably took place. After leading youngsters to determine that the story took place a long time ago, discuss the differences between life nowadays and life as depicted in the story. Which time period do your youngsters think they'd prefer and why?

The Best Breakfast Book
If the story of Jack and his pancake ordeal has incited a yen for breakfast foods—seize the moment! Mix the pancake yen together with a pinch of brainstorming and a cup or two of reading, writing, and categorizing—and your youngsters are thoroughly prepared to author "The Best Breakfast Book." Ask each child to write about and illustrate the very best breakfast he can think of. Bind all of the finished pages together between construction-paper covers titled "The Best Breakfast Book." Then have each child share his page during a group reading time.

The Best Breakfast Book

my best breakfast is pancakes with yogurt.
Jackson

We Are Little Pancakes

Cook up a little pancake fun with this song adapted to the tune of "I'm A Little Teapot."

We are little pancakes,
Round and flat.
Stack us together
Just like that.
Add a pat of butter
On the top.
Then pour on the syrup
'Til we say "stop!"

3

4

5

1

2

Stacks And Pats

Stacks of pancakes and pats of butter team up to reinforce the skills of your choice. To prepare this activity, photocopy a supply of the pancake pattern (page 145) on tan construction paper. Then photocopy a supply of the butter pattern (page 145) on yellow construction paper. Program the pancakes and the butter pats with corresponding skills (see the illustration for suggestions). To do this activity, a child either matches a pat of butter with the corresponding pancake or—in the case of a counting activity—stacks the appropriate number of pancakes to match the numeral on a pat of butter.

Assorted Syrups

Here's a pancake center that's just dripping with color-word practice. To prepare, duplicate a syrup and stack of pancakes pattern (page 145) for each desired color. Color each syrup pattern a different color; then cut out all the patterns. Glue the stack of pancakes cutouts onto a large sheet of construction paper; then label each cutout with a different color. If desired, label the back of each syrup cutout with its color to make this a self-checking center. Then laminate all the pieces. To do this activity, a child reads the color word on each pancake stack, then places the corresponding syrup color on top of that stack. To check his work, a child simply flips the syrup cutout over to see if the color words match.

143

"Flippety" Flap

Flip these pancakes to reinforce eye-hand coordination, measurement, counting, and greater-than/less-than skills. To make pancakes for flipping, photocopy the pancake pattern (page 145) on tan construction paper. Sandwich a safe-edged metal lid (such as those used for canning) between each set of two back-to-back pancakes; then glue the pancakes together. Arrange the pancakes on a plate and place them on a table with a spatula, paper, and crayons. To do this activity, have a child use the spatula to scoop up a pancake. Then encourage him to flip (toss) the pancake. After the pancake lands, have the child use his feet to measure that pancake flip by measuring the distance from where he executed the flip to where the pancake landed. Have the child write down the distance of his flip. Then encourage him to flip another couple of pancakes, repeating the measuring and recording process.

When a child has finished flipping, ask questions or give directions to help him analyze his written information, such as:

- Which pancake went the greatest distance? Draw a circle around that numeral.
- Which pancake went the shortest distance? Draw a square around that numeral.

The Real Thing—Topped!

Of course no pancake unit is complete without whipping up a batch of the real thing. To prepare for this pancake-cooking event, ask for donations of pancake toppings such as different flavored syrups, jams, fruits, and butter. Then draw a graph on poster board labeled with each of the toppings. Arrange all the toppings on a table. Using a simple pancake mix, have your students help you make enough pancakes for each child to have a few small pancakes. Encourage each child to try a different topping on each of his pancakes. Afterward ask each child to write his name on a sticky note, then attach the note to the graph in the column showing his favorite pancake topping. Then discuss what the graph reveals.

More Pancake Books

Pancakes For Breakfast by Tomie dePaola
The Pancake by Anita Lobel
Pancake Pie by Sven Nordquist

Syrup And Stack Of Pancakes Patterns
Use with "Assorted Syrups" on page 143.

Pancake And Butter Patterns
Use with "Stacks And Pats" on page 143
and " 'Flippety' Flap" on page 144.

Get Ready For Rabbits!

This bunch of rabbit-themed learning activities will have your little ones hopping! Use the ideas in this unit to introduce your youngsters to the real basics of bunnies; then turn your focus to some *imaginary* rabbits with the literature selections at the end.

ideas by Lucia Kemp Henry and Jan Trautman

Let's Get Hopping!

Before you begin these rabbit activities, cut three large rabbit shapes from construction paper. Title one rabbit "What We Know"; the second, "What We Want To Know"; and the third, "What We Learned." Post the rabbits on a wall. Then encourage children to share facts they already know about rabbits. As they share, record their comments on the first rabbit. Next ask students what they would like to know about rabbits. Record the questions on the second rabbit. At the conclusion of the unit, ask students to recall what they have learned. Write these facts on the third rabbit.

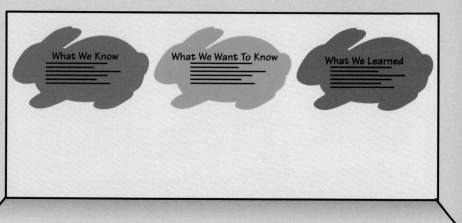

What We Know

What We Want To Know

What We Learned

Rabbit Vocabulary
- **buck**—a grown-up boy rabbit
- **doe**—a grown-up girl rabbit
- **warren**—the rabbits' tunnels that are underground
- **kittens**—baby rabbits

Baby rabbits are born with no fur.
Ben

Some rabbits have ears that flop down.
Lexa

Getting To Know All About You

Introduce some solid, scientific rabbit information with *Rabbit* by Stephen Savage (Thomson Learning). In advance, title a sheet of chart paper "Rabbit Vocabulary." As you share the book and run across new vocabulary words, write them on the chart. Then have children dictate definitions for the new words as you record their comments. Afterward stock your science center with other nonfiction rabbit books (see the literature list on page 149). Encourage children to examine the books at their leisure to discover new information. When a child discovers a rabbit fact, encourage him to write about and illustrate it. Then post his page near your vocabulary list. Discuss each new entry during a group time.

A Rabbit Poem

To reinforce some basic rabbit concepts, write the poem at right on a sheet of chart paper. After reading/reciting the poem together, place the poem in your art area. Encourage children to illustrate the poem during your center times.

Rabbits
A rabbit is a **mammal**.
That's kind of like you and me.
But a rabbit is not a **human**
As you can plainly see!

A male is called a **buck**.
The females are called **does**.
The babies are called **kittens**.
When they're born their eyes are closed.

Rabbits live in **warrens**.
Those are "tunnel-y" homes underground.
So when their enemies come looking,
The rabbits cannot be found!

When you think about the looks
Of all the rabbits far and near,
The way to tell a rabbit
Is pretty much by its ears!

Every Bunny's Different; Every Bunny's Special

Here's a chance to spread your equity lessons across the rabbit curriculum! Gather together several books that show various types of rabbits. (*Rabbit* by Mark Evans is a good choice. Also see the list on page 149.) After studying the pictures, have each child draw and cut out a rabbit shape from art paper. (If desired, enlarge and duplicate the pattern on page 149 to use for this activity.) Have each child use his cutout or the remaining stencil for this project. Provide paints, paintbrushes, sponge pieces, crayons, and colored pencils. Encourage each child to select a certain type of rabbit and paint/color his rabbit to resemble that rabbit type. Have each child copy the name of his rabbit on a sentence strip. Then display the rabbits and their names nestled among some construction-paper grass on a bulletin board.

Little Rabbit Action Poem

Here's a little rabbit poem to keep things hopping in your classroom.

One little rabbit	*Hold up one finger.*
Underneath a tree.	*Hold arms up like tree branches.*
One little rabbit	*Hold up one finger.*
As "hoppy" as can be.	*Hop.*
Two long ears.	*Hold hands at back of head.*
Two big back feet.	*Raise and touch feet one at a time.*
One wiggly nose	*Wiggle nose.*
And whiskers so neat.	*Stroke fingers along cheeks.*
Two front paws.	*Hold hands under chin, fingertips down.*
Two eyes that shine.	*Point to eyes.*
One furry body	*Hug body.*
And a fluffy tail behind.	*Wiggle bottom!*

lettuce
cauliflower
cucumber
celery
snow peas
cabbage
alfalfa sprouts
spinach
carrots
tomatoes
apples
pears
melon

Let's Do Lunch!

Rabbits are *herbivores,* which means that they eat only plants. Both wild and pet rabbits can spend many hours in a day nibbling away. During your rabbit studies, wouldn't it be fun to have a rabbit lunch one day? Have volunteers bring in items from the list of rabbit foods (that are suitable for human consumption). Arrange the ingredients on a long table and provide bowls, forks, and napkins. Then encourage each child to take a sampling of each of the rabbit foods. If you'd like to round things off from a people point of view, add salad dressings and crackers!

The Spring Rabbit
Written by Joyce Dunbar
Illustrated by Susan Varley
Published by Lothrop, Lee & Shepard Books

Though fictitious in nature, this tender tale relates the hardships of waiting—whether it be for a new sibling, or just for the arrival of spring. After discussing this story, tell youngsters that baby rabbits are born in the spring or summer when the weather is warm enough for them to survive. Looking at your months chart, determine together which months your class thinks are warm enough for baby rabbits where you live. Then share a fascinating, nonfiction book about the birth and growth of rabbits—See How They Grow: *Rabbit* by Angela Royston (Lodestar Books). After sharing this book, be sure to keep it available for close individual observation.

My Rabbit Book

Help summarize some of the rabbit information that your little ones have acquired with this little rabbit book. For each child, duplicate pages 150 and 151. Have each child cut apart her pages. Read page 1 together; then encourage her to complete the page as she likes. Next read page 2 together. Guide each child to determine that the pictured rabbit is a pet rabbit. From memory, or by looking in one of your nonfiction rabbit resources, have her draw foods that are suitable for a pet rabbit. Then read page 3 together. Encourage each child to look through your resources to find a particular kind of rabbit. Paying close attention to the chosen rabbit's features, encourage each child to illustrate that rabbit and copy the name of it on the page. Invite her to also give her rabbit a name and write it in the blank. To finish the book, color the title page, sequence the cover and pages, and staple them together along the left edge. Have each child share her rabbit book during a group time.

My Rabbit Book

by Nicholas Bruck

There are many different kinds of rabbits. Here is one that I like.

It is called ___ English Lop Spot

I will name it ___

More Rabbit Reading

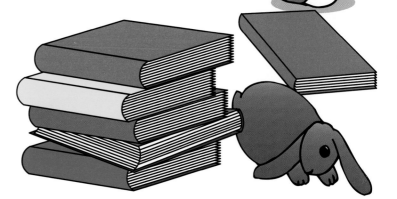

Fiction

Goldilocks And The Three Hares
By Heidi Petach
Published by Putnam & Grosset

Jackrabbit
Written by Jonathan London
Published by Crown Publishers, Inc.

Rabbit's Good News
By Ruth Lercher Bornstein
Published by Clarion Books

To Rabbittown
By April Halprin Wayland
Published by Scholastic Inc.

The Spring Hat
By Madelaine Gill
Published by Simon & Schuster

The Tale Of Rabbit And Coyote
By Tony Johnston
Published by G. P. Putnam's Sons

Nonfiction

See How They Grow: Rabbit
By Barrie Watts
Published by Lodestar Books

Pet Care Guides For Kids: Rabbit
By Mark Evans
Published by Dorling Kindersley, Inc.

First Pets: Rabbits
By Kate Petty
Published by Gloucester Press

Rabbit Pattern

Use with "Every Bunny's Different; Every Bunny's Special" on page 147.

My Rabbit Book

by

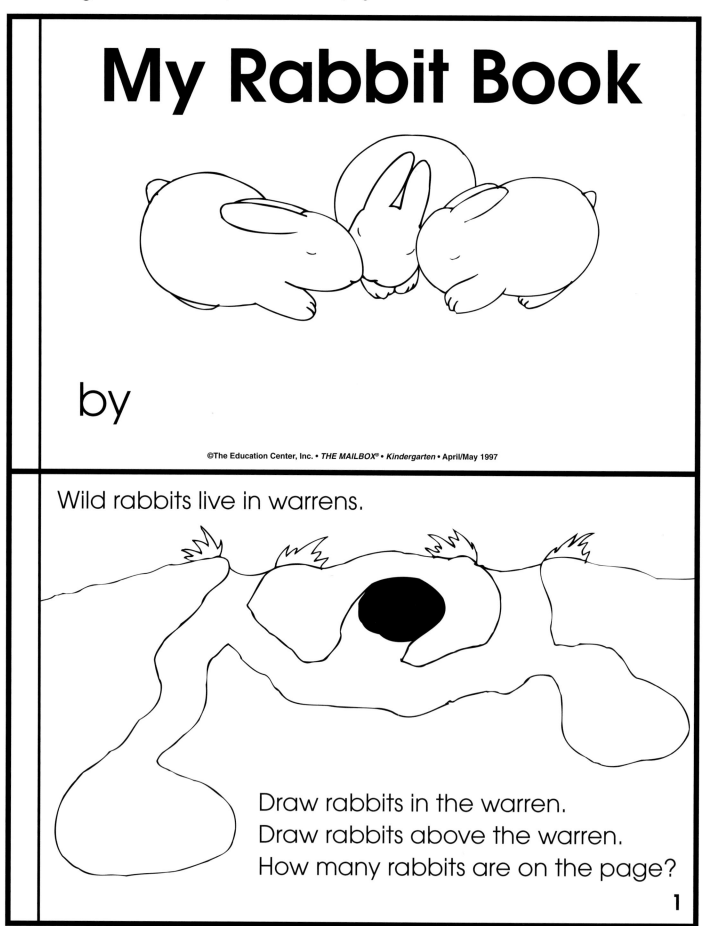

©The Education Center, Inc. • THE MAILBOX® • Kindergarten • April/May 1997

Wild rabbits live in warrens.

Draw rabbits in the warren.
Draw rabbits above the warren.
How many rabbits are on the page?

1

What can this rabbit eat?
Draw it on the page.

2

There are many different kinds of rabbits.
Here is one that I like.

It is called _____.

I will name it _____.

3

Down At The Pond

What's happening down at the pond? Plenty! Use this multidisciplinary unit to discover the natural wonders of animal life at the pond.

ideas by Lucia Kemp Henry and Mackie Rhodes

"Pond-erables"

To get things started, arrange a well-supervised trip to a pond that offers lots of hands-on experiences to ponder. Encourage students to identify, photograph, and observe as many different animals as they can. If a trip to a pond is not possible, use a resource book such as *Pond Life* by Barbara Taylor (Dorling Kindersley, Inc.) or *Pond & River* by Steve Parker (Alfred A. Knopf, Inc.) to introduce students to various pond animals. Extend your introduction by inviting resource personnel—such as a naturalist, a park ranger, or a Cooperative Extension agent—to bring in some common pond dwellers. Youngsters will find pond life fascinating—naturally!

A Pond With A View

Ever wonder what it's like to be right on a pond? Give youngsters a duck's-eye view of a pond with Nancy Tafuri's *Have You Seen My Duckling?* (Greenwillow Books). As you share this story, ask students to search each illustration to find the many different pond inhabitants. Then write a child-generated list of pond animals on chart paper. After naming as many animals as they can remember from the book, have youngsters brainstorm other pond dwellers. Then invite a few students at a time to illustrate some of the listed animals in the margins and open spaces on the paper. What a view!

ducks
fish
frog
beaver
turtle
birds
snail

Critters At The Pond

Reinforce the identification of pond creatures and their printed names with this song. To prepare, duplicate, color, and cut out the patterns on page 160. If desired, create a pond scene as shown. Then laminate each piece and prepare it for magnetboard use. (If you don't have a magnetboard, use Sticky-Tac to attach the animals to the pond.) Photocopy the name cards (page 160) on construction paper; then also prepare them for magnetboard use. Display the pond on your magnetboard; then add each pond creature and its name card as you sing about it.

(sung to the tune of "Are You Sleeping?")

[Beavers] live here. [Beavers] live here.
At the pond. At the pond.
[Beavers] eat and rest here.
[Beavers] feel the best here.
At the pond. At the pond.

Repeat the song, each time replacing the underlined word with one of the following: *dragonflies, crayfish, turtles, snails, fish, ducks,* or *frogs.*

beaver

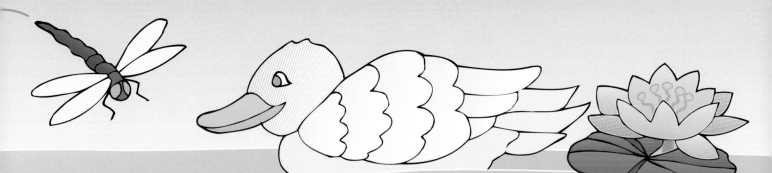

Pond Pizzazz

Create a dazzling pond display with these specialized finger paintings. Have each child create a pond-water effect by swirling blue and green finger paints on finger-paint paper. Invite her to sprinkle iridescent glitter or salt over her wet painting. Then arrange the dry, sparkly paintings on a bulletin board—overlapping the edges—to resemble a pond. Encourage children to decorate the area surrounding the pond with various plant cutouts. Use this pond display as a background for "Pond Spies." The result? A pond with pizzazz!

Pond Spies

This daily pond-inspection center will keep youngsters "ac-count-able" for their visual skills and counting practice. To prepare, duplicate a supply of the graph (page 161). Also duplicate and color a supply of the animal patterns (page 160). Cut out and laminate each pattern. Each day, choose a small group of students to pin a desired number of each animal to the pond scene created in "Pond Pizzazz." Have students count, then graph, the number of each animal type. If desired, enlarge the graph and do this activity as a whole-group project. Let's see…"Today at the pond, I spy…."

Wiggle, Waddle, Whirl

Youngsters will discover that movement is a way of life down at the pond when you share *In The Small, Small Pond* by Denise Fleming (Henry Holt And Company). In advance, convert your water table into a simulated pond. Then gather an assortment of waterproof craft items—such as small plastic lids, sheets of craft foam, foam trays, egg cups, and packing pieces. Also provide wiggle eyes, pipe cleaners, fabric paints, and a waterproof glue, such as Plaid® Tacky Glue. After sharing the story, discuss the different pond animals and their movements. Then invite each child to create his own pond creature using the provided materials. Have him experiment— moving his creature in various ways in your pond. Then invite each child to snap a photo or draw a picture of his creature. Mount each picture on paper; then have the child write/dictate a description of his creature's movements, such as "Wiggle, wobble. Tadpoles are wiggly!" Bind the pages into a class book titled "In Our Small, Small Pond." Share the book, inviting each child to tell about his page.

Wiggle, wobble. Tadpoles are wiggly!

by Tim

Wake Up, Pond!

Engage students in some organized "pond-emonium" with this activity. To begin, read aloud *Good Morning, Pond* by Alyssa Satin Capucilli (Hyperion Books For Children). Then discuss the different sounds and movements that indicate that it's wake-up time at the pond. Invite each child to select an animal to imitate. Have the students group themselves according to where each animal would be found at the pond—*on, around,* or *in* the pond. Have students who select animals that can be found in more than one pond location decide which group they will join. After the groups are formed, call one of the locations—"On the pond," "In the pond," or "Around the pond"—and have the animals in that group "wake up" and perform their distinctive movements and noises. When you say, "Good night," have that group go back to its place. Continue in the same manner with the other groups. When you say, " 'Pond-emonium,' " *all* the animals will "wake up" and begin their activities. It's wake-up time at the pond—let the "pond-emonium" begin!

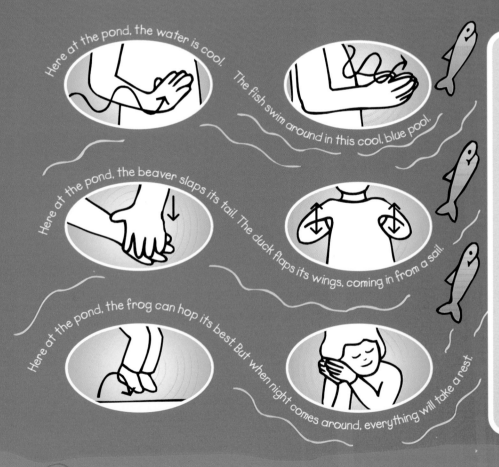

Here at the pond, the water is cool. The fish swim around in this cool, blue pool.

Here at the pond, the beaver slaps its tail. The duck flaps its wings, coming in from a sail.

Here at the pond, the frog can hop its best. But when night comes around, everything will take a rest.

Pond Action Poem

Use this poem and the corresponding motions to get students into reading, science, oral language, and movement. First write the poem on a sheet of chart paper. After you've introduced the poem to your students, put it in your art area during center time. Encourage children to drop by and contribute to illustrating the page.

Here at the pond,
The water is cool.
The fish swim around
In this cool, blue pool.

Here at the pond,
The beaver slaps its tail.
The duck flaps its wings,
Coming in from a sail.

Here at the pond,
The frog can hop its best.
But when night comes around,
Everything will take a rest.

My Little Pond Book

Here's a book for little ones to prepare and ponder. For each child, duplicate pages 157–159. Have each child cut out his animal patterns, cover, and pages. Help the child read each page and name the pictured animals. Have him complete each page by gluing each animal in the appropriate space and writing the correct numeral in the box. Then have him sequence the pages behind the cover and staple the book along the left edge. Invite him to color each page as he likes. Then encourage youngsters to take their books home to share with their families.

Paper-Plate Pond Craft

These 3-D pond crafts are fun to make and impressive to look at. To make one, you will need a thin white paper plate, green wrapping paper or magazine scraps, blue and green tempera paint, paintbrushes, crayons, scissors, glue, and a stapler. (Optional materials: sand, pipe cleaners, small sticks or twigs, and the pond animal patterns from page 160.)

1. Cut the plate so that one section is approximately one inch wider than the other. Color the top portion of the front side of the wider piece brown. (Or, if desired, apply glue to that portion and sprinkle on sand. When the glue is dry, shake off the excess sand; then glue on pieces of twigs or sticks.)

2. Cut green paper scraps to resemble pond plant life. Glue these cutouts to the colored plate. Also add pipe-cleaner accents, if desired.

3. Paint the back side of the smaller plate piece with blue/green tempera paint. When the paint dries, staple the painted piece to the larger piece, as shown.

4. Use art supplies to make pond animals. Or duplicate, color, and cut out the animal patterns from page 160. Glue the animals to the scene as you like.

Display each child's finished project on a board titled "Down At The Pond."

A Pool Of Pond Literature

All Eyes On The Pond
Written by Michael J. Rosen
Illustrated by Tom Leonard
Published by Hyperion Books For Children

In The Pond
By Ermanno Cristini and Luigi Puricelli
Published by Picture Book Studio USA

Jump, Frog, Jump!
Written by Robert Kalan
Illustrated by Byron Barton
Published by Greenwillow Books

Lily Pad Pond
Written & Photographed by Bianca Lavies
Published by E. P. Dutton

Pond Life: A New True Book
Written by Lynn M. Stone
Published by Children's Press

Pond Year
Written by Kathryn Lasky
Illustrated by Mike Bostock
Published by Candlewick Press

Splash!
Written & Illustrated by Ann Jonas
Published by Greenwillow Books

Book Cover

The Pond

by _____

Book Pages

Use with "My Little Pond Book" on page 155.

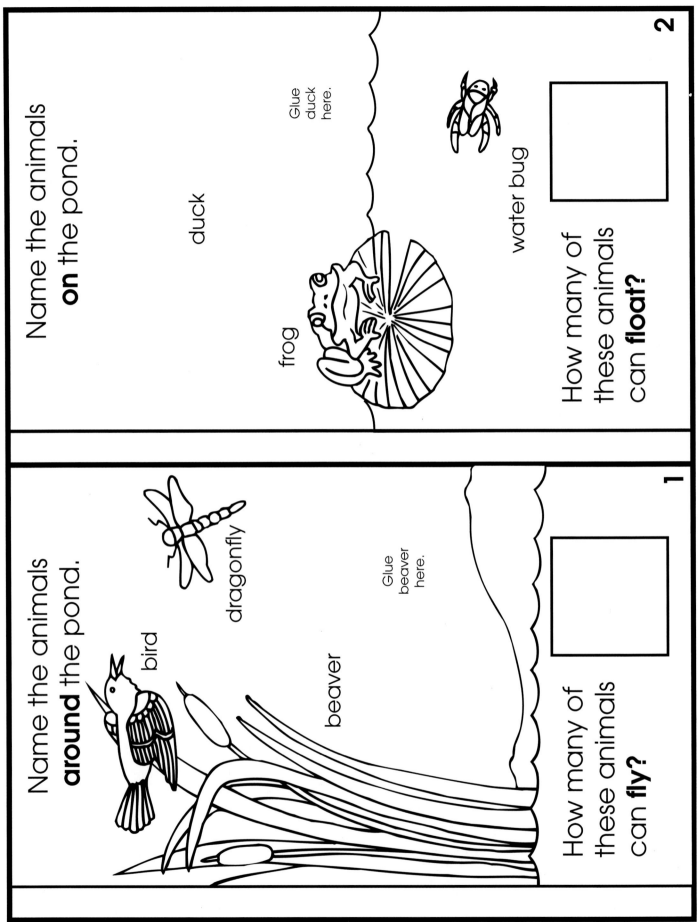

2

Name the animals **on** the pond.

duck

Glue duck here.

frog

water bug

How many of these animals can **float?**

1

Name the animals **around** the pond.

dragonfly

bird

beaver

Glue beaver here.

How many of these animals can **fly?**

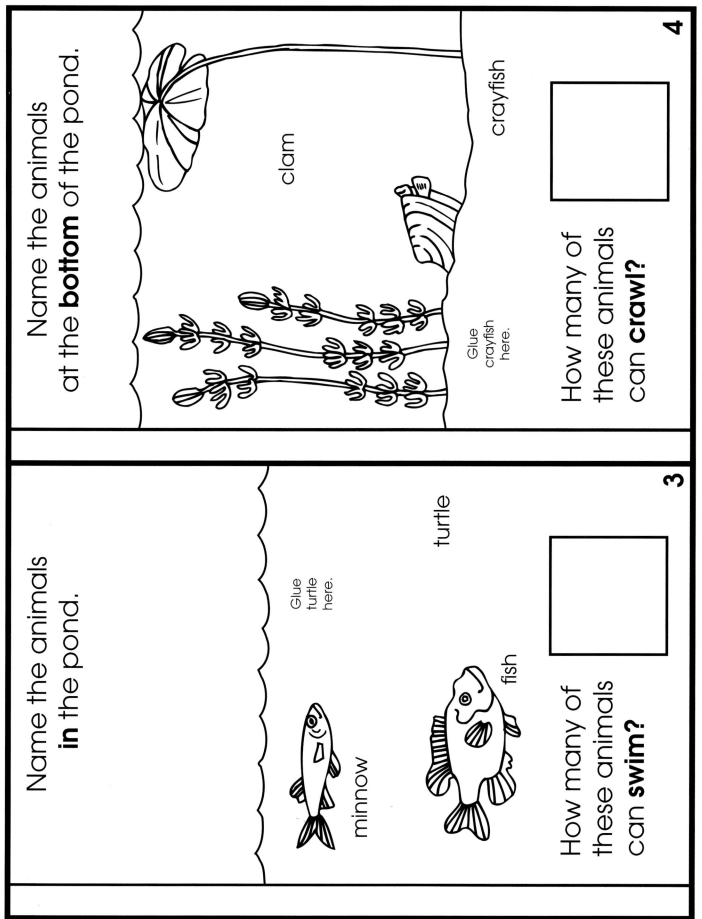

Name the animals at the **bottom** of the pond.

clam

crayfish

Glue crayfish here.

How many of these animals can **crawl?**

4

Name the animals **in** the pond.

turtle

Glue turtle here.

fish

minnow

How many of these animals can **swim?**

3

Flannelboard Pieces

Use with "Critters At The Pond" on page 152, "Pond Spies" on page 153, and "Paper-Plate Pond Craft" on page 155.

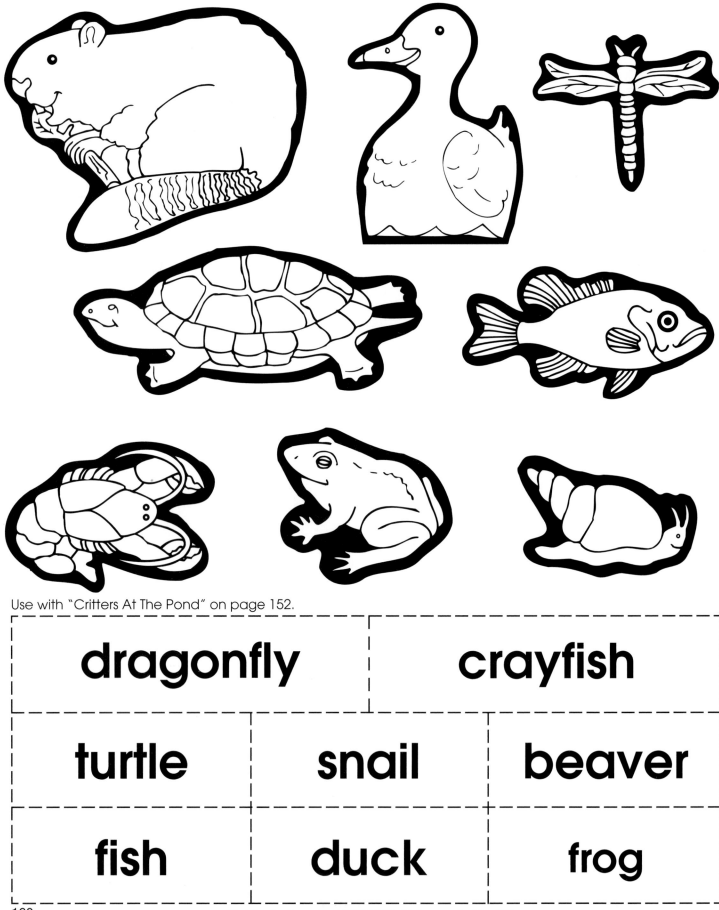

Use with "Critters At The Pond" on page 152.

dragonfly	crayfish
turtle	snail	beaver
fish	duck	frog

snail

frog

crayfish

fish

turtle

dragonfly

duck

beaver

©The Education Center, Inc. • THE MAILBOX® • Kindergarten • April/May 1997

All Aboard Boats

Your seafaring students will enjoy a cross-curricular cruise as they navigate these boat-related activities. Anchors aweigh!

ideas contributed by Lucia Kemp Henry

Boats We Know

Launch your boat unit with a brief inquiry to discover what youngsters already know about boats and their power sources. Record student responses on a large boat-shaped cutout. Then read aloud *Boat Book* by Gail Gibbons (Holiday House). Afterward invite youngsters to add any additional information to the list. Now that youngsters are on board, it's launch time. Bon voyage!

Drifting Along

Launch youngsters into the sea of make-believe with this boat converted from a large refrigerator box. To make the boat, cut off the top and two opposing sides of the box. Cut the remaining two opposing sides to resemble the shape of a boat as shown (fig. 3); then gently curve and tape the bow together. Invite small groups of students to take turns painting the boat. Print a class-generated name on the boat's bow. Then equip the boat with toy oars and flotation cushions or life jackets.

During center time, invite youngsters to take an imaginary voyage on the boat as you play a recording of gentle, flowing music such as Greg and Steve's "Quiet Time" on *We All Live Together, Volume I* (Youngheart Records: 1-800-444-4287). Have each student illustrate his voyage; then ask the children to share their illustrations with the class. Afterward move the boat to the reading center and invite students to use it as a cozy reading refuge.

Go Boats, Go!

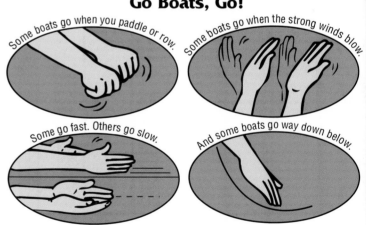

Some boats go when you paddle or row.

Some boats go when the strong winds blow.

Some go fast. Others go slow.

And some boats go way down below.

Reinforce students' nautical knowledge with this action rhyme. Invite the children to perform the actions suggested for each line; then ask them to name one or more boats that travel in each way mentioned. If desired, have youngsters use *Boat Book* to find pictures representing each line of the rhyme.

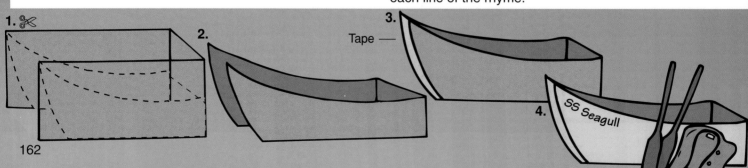

1. ✂
2.
3. Tape —
4. SS Seagull

Boatbuilder's Workshop

Cultivate some watercraft creativity with this simple idea. Provide an assortment of lightweight, waterproof craft items—such as foam meat trays, craft foam sheets, balsa wood pieces, sponges, film canisters, and craft sticks. Invite each child to use the craft materials and Plaid® Tacky Glue to create her own boat. Have each child write/dictate a description of her boat; then display each boat with its description in a special maritime museum.

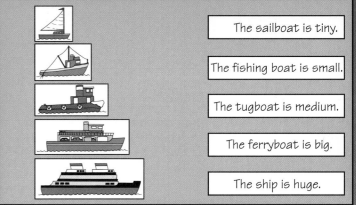

The sailboat is tiny.

The fishing boat is small.

The tugboat is medium.

The ferryboat is big.

The ship is huge.

All Kinds Of Boats

Coast into some size comparisons with this boat sequencing activity. To prepare, duplicate the boat picture cards on page 165 on tagboard. Color each picture card; then laminate the cards for durability. During a small-group activity, write a student-dictated description of the size of each boat on a separate sentence strip. Have youngsters sequence the cards according to boat size, then match each sentence strip to its corresponding card. Students are sure to stay on course with this concept-building activity.

Hey-Ho, On A Boat!

Harbor your class boat (from the activity "Drifting Along" on page 162) in the dramatic play area for additional make-believe fun. Teach youngsters this song to sing as they incorporate the boat in their imaginary play. Encourage them to replace the bold-face word with a different boat name—such as *sailboat, tugboat,* or *speedboat*—each time the song is repeated.

Water-Table Harbor

Entice youngsters to investigate the floating abilities of their boats (see "Boatbuilder's Workshop") with *My Boat* by Kay Davies and Wendy Oldfield (Gareth Stevens Publishing). Prepare a harbor by partially filling your water table; then use mounting tape to attach several plastic hooks above the water level. After sharing the book, have each child in a small group attach a length of yarn to the bow of his boat, then put his boat into the harbor to test its buoyancy. Does the boat float? If not, can adjustments be made so that it will float?

To expand this activity, encourage youngsters to use small plastic people, animals, and cars as cargo for their boats. Invite them to dock their boats by tying them to the hooks along the sides of the harbor. If desired, videotape/photograph youngsters as they immerse themselves in their world of watercraft.

(sung to the tune of "Bingo")

I wish I had a special boat,
A **rowboat** made for me-O!
Hey-ho, on a boat.
Hey-ho, on a boat.
Hey-ho, on a boat.
A **rowboat** made for me-O!

A Boat Poem

Introduce the names of some different bodies of water when you teach students this poem about boat sizes.

A great big fishing boat sails on the sea
And rides the waves all day.

A tall sailboat coasts smoothly along
The water in the bay.

A little rowboat glides on the lake,
Steered by its wooden oars.

A small raft drifts slowly on the pond
Close to the grassy shores.

A tiny boat bounces in the tub
With bath-time fun for me.

So many boats, both big and small,
On pond and lake and sea!

My Boat Book

Navigate each youngster through this book-making activity. For each child, duplicate the book pages and patterns (pages 166–168) on construction paper. Have each child cut out each book page and pattern piece. Then give her two 7 1/4" x 6" pieces of construction paper for book covers. Have her glue the title pattern to one cover, then draw or sponge-paint boat shapes around it. Instruct her to color the picture on each page, adding details—such as waves, fish, and seagulls—as desired. Then have the child glue each remaining pattern onto its corresponding page. Ask her to draw a picture of herself on the dock on page three. Staple the sequenced pages between the covers; then invite each child to take home her book to share with her family. Ships ahoy!

Shipshape Stories

Boats
Written and Illustrated by Anne Rockwell
Published by E. P. Dutton, Inc.

The Boats On The River
Written by Marjorie Flack
Illustrated by Jay Hyde Barnum
Published by The Viking Press

I Love Boats
Written and Illustrated by Flora McDonnell
Published by Candlewick Press

Big City Port
Written by Betsy Maestro and Ellen DelVecchio
Illustrated by Giulio Maestro
Published by Four Winds Press

My Blue Boat
Written and Illustrated by Chris L. Demarest
Published by Harcourt Brace & Company

Tugboat Parade

Use this activity to gently tug youngsters into some sequencing practice. Mask the word *tugboat* on the tugboat picture card on page 165; then enlarge the card. Make 26 construction-paper duplicates of the enlarged copy. Write a different letter or glue a different letter cutout on each card; then laminate the cards. Invite each youngster, in turn, to create a tugboat parade by alphabetically sequencing the cards. For a variation, program the cards with numerals. Here comes the tugboat parade. Toot! Toot!

My Boat Book

Cheri

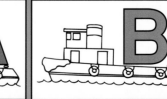

Hop aboard and take a trip.

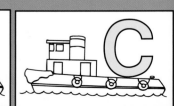

Boat Picture Cards

Use with "All Kinds Of Boats" on page 163 and "Tugboat Parade" on page 164.

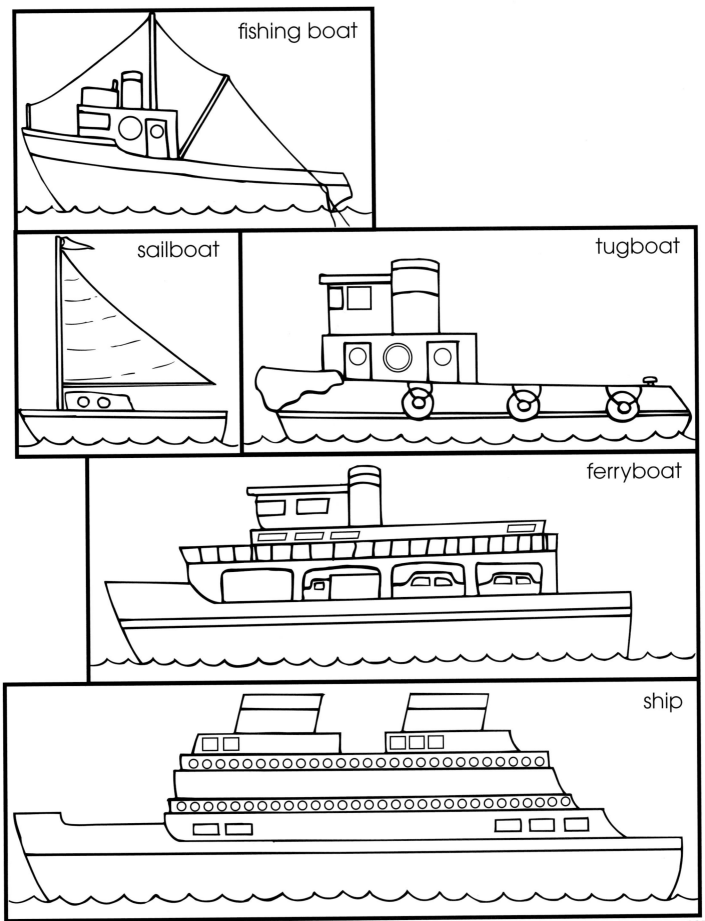

fishing boat

sailboat

tugboat

ferryboat

ship

Book Page And Patterns

Use with "My Boat Book" on page 164.

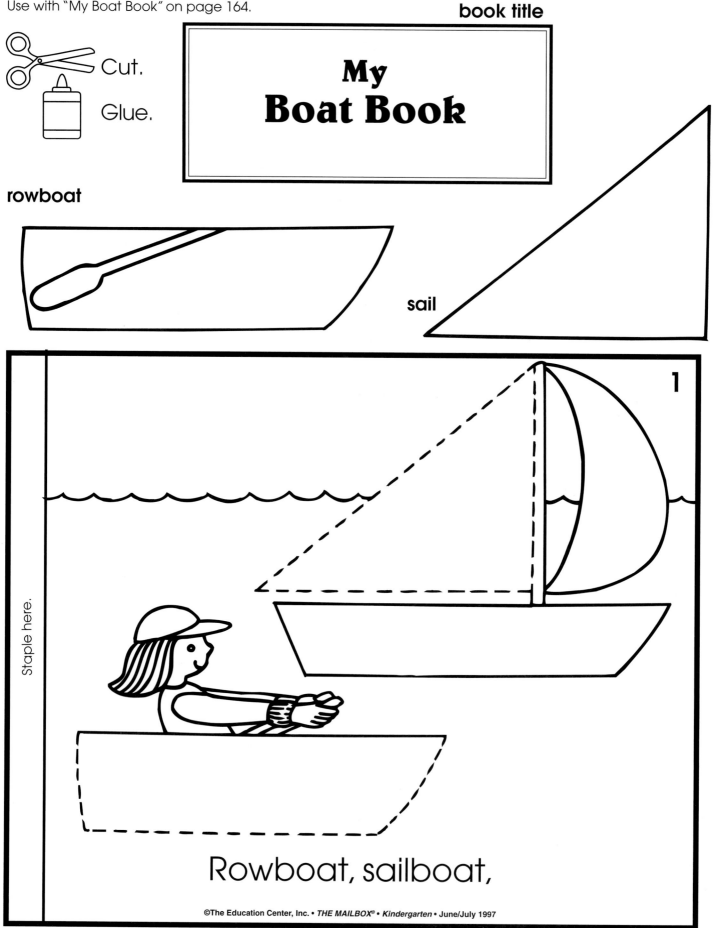

Cut.

Glue.

book title

My Boat Book

rowboat

sail

Staple here.

1

Rowboat, sailboat,

Cut.

Glue.

ship top

tugboat top

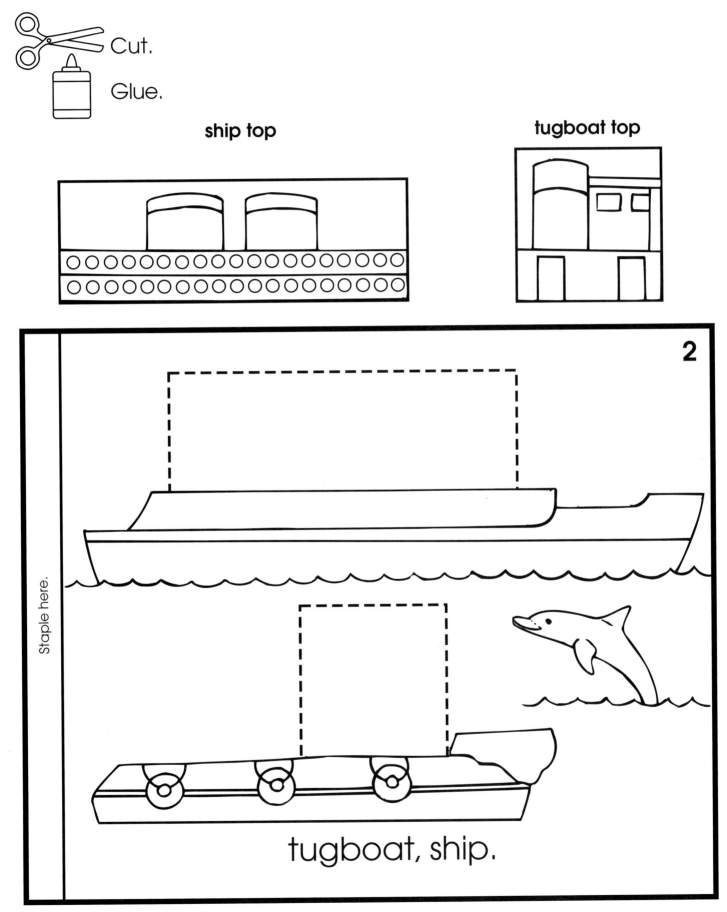

2

Staple here.

tugboat, ship.

Book Page And Patterns

Use with "My Boat Book" on page 164.

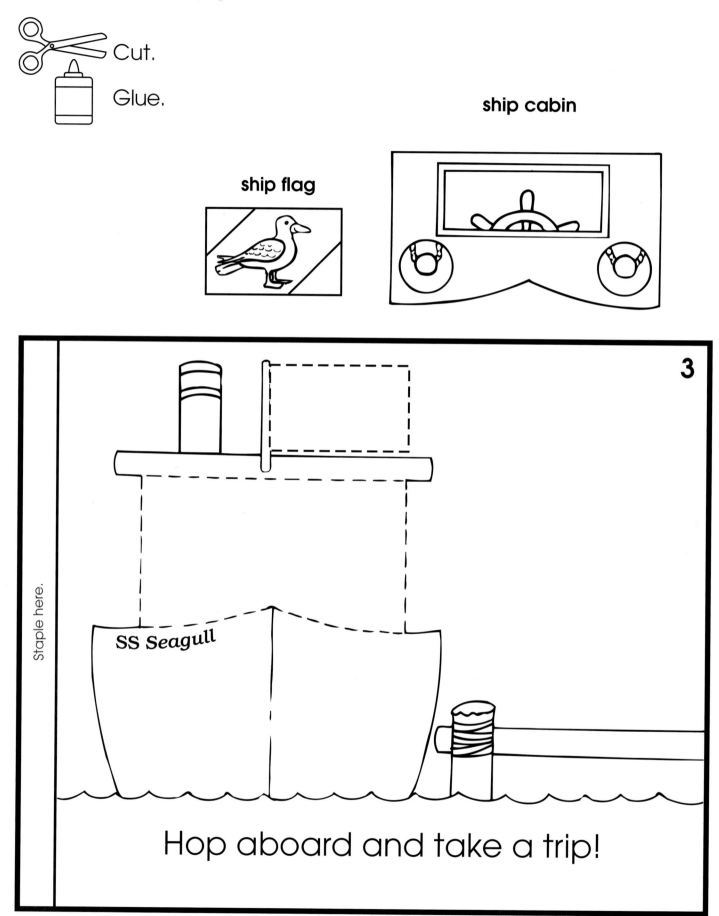

Cut.

Glue.

ship flag

ship cabin

3

Staple here.

SS *Seagull*

Hop aboard and take a trip!

flipper

**Pattern
Dolphin Puppet And Book Cover**
Use with "Dolphin Puppet" and "One Little Dolphin"
on page 172, and "Dolphin Books" on page 173.

Dolphin Delights!

Dive into the delights of dolphins—and lots of learning fun—with this collection of multidisciplinary activities.

ideas contributed by Lucia Kemp Henry

Dancing With Dolphins

Begin your dolphin studies by reading aloud *The Girl Who Danced With Dolphins* by Frank DeSaix (Farrar Straus Giroux). In this dream-like, underwater world, the author and artist entice youngsters to experience the mysteries and the comforts of these fascinating marine mammals. After discussing the story, dive into fact and fantasy by asking your students to discuss which parts of the book they think could have happened and which parts are strictly imaginary. Are there any parts of the story that students are unsure about? If so, record the parts in question on a sheet of chart paper. Encourage students to watch for related information that might answer their questions as you continue your study of dolphins.

Commerson's dolphin (4–5 feet)
Dusky dolphin (4–6 feet)
spinner dolphin (5–7 feet)
spotted dolphin (6–9 feet)
bottlenose dolphin (9–15 feet)
Risso's dolphin (10–14 feet)

Meet The Family

Much to the surprise of many people, dolphins are part of the family known as *toothed whales*. There are more than 60 species that belong to this family, ranging from the small *Amazon River dolphin* to the very large *sperm whale*. (*Dolphins: Our Friends In The Sea* by Judith E. Rinard, published by National Geographic Society, comes with a large, color poster depicting many of the species.)

Since rhythm and rhyme always aid in absorbing information, use the poem at right to introduce your youngsters to just a few of the members of this family. In advance, write the poem on a sheet of chart paper. As you read the poem with your students, display the dolphin pictures (pages 174–175). Prompt children to try to identify each dolphin featured in the poem. Then discuss the similarities and differences among the other dolphins.

Many Different Dolphins

Many kinds of dolphins
Swim the oceans blue.
And here you'll see some dolphins
Swimming by for me and you!

First a **spotted dolphin**
With spots upon its skin.
It leaps out of the water,
Then arcs to dive back in.

Next a **spinner dolphin**,
That has a certain flair,
For leaping from the water
And spinning in midair!

Next a **Commerson's dolphin**
With skin of white and black.
Its dorsal fin is rounded
Past the middle of its back.

And now a **bottlenose dolphin**.
He's just as smart as he can be!
Whether he's clowning for a crowd,
Or swimming—wild and free!

Long On Dolphins

Since most of your youngsters have never been up close—and—personal with a dolphin, use this activity to bring them a little closer together. Use an opaque projector to project the bottlenose dolphin pattern (page 175) onto a long sheet of mural paper. Position the projector so that the dolphin image reaches approximately nine feet in length. Trace the pattern; then color and cut it out. After laminating the cutout, place it on the floor in a carpeted area or mount it on a wall. Encourage children to interact with the dolphin pattern, then talk about their sizes and its size. If desired, use a permanent marker to record children's responses on the dolphin pattern.

Pam Crane

Hey, Buddy—I'm *Not* A Fish!

Here are some facts that, when learned, your young scientists will be only too proud to share with others. Explain that although dolphins are right at home in the water, they are not fish. In fact, dolphins are mammals—like dogs, cats, cows, and even people! There are two easy ways to tell:

1. Dolphins breathe air. A dolphin breathes through a *blowhole* on the top of its head. An adult dolphin can stay underwater for up to seven minutes, but it must eventually surface to breathe air.

2. While swimming, dolphins move their tails up and down. Fish move their tails from side to side. To demonstrate this fact, teach your youngsters the following chant, along with the accompanying motions.

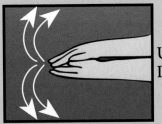

Up and down. Up and down.
Dolphin tails go up and down.

Side to side. Side to side.
Fish tails move from side to side.

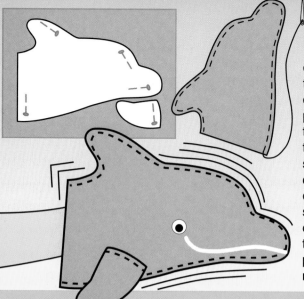

Dolphin Puppet

Enlist the help of your students to create one—or many!—of these dolphin puppets and you'll have a wonderful manipulative to use throughout your study of dolphins. First make a paper tracer from the dolphin pattern on page 169. Pin the body and flipper patterns to a piece of felt; then cut them out. Repeat the process so that you have two of each piece. Then stitch or glue (using craft glue) the edges of the two body pieces together, leaving the straight edge open. Next stitch or glue a flipper onto each side of the body. (If you're sewing, be careful not to sew the pattern together!) Glue a wiggle eye to each side of the body; then use dimensional fabric paint to paint a mouth on each side. If desired, gently stuff the dolphin's forehead and beak with a bit of tissue paper. To use the puppet, have a child insert her hand into the puppet with her fingers closed and her palm down. Holding the puppet this way will help youngsters imitate lifelike dolphin movements.

One Little Dolphin

This little poem will provide your youngsters with some dolphin information and it will also help reinforce position words. Have a child manipulate a dolphin puppet (see "Dolphin Puppet" above) in accompaniment to the poem. If desired, a child may hold his free arm parallel to the floor to represent the surface of the ocean or to mimic the motion of a wave.

One little dolphin swims all around.
First she swims **up.** Then she swims **down**.

One little dolphin likes to jump and spin.
First she jumps **out.** Then she dives back **in.**

One little dolphin finds a wave to ride upon.
First she is **off**. And then she is **on.**

One little dolphin so sleek and trim,
Leaps **over** the sea, then **under** again.

Dolphin Action Song

The melody is familiar, but you'll want to coax your youngsters to provide some of the action lyrics to this song. Write the song on a sheet of chart paper. Then sing the song with your youngsters. Afterward ask them to name other action words that a dolphin might do, such as *diving, leaping, floating, splashing, gliding,* and *eating*. Each time you sing the song, insert a new action word.

(sung to the tune of "Twinkle, Twinkle, Little Star")

Dolphin, dolphin, in the sea,
Dolphin, dolphin, wild and free.
Swimming, swimming in the sea.
Just as free as you can be.
Dolphin, dolphin, in the sea,
Swimming, swimming wild and free.

Dolphin Books

By using the patterns on page 169, your youngsters can create adorable dolphin books. Scan the options below and choose the ones that best suit your classroom needs. To make one book, duplicate the cover and flipper patterns on construction paper. Cut out the patterns; then use the body pattern as a tracer to make several book pages and a back cover. Staple the pages between the two covers along the left edge, then glue on the flipper.

All About Dolphins: Youngsters will be proud to record and share their newly acquired knowledge in their very own dolphin-shaped books. As each child makes new dolphin discoveries, suggest that he write about and illustrate each new fact on a page of his book. Encourage children to share their books during group time.

Dolphins can jump real high.

Dog

D Is For Dolphin: When your students make this book, all ears will endeavor to discover the sound of *D*—sometimes when you least expect it! Encourage youngsters to be on the lookout for pictures of words that begin with *D.* Then have each child glue her pictures or write/draw *D* words in her dolphin book. If necessary, add more pages to the dolphin books and see who can make the biggest dolphin around!

Dolphin-Dinner Counting: Math skills will make a new splash when your students create books that feature a dolphin's favorite food. Program the bottom of each page with "fish for dinner." Have each child create a book page for each of the numbers *one* to *ten.* Encourage the child to write a large numeral on each page and illustrate that many fish. Fish may be made by coloring, painting, rubber stamping, using stickers, or gluing on magazine pictures. What a dolphin delicacy!

1 fish for dinner.

2 fish for dinner.

Pelorus Jack was a pilot for ships.

Nine True Dolphin Stories

By Margaret Davidson
Illustrated by Roger Wilson
Published by Hastings House

In this book, Margaret Davidson offers a collection of fascinating dolphin stories. Although they are not colorfully illustrated, they make wonderful read-alouds. As you share a story with your youngsters, encourage each child to illustrate a part of the story. Afterward bind all of the illustrations together with a title page labeled for that particular story. During a group time, have each child share his page.

Commerson's dolphin
(4–5 feet)

Dusky dolphin
(4–6 feet)

spotted dolphin
(6–9 feet)

spinner dolphin
(5–7 feet)

bottlenose dolphin
(9–13 feet)

Risso's dolphin
(10–14 feet)

Moo-oo-ve Over For Milk

Since June is National Dairy Month, what better time could there be to teach your youngsters a few interesting tidbits about this particular food group? Use the cross-curricular ideas in this unit to get "moo-oo-ving"!

ideas contributed by Rachel Meseke Castro

It's All About Milk

Introduce your dairy studies by reading aloud *No Milk!* by Jennifer A. Ericsson (Tambourine Books). After discussing the story, ask students whether or not they think it would be a big deal if the cow in the story—or any cow, for that matter—were never able to give milk again. Why or why not? As students discuss the question, prompt them to brainstorm a list of foods that are made from milk. Record their responses; then read the list together. After seeing the list of dairy foods, do any of your students want to change their opinions? Summarize the discussion by explaining that all foods that are made from milk are called *dairy products*.

Note: *If you have students with milk allergies, it might be interesting (if they are willing) to have them share what kinds of foods they eat instead of dairy products.*

Pizza Possibilities

In *Extra Cheese, Please! Mozzarella's Journey From Cow To Pizza* (Boyds Mills Press), author Cris Peterson explains the step-by-step process of how milk from her farm becomes the cheese that tops her traditional, Friday night pizza. After sharing this story with your students, use the author's recipe at the end of the book to make pizzas in your classroom. Or use the individual pizza recipe in "Kindergarten Café" (page 299) and have each child make her own single-serving pizza. When your students make and eat their pizzas, prompt them to remember that the cheese started with Annabelle and the dairy farm.

Dairy-O!

Here's a song to help reinforce the dairy basics. In advance, write the song on chart paper. (Since your emergent readers will probably like to track the print as they sing along, you might like to write out "D-A-I-R-Y" three times in each verse.) As you sing together, encourage children to join in as they are able. When the song is familiar to your students—and they are able to identify a variety of dairy foods—place the chart in your art area during center times. Encourage children to illustrate the chart page by coloring pictures—or cutting out and gluing on magazine pictures—of dairy products.

(sung to the tune of "B-I-N-G-O")

There is a food group made from milk,
And dairy is its name-o.
D-A-I-R-Y *(Repeat three times.)*
And dairy is its name-o!

Dairy foods help our bones grow strong
So we will all be healthy.
D-A-I-R-Y *(Repeat three times.)*
And dairy is its name-o!

So we'll drink milk for meals or snacks,
At least two times a day-o.
D-A-I-R-Y *(Repeat three times.)*
And dairy is its name-o!

A Musical Review

Here's a song with a little puppet panache that will reinforce the key concepts in the cheese-making process (see "Pizza Possibilities"). Before you introduce the song to your class, write it on a sheet of chart paper. Also enlarge and photocopy the patterns on page 180. Color, cut out, and laminate the patterns. Then glue each pattern to a wide craft stick. When you introduce the song to your youngsters, show the stick puppets at the appropriate times. When your students are familiar with the song, choose six students at a time to each hold a different puppet. Have those students stand side by side in a line. As the whole class sings the song, encourage those students who are holding puppets to raise them at the appropriate times.

The cheese goes to you.
The cheese goes to you.
You buy it at the grocery store.
The cheese goes to you.

A Food Chain

Visually link your students into understanding the science concept of the food chain. After singing the song from "A Musical Review," give each child six wide construction-paper strips (each approximately 3" x 11"). Prompt children to discuss the main steps in making cheese. (If your students break the process down into more than six steps, give them extra construction-paper strips!) Have each child write or draw a different picture on each of the strips to resemble each step in the process. Then have each child glue his first strip (illustrated with a sun) together to form a link. Encourage each child to make a chain by linking the remaining strips in order. Referring back to and singing the song are allowed! After the chains have been made, discuss how a chain needs every link in order to stay together. (If desired, make an extra chain and use it to demonstrate how the whole chain falls apart if one link is torn apart.) Then encourage each child to take his food chain home and share what he has learned with his family.

sun
hay
cow
cheese
milk
kids

177

Pudding Power

If the proof is in the pudding, this dairy-related, taste-testing activity will be a hit! First arrange several flavors of prepared puddings on a table. Place a serving spoon in each bowl. Also provide a plastic plate, a spoon, and a paper plate for each child. Ask students to predict which flavor will be the class favorite. Next have each child scoop a small amount of each pudding flavor onto his plastic plate, then taste them all. Encourage each child to choose his favorite flavor, then write his name on the paper plate and color it to resemble that flavor. Use sentence strips to label your floor with the pudding flavors; then have each child graph his favorite flavor by placing his colored plate in the appropriate place on the graph. Prompt your students to discuss what the graph reveals.

Hidden Milk

Come out, come out, wherever you are! With this activity, your youngsters will discover that milk is hiding in all kinds of places. In advance, cut out a classroom supply of magazine pictures of dairy foods, being sure to include some tricky ones such as tacos (with cheese) and cheesecake. Mount each picture on a piece of construction paper. Hide the pictures around your classroom. Then inform youngsters that you have hidden pictures of dairy foods around your classroom. At your signal, have each child try to find and bring back one dairy-food picture. When all the children are gathered, have each child share his picture with the group and try to identify where the milk is "hiding." Save the pictures for "Refrigerator Game."

Refrigerator Game

Here's a cool idea to reinforce dairy-related vocabulary and work on following directions at the same time. To prepare, back each of the pictures from "Hidden Milk" with a piece of magnetic tape. Then draw a large refrigerator shape—with horizontal shelves—on a magnetic board. Depending on each child's abilities, give a series of one-, two-, or three-step directions including concepts such as position words and ordinal numbers. For example, you might say, "Please place the ice cream on the top shelf, the yogurt on the middle shelf, and the cream cheese on the bottom shelf." Afterward discuss with your youngsters the importance of refrigerating dairy products.

Swiss Cheese, Please!

Any way you slice it, this center provides great counting practice. For each number that you'd like to include, cut out a tan square of construction paper—these will be bread slices. Program each bread slice with a numeral or number word. Next cut out the same number of slightly smaller squares from manila folders or construction paper—these will be slices of Swiss cheese. For each numeral or number word on a bread slice, punch that many holes in a different slice of cheese. Laminate all the pieces; then place them in a decorated string-tie envelope. To use this center, a child chooses a slice of cheese, counts the holes, and matches it to the corresponding bread slice. For a job well done, you might like to have some crackers and cheese available for this center's participants.

Milk-Shake Surprise

Perhaps one of the most irresistible dairy products is a thick-and-creamy milk shake. Your little ones will be surprised to see what secret ingredient lies in each of these enticing secret shakes. In advance, cut out a classroom supply of white construction-paper milk-shake glasses. On each glass, use a white crayon to secretly write a numeral, letter, or dairy-related message. Begin a discussion by asking students to share what their favorite milk-shake flavors are. Then give each child a cutout. Explain that she may use watercolors to make her shake whatever flavor she'd like. No matter what flavor the child selects, the message will magically appear! Afterward have each child describe her milk shake for the class and tell what her secret message says.

Dairy-Related Literature

Belinda
By Pamela Allen
Published by Puffin Books

The Milk Makers
By Gail Gibbons
Published by Macmillan Publishing Company

From Milk To Ice Cream
By Ali Mitgutsch
Published by Carolrhoda Books, Inc.

Milk Rock
By Jeff Kaufman
Published by Henry Holt And Company, Inc.

No Moon, No Milk!
By Chris Babcock
Illustrated by Mark Teague
Published by Crown Publishers, Inc.

Patterns

Use with "A Musical Review" on page 177.

sun

hay

cow

farmer/milk

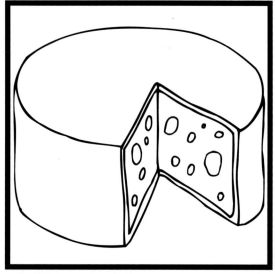

cheese

you

Special Features

Make Way For Manners!

After you...

No, after you...

No, no, I wouldn't even consider it. Please, after you...

Tut, tut, not at all...

Oh, but I must insist!

In those getting-to-know-you stages of the new school year, are your youngsters' manners sometimes a little *less* than desirable? Then start things off on the right foot to get your little ones heading in the right direction for the rest of the school year. Use the ideas and suggestions in this unit to start your classroom running smoothly.

ideas contributed by Lucia Kemp Henry

Mixed-Up Manners

Joanna Cole's *Monster Manners* (Scholastic Inc.) delightfully captures the attention of children, and before you know it—a lesson on manners has slipped on in there! Before sharing the book, ask youngsters to discuss what they think good manners are. Write their responses on chart paper. Then read the book aloud. Through the giggling that is bound to occur, ask youngsters to tell you when they see an example of good manners in the book that you could add to their dictated list. Afterwards discuss the book and your list of good manners.

The Magic Of Manners

If you've introduced and discussed manners (see "Mixed-Up Manners"), your youngsters are ready to do some critical thinking as they search for cause-and-effect situations that occur in *The Bossy Gallito,* retold in English and Spanish by Lucia M. Gonzalez (Scholastic Inc.). Be sure to preview this book so that you'll read it with the appropriate tones of voice! As you share the book, ask youngsters to discuss the behavior of the little gallito and the effects thereof. Then review the story by asking children to state the little gallito's problem and the mounting complications. Ask children what they think changed the tide in the story.

After your discussion, select students to role-play the characters. As you read aloud and the actors act, encourage the audience members to give the thumbs-up sign when they see good manners and the thumbs-down sign when they see bad manners. Repeat the performance until each child has had a chance to be a cast member and an audience member.

More tea?

Please.

OOOHHH... *AAAHHH...* *OOOHHH...* *AAAHHH...*

QUI-QUI-RI-QUI

Oooh! Aaah!

You won't have any trouble keeping your youngsters' attention with this interactive version of a manners lesson. Choose a scenario to enact—in this case, a pretend tea party—and set up any desired props in front of the class. Choose a few students to be your guests. Tell the audience members that as you role-play they are to say, "Buzz!" when they see an example of bad manners, and say, "Oooh! Aaah!" when they see an example of good manners. As you role-play, intentionally use exaggerated bad manners. When you get buzzed, ask a child volunteer to suggest or role-play an example of good manners in the same situation. Then continue acting where you left off.

Making Big Books From Songs

Who can resist the good, old-fashioned songs that have held their ground for years and years? Teachers sang them as children, and your little ones will be eager to do the same. So grab onto this opportunity and turn some of those oldies-but-goodies into classroom literature favorites.

Baa, Baa
Black Sheep!

Baa, Baa, _blue_ sheep,
Have you any wool?
Yes, sir. Yes, sir,
Three bags full.
One for my master.
One for my dame.
And one for the little boy
Who lives down the lane.

Are you sleeping?
Are you sleeping?

Brother John
Brother John

Morning bells are ringing

Morning bells are ringing

Ding, Dong, Ding!

Ding, Dong, Ding!

Colorful Sheep

This appealing takeoff on "Baa, Baa, Black Sheep" helps reinforce a whole flock of language-arts skills and highlights color-word recognition. You can make one big book for the class to share and/or have each child make his own smaller version. Either way, this is an interactive book that's just right for kindergartners.

To make one big book, decide how many colors you would like to include in your book. That will be the number of pages in your book and the number of bows you will need to cut out. Copy the text as shown in black above, leaving a space to insert a color word. Photocopy that text for each page in your book. Then cut a large, white, scalloped construction-paper circle—this will be the sheep's body—for the cover and each page of the book. To each sheep shape, glue on black construction-paper legs and a black face. Use paper hole reinforcements for the eyes and a white circle for the nose.

Bind all of the pages together along the left edges. Next cut out a construction-paper bow (or use real ribbon) in each color that you will include in your book. Laminate the bows. Then attach a small piece of Velcro® to the back of each bow and to the top of each sheep's head. Store the bows in a press-on pocket on the back of the last page of the book. Finally program a different color word—corresponding to the color of the bows—in the text on each page of the book. Write a title on the cover; then you're ready to go!

When you share the book, encourage youngsters to read and/or sing along with you. Also choose a volunteer to find the correct bow to attach to each different sheep.

Jackie Wright—Gr. K and Preschool, Summerhill Children's House, Enid, OK

Rise And Shine

A little musical spark draws children into reading this big book made from the text of "Are You Sleeping?" You will need three large sheets of construction paper. Program them as shown. On the first page, glue on fabric scraps to make a quilt. On the second page, attach a ribbon with a small bell tied to the end. On the last page, draw a boy who is wide awake. When you read this book aloud, ring the bell at the appropriate time. After sharing the book with your class, you might like to offer the supplies for youngsters to make individual books as a center option. Ding! Dong! Ding!

Five green and speckled frogs,
Sat on a speckled log,
Eating some most delicious bugs.
(Yum! Yum!)
One jumped into the pool
Where it was nice and cool.
Now there are...

I know an old lady who
swallowed a three.
How could that be?
She swallowed a three!

She swallowed the three to
catch the two.
She swallowed the two to
catch the one.
But what can be done?
She swallowed a one!
Perhaps she'll die.

four green speckled frogs.
(Ribbit, Ribbit, Ribbit, Ribbit.)

Four green and speckled frogs,
Sat on a speckled log,
Eating some most delicious bugs.
(Yum! Yum!)
One jumped into the pool
Where it was nice and cool.
Now there are...

three green speckled frogs.
(Ribbit, Ribbit, Ribbit.)

Three green and speckled frogs,
Sat on a speckled log,
Eating some most delicious bugs.
(Yum! Yum!)
One jumped into the pool
Where it was nice and cool.
Now there are...

Eat It All Up

Take that old lady who swallowed a fly, give it a twist, and you've got a motivating, math-related big book! Enlarge and photocopy the old-lady pattern (page 185) five times on different sheets of construction paper. Color; then laminate each page and a cover page. Bind the pages together. Then use a permanent marker to write the appropriate text across from each picture (see below).

Before you share your book, read aloud *I Know An Old Lady Who Swallowed A Fly* retold and illustrated by Nadine Bernard Westcott (Little, Brown And Company). Then introduce *your* big-book version. As you read the text on each page, ask a child to use a dry-erase marker to write the indicated numeral on the old lady's apron. Also encourage children to use the book independently and write numerals in the blank spaces on the rest of the pages for additional numeral-writing practice. When a child is through with the book, he simply wipes his writing off with a tissue.

Brenda Hume, Sangaree Elementary School, Summerville, SC

I know an old lady who swallowed a one.
What can be done? She swallowed a one!
Perhaps she'll die.

I know an old lady who swallowed a two.
What will she do? She swallowed a two.
She swallowed the two to catch the one.
But what can be done? She swallowed a one!
Perhaps she'll die.

I know an old lady who swallowed a three.
How could that be? She swallowed a three....

I know an old lady who swallowed a four.
Her throat must be sore if she swallowed a four....

I know an old lady who swallowed a five.
She's no longer alive!

Disappearing Frogs

This big book is a countdown of frog fun to the tune of "Five Green And Speckled Frogs." To make the book, photocopy the frog strips (page 186) on construction paper; then color the frogs and cut out the strips. Next cut out two identically sized construction-paper logs. Write the text on the pages as shown. Next glue the appropriate frog strip to the top of each page. Then staple the pages together. Your kids will be jumping at the chance to be the reader of this big book.

No green speckled frogs.

(Glub, Glub.)

Ribbit

Ribbit

Frog-Strip Patterns

Use with "Disappearing Frogs" on page 184.

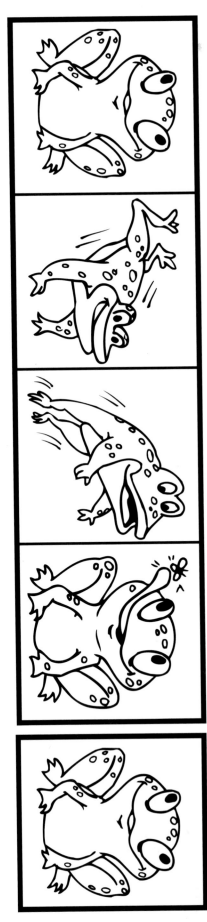

Monkeying Around With Measurement

What do you get when you give measurement tools to a group of fun-loving children? Youngsters who go wild over measuring! So pull out a variety of standard and nonstandard measurement tools to equip your little ones for these measurement explorations. Then let the monkey business begin!

ideas by Mary Rice

Why Measure?

Help students swing smoothly from one branch of thought to another as they discover the answers to the question, "Why measure?" To begin, give each child a sugar cookie. As the students enjoy their treats, ask them what ingredients go into sugar cookies. As children speculate, list the named ingredients on chart paper. Then involve children in pretending to make a batch of cookies following their dictations. (For example, if sugar was named, ask a child to pretend to bring you some sugar.) As you pretend to pour *all* of the sugar into a bowl, prompt thinking by making comments such as, "This sure looks like a lot of sugar!" or "Will all of our ingredients fit in this bowl?" When students come to realize that the ingredients must first be measured, ask them to explain why. Then have them decide on the amount of each ingredient needed. Write the completed student-generated recipe on a sheet of chart paper and an actual recipe on another sheet. Compare the two recipes.

At another time, have students help make a batch of cookies according to their class recipe (if it's within reason!); then do the same using a proven sugar-cookie recipe. As the doughs are being prepared, emphasize the measurement terms used. After the cookies have been baked and have cooled, give each child one cookie made from each recipe to sample. And the judges say....

Some Serious Business

Monkey business has never been so serious as when youngsters experiment and explore with dry and liquid measurements. To help your little ones get serious about measurement, stock your classroom sand and/or water table with a variety of containers, scoops, funnels, and measuring cups and spoons. Also keep a supply of paper and writing utensils nearby to encourage writing skills.

As small groups use the materials at the table, invite them to talk about their discoveries and observations. (For instance, have a child predict and then find out how many scoops of sand are necessary to fill a certain type of container. Or prompt him to compare the amounts of water in different containers.) Then invite the children to record their findings on paper. Periodically add a few drops of food coloring to your water table or replace the sand in the sand table with colored rice, pasta, or beans. It's time to get down to some serious business—by monkeying around with measurement!

Tall, Taller, Tallest

Constructive chatter will fill your classroom as students cooperate in this activity that requires a sharp eye for height comparisons. Divide your students into two groups. Challenge each group to work together to line up according to their heights. (Take care to avoid offending children who may be sensitive about their heights.) Invite each child in each group to consider his own height and decide, along with his classmates, where his position in the line should be. Encourage students to use comparative terms such as *tall, taller,* and *tallest.* After students have completed their lines, have them stand across from each other so each group can observe the other group's work. Record the order of the students on a sheet of chart paper. Later in the year, repeat this activity and compare the new results with the old.

A Tale Of Length

Students will have a tale to tell when they explore how things measure up to the monkey's tails in these little booklets. For each child, duplicate page 191 on construction paper. Have each child cut the pages apart, then color the cover of his booklet as desired. Stack the cover and pages of the booklet; then staple them together along the top edge. Punch a hole on the cover for the monkey's tail. Then have each child create a monkey's tail by looping one end of a pipe cleaner through the hole and twisting it securely around itself. Encourage each student to compare the length of his monkey's tail to different items in the classroom. Then have him complete each page of his booklet. After the booklets are completed, have youngsters share them with a partner.

Get Into The Swing!

These motivational monkey vines will have your little ones swinging around the room to make height comparisons. For each child, photocopy one of the monkey patterns (page 192) on construction paper. Have each child color and cut out his monkey, then glue it on a tagboard card. Use a measuring tape to determine each child's height; then record his height on his monkey. Next, cut a length of green or brown streamer equal to the child's height. Staple the streamer to the tagboard card so that it resembles a vine in the monkey's hand. Challenge each child to use his monkey vine to measure items in the classroom. Can he find something that is taller than he is? Shorter? How about just the same? Afterwards, invite each youngster to take his monkey vine home to find objects there that are equal to his height.

188

In The Balance

Youngsters will go bananas over this balancing activity that culminates in a tasty treat suitable for any primate. In advance, purchase some small fresh fruits (or cut larger fruits into small pieces). Arrange a variety of manipulatives—such as Unifix® cubes and teddy bear counters—and a simple balance scale in a center. Duplicate page 193; then cut the page in half along the bold line. Program each box in the left column of the weight chart with a simple drawing of a different piece of fruit that you have. On whole sheets of paper, copy the programmed page for each child.

To do this activity, have a child decide which manipulative he would like to use, then draw that manipulative on the blank half of the page. Next have him place a small piece of fruit on one side of the scale. Encourage him to balance the scale using the chosen manipulatives. When the scale is balanced, explain that the weight on both sides is the same. Ask the child to count the number of items needed to create the balance. Have him record that number in the appropriate box on the chart. Prompt him to continue in this manner until his chart is complete. Post the completed charts near the center; then encourage students to compare the numbers of different items needed to balance each type of fruit.

After taking care of such weighty matters, don't leave your youngsters' appetites in the balance! Invite them to prepare the unhandled fruits for a tasty fruit salad. To serve the salad, scoop a serving of the salad on a small plate. Place the plate on the scale; then place an empty plate on the other side. Encourage a child to spoon fruit salad onto the empty plate until the scale is balanced. Then invite everyone to enjoy the fruits of their labor!

Weight

Measure this	How many?
🍉	5

45 Jon	40 Mary	45 Ken	47 Kevin	43 Jill

Weighing In

Although your youngsters may appear to be light and spry, you may be surprised to discover just how much each child actually weighs! Obtain a bathroom scale for your classroom. Weigh each child; then record her weight on a sticky note labeled with her name. Divide the class into several groups. Have the students in each group sequence themselves according to weight; then have them place their sticky notes in that same sequence along a sentence strip. Display the sentence strips one above the other. As a class compare the weights of the children posted on each sentence strip. Which child weighs the most? Which weighs the least? Then make weight comparisons of all the children posted first on each strip, then second, and so on—encouraging youngsters to use terms such as *more, most, less,* and *least.*

After the discussion, invite small groups of students to experiment with weighing common classroom objects on the scale. Encourage them to estimate which of two objects will weigh more or less and to compare the weights of the objects to their own weights.

189

Measure With Manipulatives

A variety of nonstandard units of measure and some freedom to move about the classroom are all that are necessary to give youngsters the opportunity to explore length—and, perhaps, to engage in a few monkeyshines along the way! Make a copy of the length chart on page 193. Then cut the page in half along the bold line. Program the page with additional pictures of objects in your classroom, if desired. Then duplicate the chart for each child. Provide containers of different sets of objects, such as blocks, paper clips, index cards, and markers. Have each child select a set of manipulatives; then ask him to draw a picture of that manipulative on the blank side of his paper. Invite youngsters to move around the room from one pictured object to another, determining the length of each object by measuring with his chosen manipulatives. After measuring each item, have the child write the number of manipulatives needed in the appropriate box on the chart. When the charts are completed, encourage youngsters to compare their charts with those of classmates who used the same manipulatives.

Length	
Measure this	How many?
🪑	37
🚰	18
🗄	2?

Going The Distance

Lure your little monkeys out of their barrels and into some head-scratching, thought-provoking rounds of reasoning when they measure and compare the distances between different school locations. In advance, prepare a sheet of chart paper with several columns. Label each column with a different school location that your class visits on a regular basis (such as "Art," "Music," "Lunch," and "Media."). Then trace around each child's shoe on a sheet of construction paper. Have each child cut out his shoe outline and label it with his name. Set the cutouts aside for later use.

As your class prepares to leave the classroom for another location, designate one child to be the official Walker and another to be the Counter. Ask the Walker to lead the line to the new location as the Counter counts the number of steps taken. Have the Counter write that number on a sticky note. Designate a different Walker and Counter for the return trip, following the same procedure. When the class returns to the room, have each Walker find his shoe cutout and tape it to the chart paper under the appropriate column. Then invite each Counter to attach the sticky note to its corresponding cutout. As more cutouts are added to the chart, encourage students to compare the numbers of steps taken to reach each location. Ask, "Why do you think the numbers differ?" Have them compare the sizes of the cutouts. Ask, "Is there a relationship between the size of the shoe and the number of steps taken?" Ask the children whether an adult or a smaller child would take more steps to reach a specified location. Hmm, now there's a bushel of thinking for a barrel of monkeys!

ART	MUSIC	LUNCH
Joe 52	Amy 33	
Kim 61		

A Tale Of Length

©The Education Center, Inc.

My monkey's tail is shorter than…

My monkey's tail is longer than…

My monkey's tail is the
same length as…

Monkey Patterns

Use with "Get Into The Swing!" on page 188.

©The Education Center, Inc.

©The Education Center, Inc.

©The Education Center, Inc.

©The Education Center, Inc.

Charts

Use the weight chart with "In The Balance" on page 189.
Use the length chart with "Measure With Manipulatives" on page 190.

Weight		Length	
Measure this:	How many?	Measure this:	How many?

CALENDAR

Are you looking for some neat ideas for teaching calendar concepts? Then try some of these creative activities to help your youngsters learn the days of the week, months of the year, and other calendar skills.

"TODAY IS MONDAY"

Reinforce the days of the week with the traditional song "Today Is Monday." After sharing this song with your class, invite students to make their own books that pair each day of the week with a food. Program seven separate sheets of paper with "Today is [Name of day]. [Name of day], _____." so that each sheet names a different day of the week. Duplicate a class quantity of each page. Have each student illustrate each page with a different food. Or have him glue a food picture cut from a magazine or grocery-store advertisement onto each page. Have him write/dictate the name of that food on the line provided. Sequence the completed pages between two construction-paper covers; then staple the book together along the left edge. Encourage each youngster to write the title "Today Is Monday" on his book cover and to decorate his cover as desired. Invite pairs of students to read or sing the texts of their books to each another.

Judy McCann—Pre-K
Promiseland Preschool
Euless, TX

Today is Tuesday.
Tuesday ice cream.

MIXED-UP DAYS

Here's a hands-on activity that helps children learn to recognize the days of the week in print as well as to sequence them. To make word cards, label seven sentence strips each with a different day of the week. Laminate the word cards; then back each card with pieces of magnetic tape. To use the cards, have a different child hold each one. Ask a child volunteer to sequence those children by the days on their cards. Have students take turns holding the cards and sequencing them until every child has had an opportunity to do both. Then place the word cards randomly on a magnetic board in a learning center. As each student visits the center, challenge him to sequence the cards. For a variation, place one card on the board; then have the child find the two cards labeled with the days of the week which precede and follow that day. Ask him to identify which day would be *yesterday,* and which would be *tomorrow.* Lots of calendar-connections practice here!

Jennifer Strathdee
Palmer Elementary
Syracuse, NY

Monday

CONNECTIONS

SING A SONG OF DAYS

Have you found that one of the best ways to help little ones learn is to capture the concept in song? Then teach your youngsters the days of the week using these words sung to the tune of "Are You Sleeping?"

Every week has seven days.
See how many you can say.
Sunday, Monday, Tuesday,
Wednesday, Thursday, Friday,
Saturday. What's today?

Teri Buck—Gr. K
Unity Christian School
Momence, IL

PATTERNING THE DAYS

These individual calendars can be used now to help students understand patterning and later to practice counting the days in a month. Make one copy of the calendar on page 198 and fill in the month name, but not the numerals. Then duplicate a calendar for each child. Each day, while working with small groups of students or in a learning center, have each student mark that day on her calendar using a specified color. At first encourage her to mark each day with one of two or three different colors. After each color is used once, have the child repeat the color sequence on subsequent days so that a color pattern develops over the course of the month. While reviewing the calendar each day, be sure to emphasize the order of the days of the week and reading the color pattern in a left-to-right, top-to-bottom progression. After one calendar is complete, invite each child to begin a new calendar for the next month. As the year progresses, have her increase the number of colors used in the pattern to correspond to her abilities. Later in the year, encourage the student to number her calendar too. Encourage the child to take each of her completed calendars home to share with her family.

Tina Costello—Developmental K
Lincoln Titus Elementary
Crompond, NY

CALENDAR HELPER

If your daily routine includes a time to review the calendar, invite a different student to be your calendar helper each day. Guide the calendar helper to ask the class questions about the calendar such as, "What day of the week is today?" and "What is the name of this month?" Then have the helper lead the class in counting each of the previous days in the month. Next have him place that day's number in its appropriate place on the calendar. Afterward invite all the youngsters to participate in singing the song "Months Of The Year" by Greg and Steve on the album *We All Live Together: Volume 2* (Youngheart Records). Have the calendar helper name an action—such as *stand* or *jump*—for students to perform when they hear their birth months mentioned in the song. As the Spanish verses are sung, encourage students to listen closely and to perform the actions when they *think* their birth months are named. Was the name of that month *January* or *Enero?*

Tara DiNuzzo—Gr. K
Our Lady of Fatima School
Piscataway, NJ

THE MONTHS IN REVIEW

Students will enjoy repeated glances at these personalized books about the months of the year. Have each child decorate a 9" x 12" sheet of construction paper to create a front cover. Title each child's cover "The Year In Review." Then laminate the front cover and a construction-paper back cover for each child. Each month, engage students in a discussion about holidays, special days, and events or activities that occurred during that month. Then provide each child with a 9" x 12" sheet of construction paper. Assist him as necessary to write the name of the month at the top of the page; then have him illustrate some of the events associated with that month. Or have him glue on magazine and catalog cutouts of things related to that month. Each child might choose to include illustrations of personal and family activities that occurred during that month, such as a visit to grandparents or a vacation. Write the child's dictated sentence about his pictures on each page. (If your class does not attend school over the summer months, you might have students complete the pages for those months before school ends for the year.) Laminate the monthly pages as they are completed. Punch three holes along the left edge of each page. Have the child sequence his pages between the covers, adding each page as it is completed. Help him fasten the pages together with brads. At the end of the year, invite youngsters to take their completed books home to share with their families and to keep as treasured memories of their kindergarten year.

Tracey Rebock—Gr. K
Temple Emanuel
Cherry Hill, NJ

November
I'm going to my Grandma's in Florida.

CHICKEN SOUP FOR EVERY MONTH

A healthy serving of *Chicken Soup With Rice* awaits your youngsters each month! This book of poems, authored and illustrated by Maurice Sendak (Scholastic Inc.), ladles out a serving of fun and entertaining thoughts for each month of the year. Prior to sharing the monthly poems with your students, draw and cut out a large ladle and soup bowl from bulletin-board paper. Display the cutouts on a bulletin board with the title "It's 'Chicken Soup With Rice' Month!" Then read the poem for the present month to your students. If desired, copy the poem onto a sheet of chart paper and lead a choral reading of the poem with your students. Engage students in a discussion about the month's poem; then discuss the various events and adventures that await your students during that month. Invite each child to illustrate an adventure—imaginary or real—that he would like to embark on during that month. Then write his dictation on his paper. Display each child's picture on the bulletin board. During the next month, continue in the same fashion, having students create new pictures to display. You'll find that there's plenty of chicken soup and rice for every month of the year!

Lori Gordon-Dworsky—Gr. K
St. Catherines of Sienna
Wilmington, DE

I will eat chicken soup out of a jack-o'-lantern.

RAPPIN' UP THE MONTHS

Use this rollicking, repetitious rap to teach youngsters the months of the year! Begin a rhythm by snapping your fingers, clapping your hands, or tapping your knees; then add the words to the rap. For the first verse, keep the rhythm going and pause after saying each month. Have students repeat the month in that pause. The rhythm and rhyme of a rap may be just what your students need to keep the months rolling through their minds.

There are twelve months in a year, it's true!
Listen now. I'll say 'em for you:
January, February, March, April, May, June,
July, August, September, October,
November, December.

These twelve months make up a year!
Let's say 'em again, loud and clear:
Repeat the name of each month.

Elizabeth Shiry—Gr. K
Mark Twain School
Buffalo Grove, IL

LITERATURE LINK
Today Is Monday
Illustrated by Eric Carle
Published by Philomel Books

Cookie's Week
Written by Cindy Ward
Illustrated by Tomie dePaola
Published by Putnam Publishing Group

All Year Long
Written & Illustrated by Nancy Tafuri
Published by Greenwillow Books

Seven Blind Mice
Written & Illustrated by Ed Young
Published by Philomel Books

Come Out And Play, Little Mouse
Written by Robert Kraus
Illustrated by Jose Aruego and Ariane Dewey
Published by Mulberry Books

Calendar

Use with "Patterning The Days" on page 195.

Sunday	Monday	Tuesday	Wednesday	Thursday	Friday	Saturday

Winter Celebrations

Use this collection of ideas to introduce and celebrate a variety of winter holidays and special occasions.

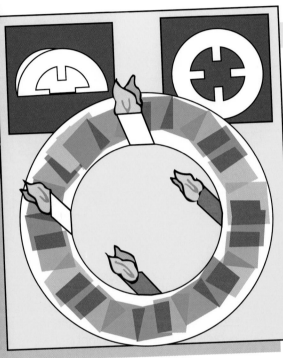

Luciadagen Crowns

In Sweden, St. Lucy's Day is widely celebrated as *Luciadagen.* The name *Lucy* means "light," and St. Lucy became known as a symbol of the preciousness of light. Traditionally this occasion is observed by dressing the family's oldest daughter in a white robe, a crimson sash, and a leaf-covered crown of candles. On the morning of December 13, she and other costumed children awaken their family members with a tray of coffee and pastries.

Commemorate this Swedish celebration by making Luciadagen crowns. Photocopy the patterns on page 202; then cut them out to make tracers. To make a crown, fold a nine-inch paper plate in half. Place the straight edge of the tracer on the center of the fold and trace around the rest of the shape. With the plate still folded, cut along the lines to cut out the interior shape—the candles. Next color the wreath and the candles. Then glue on pieces of torn tissue paper to represent leaves on the wreath and flames on the candles. When the crown is dry, fold the candles back so they stand up. Then invite each child to wear her decorative head wreath as she serves herself a pastry from a tray passed from child to child.

Michelle Weeks—Gr. K, Oxford Middle School, Oxford, AL

Dreidel Match

Provide background information about a widely observed Jewish holiday by sharing Leslie Kimmelman's informative *Hanukkah Lights, Hanukkah Nights* (HarperCollins Children's Books). Then show your students one element of the traditional holiday festivities—a dreidel. (If you don't have a dreidel, *Let's Play Dreidel!,* a book/cassette/dreidel set, is published by Kar-Ben Copies, Inc., and available to order by calling 1-800-4-KARBEN.) Next reinforce your youngsters' visual-discrimination and memory abilities with this small-group dreidel-matching game. To prepare, duplicate the dreidel cards (page 203) on construction paper; then mount the cards on tagboard. Laminate the cards. Then arrange all the cards facedown on a table. Invite a player to turn over two cards. If the cards match, the child keeps them, and play moves to the next player. If the cards do not match, have the child return them facedown on the table. Continue play with the next player until all the matches have been found.

Inside-Out Grandma

by Joan Rothenberg
Published by Hyperion Books for Children

Inside-Out Grandma offers a delightfully roundabout approach to reinforce some traditional Hanukkah customs. In advance, collect the supplies needed to make potato latkes (see the recipe at the back of the book). When you prepare to read the story, don an inside-out shirt. Read the book aloud. Afterward draw attention to your inside-out shirt. Lure children to ask you why you are wearing it. When they ask, "suddenly remember" that you have all the supplies needed to whip up a batch of potato latkes for your youngsters!

Colorful Kwanzaa Mats

These colorful Kwanzaa mats are decorative reminders of the colors and meanings of Kwanzaa. In advance, collect a class quantity of light-colored carpet samples (many carpet stores or outlets will donate these). Also gather sponge-tipped ink bottles (such as bingo daubers) in red, green, and black. Then cut out a different shape from each of several squares of sturdy cardboard or tagboard. Before introducing this craft, read aloud *The Gifts Of Kwanzaa* by Synthia Saint James (Albert Whitman & Company). Afterward discuss the Kwanzaa colors and their meanings—*black* for the people, *red* for their struggles, and *green* for hope.

Then have youngsters make these decorative mats to help them remember the special Kwanzaa colors and their meanings. Give each child a carpet sample and have him position a cardboard stencil on his carpet. Encourage him to dot the ink bottle over the shape's opening to transfer that design onto the carpet. Then have him reposition the cardboard and transfer the design again, this time using a different ink color. Invite the child to continue decorating his carpet in this manner, using all three Kwanzaa colors. Set the completed mats aside to dry; then have each student take his mat home and share the principles of Kwanzaa with his family. (By cutting out different stencil shapes and using different colors of ink, these mats can easily be adapted to suit any holiday theme.)

Adapted from an idea by Connie Mangin—Special Education, Brillion Elementary, Brillion, WI

Kwanzaa Lights

Candles play an important role in the Kwanzaa celebration. Seven candles are placed in a candleholder called the *kinara*—three red, one black, and three green. On the first night of Kwanzaa, the black candle is lit. On each night thereafter, an additional candle is lit—alternating red and green until the entire kinara is glowing on the final night of Kwanzaa. To recognize this special celebration, youngsters will enjoy creating these sparkling Kwanzaa candles. For each child, cut seven tagboard strips to represent candles. Also, for each child, cut a wide strip of brown tagboard to represent the kinara. In three separate containers, mix equal amounts of warm water and sugar; then stir the mixtures until the sugar dissolves. Add a different Kwanzaa color of tempera paint to each container. Then have each child paint his tagboard candles with the solutions. After his candles dry, have the child glue them along the top of his kinara. Then invite him to top each candle with a glued-on, torn tissue-paper flame. Display the sparkling Kwanzaa candles on a bulletin board titled "Kwanzaa Lights."

Peace Ringers

To celebrate the birthday of Dr. Martin Luther King, Jr., youngsters can follow his example and ring out the message of peace. First introduce this honored man and his beliefs by reading aloud *Happy Birthday, Martin Luther King* by Jean Marzollo (Scholastic Inc.). After discussing the book, ask children to brainstorm ways in which people can live together peacefully. Then have each child write/dictate his response on a strip of paper. Punch a hole in one end of the paper strip. Next have each child decorate the bottom side of a small paper-plate half. Help him thread a thin ribbon through the loop of a jingle bell; then tie a knot approximately 1 1/2 inches above the bell. Wrap the plate around the ribbon just above the knot, stapling the straight edges of the plate together to create a cone. Thread one end of the ribbon through the hole in the paper strip; then tie the ends of the ribbon together. Invite each child to read his statement of peace to the class, then ring his peace bell for all to hear.

We can live together in peace if we help each other. Abbey

St. Basil's Cake

In Greece, the first day of the New Year is known as the Feast of St. Basil. Celebrations for this occasion actually begin on New Year's Eve, when it is believed that St. Basil gives his blessings to the people, animals, and belongings of each home, and also brings presents to the children. On January 1, a special cake with a coin baked into it—the *Vassilopita*—is served. The person who finds the coin in his slice of cake is considered to be the luckiest family member for the New Year.

Introduce your students to this Grecian custom with individual versions of the Vassilopita—and lucky hidden surprises. To make these cakes, bake a class quantity of cupcakes according to the package directions. After the cupcakes cool, use a knife to cut a deep slit in the middle of each one. Slip a gumdrop or candy-coated chocolate into the slit of each cupcake; then spread icing over the tops of the cupcakes to conceal the slits. Encourage each child to announce when he discovers his hidden surprise. Then remind him of all the good luck that awaits him in the New Year.

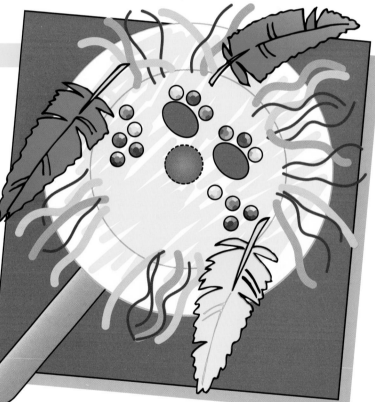

Lions On Parade

The monthlong celebration of the Chinese New Year is celebrated wherever there are substantial Chinese communities. It begins in late January or early February and includes outdoor parades and fireworks. A Lion Dance is performed to scare away evil spirits and to bring good luck for the New Year. Youngsters will enjoy creating lion masks for their very own classroom Lion Dance.

In advance, read aloud *Lion Dancer* by Kate Waters and Madeline Slovenz-Low. Then give each child a paper plate that has two eyeholes cut out of it. Have him color his mask with glitter crayons; then invite him to decorate his mask by gluing on a variety of craft items, such as colorful feathers, sequins, pom-poms, and foil wrapping-paper scraps and streamers. After the glue dries, help each child tape a wide craft stick securely in place. Then play some lively music while youngsters use their masks and perform their own versions of the Lion Dance. Your little lions will have a roaring good time.

A Clean Start

The most popular holiday celebration in Japan is the New Year festivities that take place from January 1 to 3. On this occasion, the Japanese engage in ceremonial housecleanings, visits, and gift exchanges. To celebrate the New Year Japanese-style, hold a ceremonial classroom cleaning. Gather a number of cleaning supplies, such as brooms, dustpans, carpet sweepers, dusters, buckets, festive-shaped sponges, and mild detergents. Attach ribbons or bows to the handles of the cleaning tools. Partially fill the buckets with soapy water. Then invite each child to select some cleaning supplies and an area of the room to clean. Provide a ceremonial atmosphere by playing instrumental music while the children are working. When the cleaning is done, have students bring their cleaning supplies to group time. Light a scented candle; then hold a ceremony in which each child returns her cleaning supplies to be stored. After putting away all the supplies, dedicate the classroom to a fresh, clean start for the New Year.

Pam Crane

201

Crown Patterns

Use with "Luciadagen Crowns" on page 199.

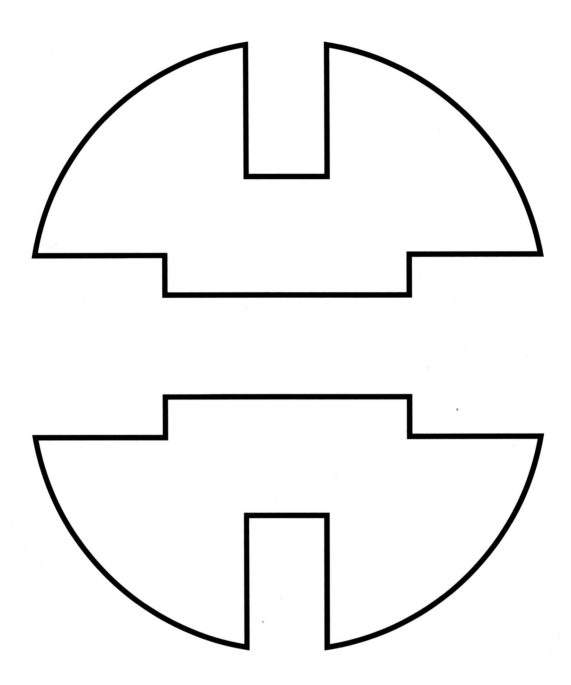

nun   gimmel   hay   shin

nun   gimmel   hay   shin

nun   gimmel   hay   shin

nun   gimmel   hay   shin

A GINGERBREAD "SENSE-SATION"

These activities add a touch of gingerbread and a flavor of fun to stir up some five-senses learning experiences for your youngsters.

ideas contributed by Kathy Curnow

AN INVITATION TEMPTATION

Stimulate the curiosity and senses of your little ones with this eye-appealing, sense-tickling door display. To make it, tape a length of brown bulletin-board paper along your classroom door frame. Trim the paper above the door to resemble a roof. Edge the house with scalloped bulletin-board trim; then paint details on the house. Next give each child a construction-paper circle and have him glue a photo of himself to the center of it. Then encourage him to decorate his cutout in lollipop-style. To add fragrance to his lollipop, have him squeeze a line of glue along the edge of his circle, then sprinkle on ground cinnamon, cloves, or a flavored gelatin mix. After the glue dries, tape the end of a wide craft stick to the cutout. Attach the completed lollipops to the gingerbread-house display to make an inviting grand entry into the "scent-sational" world of gingerbread.

GINGERBREAD LISTENING

Highlight each child's sense of hearing by presenting a hearing-oriented storytime. Read aloud Paul Galdone's *The Gingerbread Boy* (Clarion Books), but do not show the pictures. Encourage each child to close his eyes and use his sense of hearing to imagine what is happening in the story. Afterward, ask children questions about the story. As youngsters respond to your questions, ask how they knew the answers—since they couldn't even see the pictures! Guide youngsters to conclude that they could follow the story because they used their sense of hearing.

YOO-HOO! WHERE ARE YOU?

After reading the story without pictures (see "Gingerbread Listening"), invite students to participate in this game requiring sharp listening skills. In advance, duplicate one gingerbread-boy pattern (page 207) on construction paper. Cut out the pattern; then decorate it as desired. Attach a craft stick to create a stick puppet. Seat students in a circle. Designate one child to be It and to sit in the middle of the circle with her eyes closed. Then play some music and have the other students pass the puppet from child to child. Stop the music and have the child with the puppet hold it. Then instruct It, with her eyes closed, to say, "Yoo-hoo! Where are you?" Ask the child with the puppet to respond, "Here I am!" It uses her sense of hearing to identify who has the gingerbread boy. After the child is identified, she exchanges places with It. Continue in the same manner, giving each child an opportunity to be It.

GINGERBREAD VIEWERS

And now for the sense of sight! Review *The Gingerbread Boy* (see "Gingerbread Listening") with your students. Ask questions that students might only know for sure by using their sense of sight. (For example, you might ask, "What color are the Gingerbread Boy's shoes?") When you begin to get varying answers or questions, invite your youngsters to use their sense of sight as you reread the story and show the illustrations. Then ask the same questions that you asked at the beginning of this activity. Emphasize how each child's sense of sight provided him with more information.

TOUCH AND TELL

Youngsters may be quite interested to learn that hearing and seeing are not the only senses that provide us with information—the sense of touch can provide lots of information, too. Invite students to play a tactile matching game. Use the pattern on page 207 to make several pairs of tagboard gingerbread boys. Apply a different texture to each pair of cutouts. For example, to one pair, glue on sandpaper. To another pair, glue on stretched-out cotton balls. To a third pair, use craft glue to glue on aquarium gravel. To a fourth pair, glue on identical fabrics. When each set is dry, invite students to play a touch-and-tell matching game. To play, have a child close his eyes; then give him a gingerbread boy. Place its match and an additional gingerbread boy in front of the child. Encourage him to carefully feel the gingerbread boy he is holding, then feel the others to find its match. After he identifies the matching gingerbread boy, have him open his eyes and use his sense of sight to check his choice. A lot can be learned through touch alone!

THE NOSE KNOWS

Out of sight? Out of earshot? Out of touch? Then stimulate those sniffers and try smelling it out! In advance, prepare two different flavors of Jell-O® Jigglers® according to the package directions. Also follow the provided recipe to prepare a stiff batch of cinnamon-flavored gelatin. After each flavor of gelatin has set, cut out small gingerbread-boy shapes using cookie cutters. Put a spoonful of cinnamon in a paper cup. Then place a gelatin gingerbread boy of each flavor on separate paper plates. Cover each plate with a paper towel. First have a volunteer smell the cinnamon in the cup; then ask him to smell the gelatin on each plate (without looking) to determine which one matches the aroma of the cinnamon. When he discovers the match, ask him to use his sense of sight to check his selection. Afterward, invite him to eat one of the Jigglers®. Then replace the selected gelatin with one of the same flavor and repeat the exercise, giving each child an opportunity to sniff and match.

Cinnamon Gelatin

2 envelopes unflavored gelatin 1/2 Tbs. cinnamon 3 Tbs. sugar 1/2 cup cold water 1 1/2 cups boiling water	In a large bowl, sprinkle the cold water over the gelatin. Let the mix stand for one minute; then stir in the cinnamon and sugar. Add the boiling water and stir the ingredients together until the gelatin and sugar dissolve (the cinnamon will remain grainy). Chill the gelatin until firm.

FRAGRANT FRAMES

Invite students to make a gingerbread delight that's pleasing to the sight—a scented picture frame! And, as a bonus, youngsters will use most of their other senses while making these frames. To make the dough for one frame, have a child mix four tablespoons of flour, one tablespoon of salt, two tablespoons of water, and a pinch of cinnamon or ginger spice in a bowl. Have the child knead the ingredients to form a dough. Then ask her to press out her dough and cut it with a gingerbread-boy cookie cutter. Using the lid from a two-liter bottle, cut a hole in the middle of each dough cutout. Place the cutouts on a cookie sheet and bake them at 350°F for approximately 45 minutes. Then have each child paint her cooled gingerbread-boy frame with tempera paint. After the paint dries, invite her to use a fine-tipped permanent marker to draw on other features—such as a nose, mouth, eyes, and buttons. Spray the completed frame with clear varnish. If desired, hot-glue a decorative bow to the front of the frame and a looped ribbon to the back to create a frame-hanger. Position and glue a photo of the child behind the frame so that the child's face can be seen through the hole. Encourage youngsters to take their framed pictures home to give as gifts or to use as holiday ornaments.

Debbie Newsome—Gr. K
Dolvin Elementary
Alpharetta, GA

ACTIVATE ALL SENSES

With all these gingerbread activities, your youngsters will be primed for a total sensory experience resulting in a treat they can sink their teeth into—gingerbread cookies! In advance, make a chart with a column labeled for each of the five senses. With the help of students, prepare gingerbread cookies following the provided recipe. As you do, ask children to comment on the many things they see, hear, feel, smell, and taste. Record youngsters' comments on the chart. Students are sure to be motivated when their senses are activated.

touch	taste	sight	hearing	smell
• It's cold. • gooshy • soft	• yummy	• kind of tan	• smush	• Mmm! like coffee

GINGERBREAD COOKIES
(makes approximately 30 cookies)

1 cup sugar	2 tsp. baking soda
3/4 cup shortening	1/4 tsp. salt
1 egg	1 tsp. cinnamon
1/4 cup molasses	3/4 tsp. cloves
2 cups plain flour, sifted	3/4 tsp. ginger

Preheat the oven to 375°F. Combine and mix the first four ingredients in a large bowl. Add the remaining ingredients and mix well to form a dough. Roll the dough onto a sheet of waxed paper. Cut the dough with gingerbread-man cookie cutters; then place the cookies two inches apart on a greased cookie sheet. Bake the cookies 10–12 minutes. After the cookies cool, have each child use tube icing to decorate a cookie as desired. Then invite him to enjoy the sweet sensation of eating his cookie.

BOOKS THAT MAKE SENSE

The Five Senses series (A five-book set)
Written by J. M. Parramón, et al.
Published by Barron's Educational Series, Inc.

I Can Tell By Touching
Written by Carolyn Otto
Illustrated by Nadine Bernard Westcott
Published by HarperCollins Publishers

The Listening Walk
Written by Paul Showers
Illustrated by Aliki
Published by HarperCollins Children's Books

My Five Senses
Written and Illustrated by Aliki
Published by HarperCollins Publishers

Gingerbread-Boy Pattern
Use with "Yoo-Hoo! Where Are You?" on page 204
and "Touch And Tell" on page 205.

Opposites Here And There

Here's an assortment of activities that will keep your little ones delightfully engaged in learning about opposites from start to finish. To prepare, duplicate a supply of the opposite concept pictures (pages 211–212) on construction paper. Mount each picture on a 3" x 5" card. Then use the cards as directed in each activity.

Around The Circle

Circle time is the perfect place to practice matching opposites. Give each child an opposite card. Ask one child to stand up and name the concept on his card. The child holding the corresponding opposite card then stands up and names his concept. After verifying the opposite pair, invite the children to walk around the circle at the same time in opposite directions, then return to their seats. Continue around the circle in the same manner until every student has located his opposite pair.

Michelle Wolfe—Gr. K
Kennewick, WA

Find The Opposite

To further reinforce opposites, send youngsters on an opposite search. Divide the cards into two stacks so that one card from each pair is in each stack. Attach each card from one stack to an area or item in your room that represents the concept depicted on that card. For instance, attach the card for *empty* to an empty container, or tape the card for *under* to a toy positioned under a table. Give each card from the other stack to a different child in a small group. In turn, ask each child to name the concept on his card. Then have him search the room until he finds the card that pictures the opposite of his card. If the child has difficulty finding the corresponding card, give him clues to help him in his search.

Carolyn Bryant—Five-Year-Olds Pre-K
First Baptist Church Powder Springs
Powder Springs, GA

Cross The Room

Why did the kid cross the room? To get to the opposite side, of course! Separate the opposite cards so that one card from each pair is in each stack. Then spread out each stack of cards faceup on opposite sides of your floor. Divide the class into two groups. Have the groups stand on opposite sides of the room. Ask a child from one group to pick one of the cards on his side of the room. Then name an action—such tiptoe or march—for that child to do as he crosses to the opposite side of the room to locate the corresponding opposite card. After the child matches the cards, have him tag a child from the group on that side of the room to take a turn. Following each child's turn, return each card to its original position.

Adapted from an idea by Amy Spence—Gr. K
Harvest Baptist Christian School
Central Point, OR

Puzzled Pairs

Youngsters will learn about opposites piece by piece when they assemble these puzzles. Collect the fronts of seasonal and greeting cards. Cut each picture to create a two-piece puzzle. On the back of each piece of a puzzle, glue one picture of an opposite pair. Laminate the puzzle pieces for durability. To use, randomly place all the pieces on a table with the opposite pictures facing up. Have a child identify a pair of opposites; then invite him to turn over the pieces and assemble the puzzle. A correct match will result in a completed picture when the two pieces are put together.

Marcia Cannin—Speech Therapist
Robert Morris School
Batavia, NY

Remember That Opposite

Challenge little ones' understanding of opposite concepts and their visual memory skills by having them remember the placement not of the same—but of the opposite—pairs of concept cards in this memory game. Place the cards facedown on a table. Invite a player to turn up two cards. If the cards make an opposite pair, the child may keep them. If the cards are not an opposite match, have the child return them facedown to the table. Have the other players take their turns in the same manner, continuing the game until all the opposite pairs are found.

Amy Spence—Gr. K
Harvest Baptist Christian School
Central Point, OR

Do The Opposite

Now here's a game of charades that encourages youngsters to do the *opposite* of what they've been told! Put the opposite cards in a bag. Invite a child to remove a card from the bag. Whisper the name of the pictured concept to the child; then have him act out the opposite of that concept while his classmates try to guess the word. Continue the game until each child has the opportunity to act out an opposite concept.

Dianne Joseph—Gr. K
Bayou Vista Elementary
Morgan City, LA

What's The Word?

Thrill students with lots of opportunities to correct your word choices while studying opposites. At unexpected times throughout the day, give a direction or make a statement using the opposite of a word which is typically used in that context. For example, you might say, "It's time to go *inside* to the playground." Express appreciation to those students who correct your statements by commenting on how well they listen and think about the words they hear.

Tonya Y. Wright—Gr. K
Social Secur-A-Kiddie CCC
Baltimore, MD

empty

full

For The Birds

This little ditty about opposites will really fly with students! To make a bird puppet for each opposite concept, glue a construction-paper bullet-shaped cutout onto a craft stick. Attach a construction-paper wing to each side of the cutout; then glue on a construction-paper beak and wiggle eyes. Complete the bird puppet by attaching a feather to the top of its head. Glue a different opposite concept picture on each puppet. To use these, give a different puppet to each child; then recite the rhyme. Invite the children holding the appropriate puppets to move their puppets to correspond to the actions of the rhyme. Repeat the rhyme, each time substituting a different pair of opposites from pages 211–212 for the underlined words.

(recited to the meter of "Two Little Blackbirds")

Two little birds play an opposites game.
[Empty] and [Full] are the little birds' names.
Fly away, [Empty].
Fly away, [Full].
Come back, [Empty].
Come back, [Full].

Adapted from an idea by Nan Hokanson
Sheboygan Falls, WI

Lift The Flap For Opposites

Youngsters will flip over these lift-the-flap booklets. For each child, fold a sheet of construction paper in half lengthwise. On one folded side of the paper, cut three evenly spaced lines to the fold so that four sections are created—the book flaps. Have the child select four pairs of opposite pictures (from pages 211–212) or draw his own to color and cut out. Then instruct him to glue one picture from each pair on a flap. Have him glue the corresponding picture under the flap. After the glue dries, help the child fold his booklet in half. Write the title "My Book Of Opposites by [child's name]" on the front cover. Encourage the child to choose a partner with whom to share his booklet.

Cheryl Martin—Gr. K
Woodlake Elementary
San Antonio, TX

night   day   empty   front   happy

Breyanna Lynne
My Book
Of Opposites

Books About Opposites

Fast-Slow, High-Low: A Book Of Opposites by Peter Spier
Published by Doubleday & Company, Inc.

Opposites by Rosalinda Kightley
Published by Little, Brown And Company

Mr. Tall And Mr. Small by Barbara Brenner
Published by Henry Holt And Company, Inc.

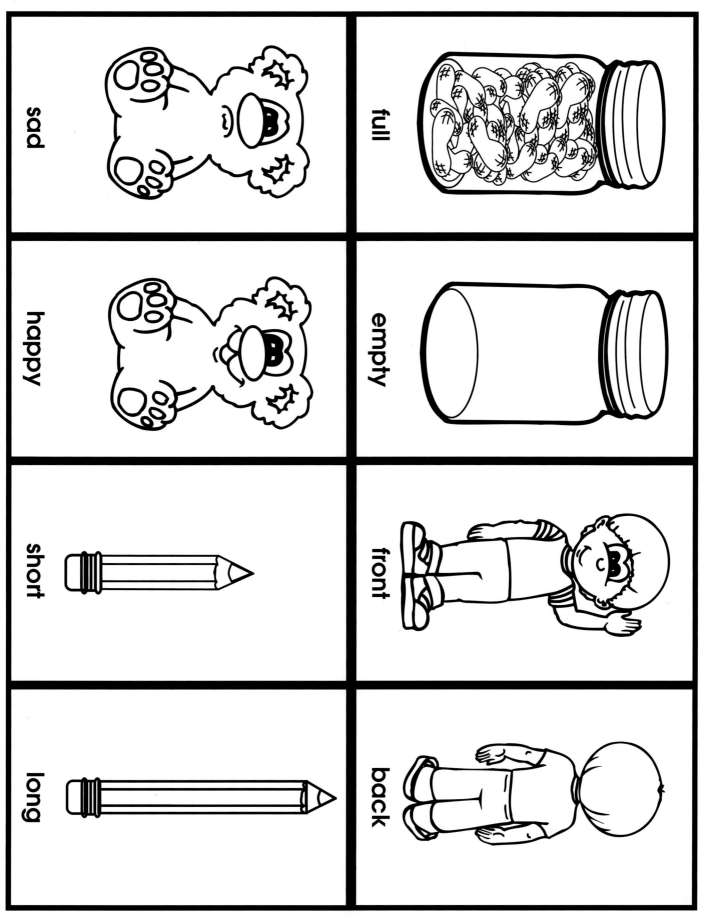

sad

full

happy

empty

short

front

long

back

Opposite Concept Pictures

Use with activities in "Opposites Here And There" on pages 208–210.

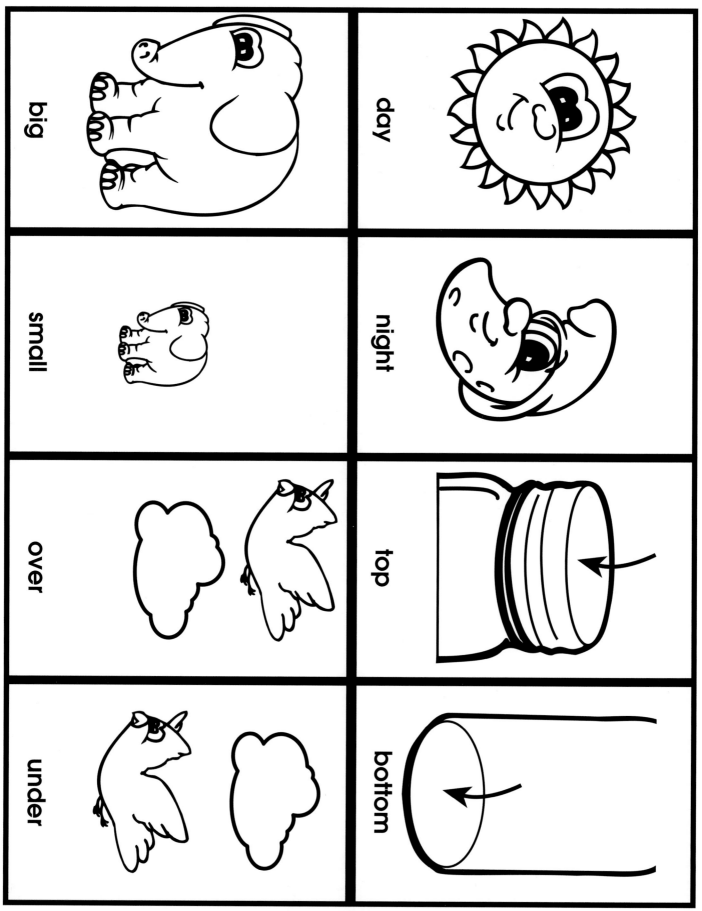

HIP, HIPPO-RAY— IT'S THE 100TH DAY!

Wow—100 days of living and learning together! *That's* certainly worth special recognition. And the day itself offers lots more opportunities for learning and fun. So use your selection of the ideas in this unit to celebrate—and learn even more—in 100-Day style!

ideas contributed by Elizabeth Trautman

BADGE OF HONOR

Your students will beam with pride when they wear these 100-Day badges of honor. On the 100th day of school, greet each child with a construction-paper badge. Invite each child to use various art supplies (such as crayons, glitter glue, and sequins) to color and decorate her badge. Then safety-pin each child's badge to her shirt to serve as a reminder of a job well done for 100 days. Hip, hip, hooray!

100-DAY DECOR

Decorate your classroom with this cooperative project that is made up of 100 paper links. To prepare, use a marker to number 100 construction-paper strips 1–100. Then put the strips in a center along with a glue stick and a counting chart that goes up to 100. During the day, encourage each child to take a turn visiting the center to glue a few links to the paper chain—in numerical order. Prompt children to refer to the counting chart if necessary. When all 100 links are intact, hang the paper chain along your classroom wall or ceiling.

HOW MUCH IS 100?

If you're talking about physical exercise, 100 can be *quite a lot!* When you have transitional moments on 100 Day, challenge your students to count to 100 by ones while they perform designated movements in unison such as jumping, hopping, shrugging, snapping, or clapping. As your students count and move, you may be urged to change the given movement after sets of 10 or 20!

CLAP
CLAP
CLAP

78, 79... WHEW!

TALLY UP THE KINDNESS

This activity encourages kindness and also offers reinforcement for tallying practice and counting by fives and/or tens. Label a sheet of chart paper "100 Acts Of Kindness." When you see a child demonstrate an act of kindness—such as sharing, helping, or saying "please" or "thank you"—subtly get that child's attention; then make a tally mark on the chart. After each row of ten tally marks, write the appropriate numeral. When you have reached 100, count to 100 together and marvel at the kindness of your class. Who knows—your youngsters just might be motivated to fill several charts with 100 acts of kindness!

100 WORDS

1. red   2. blue   3. yellow   4. green   5. orange
6. one   7. two   8. three   9. me   10. the
12. ten

READING TO 100

Little ones (and you, too!) might be amazed when they see the number of words they can read. Title a large sheet of poster board "100 Words"; then number it from 1–100. As you explore reading as a class, write words on the list that your students can read by themselves. Every time someone reads a new word independently, add it to the list. Display this impressive poster for classroom visitors to see and for your read-the-room activities.

HOW FAR IS 100?

Exactly how far is 100 feet—kindergarten feet, that is? With this activity, you'll see! Provide a supply of colorful construction paper, pencils, and scissors. Ask each child to trace and cut out his foot a given number of times. (Specify the number of times so that the total number of cutouts will be 100 or close to it. For example, if you have 24 children, have each child trace and cut out four foot cutouts; then add four extra cutouts to total 100.) As a class, decide on a long, flat place that you think might accommodate 100 kindergarten feet. Use pieces of yarn to make predictions regarding how far your collection of feet will go. Then, in turn, have each child lay his cutouts end-to-end. Well—how far is 100? (Save the cutouts to do more nonstandard measurement activities in your classroom.)

PICTURE THIS

Here's a cooperative project that reinforces counting to 100 and classification skills. In advance, draw a 100-square grid on each of three sheets of poster board. If desired, number the squares. Label one poster "100 Animals," the second poster "100 People," and the third poster "100 Foods." Also label each of three baskets to correspond with a poster label. Stock a center with a supply of old magazines, scissors, and a glue stick. As each child visits this center, have him first cut out pictures of animals, people, or foods, and sort them in the appropriate baskets. Then have him glue each picture to a square on the appropriate poster. When each poster is filled, display it in your classroom. When you have spare minutes to fill, count the items on the posters.

100-DAY MUNCHIES

This little snack requires counting, fine-motor skills, and lots of munching to the tune of 100! In advance, ask each of ten (or more) parents to donate an ingredient that you specify. (Some suggestions are listed below.) On 100 Day, put each ingredient in a separate bowl and arrange the bowls on a table. Invite each child to take ten pieces from each of ten bowls. There you have it—100-Day Munchies!

cereal pieces	chocolate candies	peanut-butter chips
raisins	banana chips	popcorn
peanuts	minimarshmallows	candy corn
pretzels	chocolate chips	yogurt-covered nuts or raisins
fish crackers	butterscotch chips	sunflower seeds

BARRY SLATE

Time Passages

An hour, a day, a season, a year—time is ticking right on by. Use the ideas in this unit to help your youngsters explore all kinds of time passages.

ideas by Lucia Kemp Henry

summer 1994 1995 1996
fall
winter

Time Goes By

Youngsters will start to associate vocabulary with familiar time concepts when you read/recite this poem together. In advance, copy the poem onto chart paper. If desired, add simple picture cues (as shown). Read the poem aloud, encouraging youngsters to join in as they are able. When your students are familiar with the words, encourage them to make up motions to go with each verse.

Time Goes By

Time goes by.
The earth spins around.
The sun comes up
And the sun goes down.

Time goes by.
Morning starts the day.
The sun arcs the sky
As we work and play.

Time goes by.
Darkness is deep.
The sun's gone down
Now it's time to sleep.

It's Time To...

Although many of your youngsters can't yet tell time by looking at a clock, most of them are aware of the passage of time throughout a day. Brainstorm a list of ways that your youngsters can "tell time" without even looking at a clock. Prompt thinking by asking students how they often know when, for example, it's almost time for lunch or close to their bedtimes. Record youngsters' comments on a sheet of chart paper; then discuss the completed list.

- We know it's time for lunch because we're hungry!

- When it's my bedtime my eyes get tired.

216

Morning, Afternoon, And Night

Most likely, your students are familiar with this trio of time designations for three distinct reasons—breakfast, lunch, and dinner! Take some time to discuss what your youngsters typically do during the morning, afternoon, and night. Then divide your class into three groups. Ask one group to draw illustrations of things that happen in the morning. Ask the second group to illustrate afternoon events, and have the third group illustrate nighttime events. Then divide a bulletin board into three sections—one section for each time designation. Title the board "What's Happening?" Have each child post his picture in the appropriate place on the board; then discuss all the pictures.

That's MY Time Of Day!

Extend your exploration of times of the day and also get to know your students a little bit better while you make this class big book. Begin a discussion by asking children if they have ever heard of someone being a *morning person* or a *night owl*. Ask youngsters to share what they think those sayings mean. After your discussion, ask each child to write/dictate about and illustrate his favorite time of day. Bind all the pages together between two construction-paper covers; then have each child share his page during a group reading time.

My favorite time of day is morning because I'm wide awake!   Frankie

My favorite time of day is is at night when everyone is quiet.   Caroline

Time It

A minute, is a minute, is a minute—but sometimes it sure doesn't seem like it! Prompt your little ones to explore the consistency of time with this activity. Obtain a timer that you can set for one minute (a sandglass timer works well to add a visual aspect). First ask your youngsters to do something that is relatively challenging or tiresome for one minute. For example, you might have them be absolutely still or try to stand on one foot. Time the chosen task for one minute. Then prompt youngsters to discuss whether that minute felt long or short. Next, time students doing something fun for one minute—such as dancing or playing. Then discuss how the passage of that minute felt. Lead youngsters to conclude that the time elapsed was exactly the same even though it might have felt very much different.

A Year Of Seasons

Help your little ones wrap up the concept of a year by studying the seasons within it. In advance, glue a torn-paper tree to each of four large sheets of poster board. Then share *Gather Up, Gather In: A Book Of Seasons* by M. C. Helldorfer (Viking) with your students. After discussing the book, divide your class into four groups. Give each group a tree poster; then assign each group a different season. Encourage each group to use art supplies to embellish its poster to depict its specific season (see suggestions below). When the posters are complete, mount them on a wall in a cyclical fashion with arrows. Use the posters to facilitate discussion about a whole year of seasons.

winter
- Sponge-paint snow on the branches.
- Glue on white foam packing pieces.

spring
- Glue on construction-paper flowers, birds, and nests.
- Color popcorn with powdered tempera paint; then glue it on for blossoms.

summer
- Glue on torn tissue-paper leaves.
- Paint lots of leaves on the tree.

fall
- Sponge-paint fall-colored leaves on the branches.
- Brush water-diluted glue on white construction-paper leaves. Overlap fall colors of tissue paper on the leaves. Glue the leaves to the tree.

Time Brings Change

Simple sequence pictures help illustrate for your youngsters how time brings change. Enlarge and photocopy the sequence pictures on page 220. Color and cut out the pictures; then mount each picture on a construction-paper card. To introduce one set of cards, show children the first card in a sequence—for example, the baby. After discussing the picture, ask children what they think might happen after some time passes. Then display the remaining cards in that set in random order. Have children direct you to sequence the cards according to what might happen over time. After this introduction, put all of the cards in a center. When a child visits the center, ask her to arrange the cards according to what could happen over time. If desired, program the backs of the cards for self-checking.

"What Time Is It?" Booklet

This telling-time booklet will give children a hands-on opportunity to practice their clock skills. For each booklet, reproduce one set of the booklet patterns (pages 221–223) on construction paper. Cut out the outside and inside covers, and glue them together back-to-back. Then cut out the clock hands and punch a hole in the cover and the clock hands where indicated. Push a brad through the cover and the clock hands so that the brad head and clock hands are on the *inside* cover. Fold the brad prongs out to resemble clock hands on the outside cover. Then cut out the back cover and the booklet pages. Staple the front and back covers together; then stack the booklet pages and staple them to the back cover (as shown).

By drawing or gluing on cut-out magazine pictures, have each child illustrate each booklet page. When his booklet is complete, encourage each child to read his booklet with a partner and set the clock hands according to the text on each page.

What time is it when...

7:00

you eat breakfast?

What Time Is It?

Sequence Pictures

Use with "Time Brings Change" on page 219.

outside cover

Booklet Patterns
Use with " 'What Time Is It?' Booklet" on page 219.

What Time Is It?

©The Education Center, Inc. • THE MAILBOX® • Kindergarten • Feb/Mar 1997

clock hands

What time is it when...

inside cover

Booklet Patterns

Use with " 'What Time Is It?' Booklet" on page 219.

back cover

booklet pages

you wake up?

1

you eat breakfast?

2

Use with " 'What Time Is It?' Booklet" on page 219.

you get to school?

3

you eat lunch?

4

you go home?

5

you go to bed?

6

Hot Off The Classroom Press!

Keep your young authors inspired with these teacher-tested ideas for child-made and classroom-published books. What better way to encourage reading and writing than by reading and writing?

Look What I Built!

Are your young architects impressed with the structures they create in your block area? If so, you've got the perfect opportunity for a class-made book! To make the book, glue construction-paper blocks to a cover page. Laminate that page and another one for the back cover. Bind blank pages between these laminated covers. When a child creates a structure of which he is particularly proud, take a photo of it. When the picture is developed, have the builder glue the photo onto a blank page of the book and write about what he built. One of the latest entries in Barbara Meyers's "Look What I Built" book is the Great Wall Of China!

Barbara Meyers—Gr. K
Fort Worth Country Day
Fort Worth, TX

Old Mac-You!

Here's a great manipulative project book that each child can work on during your farm studies. To make each book, you will need a large sheet of construction paper for the cover and for each page that you'd like to include in the book. To make the cover and each of the pages, fold the sheets of construction paper in half. Glue the sides of each sheet, leaving the top open to form a pocket. Then staple the pocket pages together down the left-hand side to form the book (see the illustration).

- On the cover, write "Old Mac [child's name] Had A Farm, E-I-E-I-O." Have the child draw herself as a farmer on a half-sheet of large construction paper, then cut it out and slide the cutout into the pocket.

- On each successive page, write or have the child write/copy "And on that farm [he/she] had a [name of animal], E-I-E-I-O." Encourage the child to create that particular animal from craft materials, being sure that the finished project is no larger than the pocket. Slide each completed animal in the appropriate pocket. If desired, have each child illustrate a scene on each of the pages of her book.

To share each book, have the author hold her book in front of the class. As the class reads chorally, have the child remove the pocketed characters at the appropriate times. No two MacFarms are exactly alike!

Debbie Newsome—Gr. K
Dolvin Elementary
Alpharetta, GA

LOOK WHAT I BUILT

It is easy to build a rocket out of blocks.

Timmy

Old Mac Emily Had A Farm, E-I-E-I-O

And on that farm she had a pig. E-I-E-I-O

The Very Hungry Kindergartner

Loosely based on the format of Eric Carle's *The Very Hungry Caterpillar,* your young authors will find this end-of-the-year publication a delight. To prepare the pages for each child, first title the front cover "The Very Hungry Kindergartner." Then, for each month that your school is in session, program a page as indicated below. (Adapt as necessary to fit your school year.)

Page 1 In September [he/she] ate one _____.
Page 2 In October [he/she] ate two _____.
Page 3 In November [he/she] ate three _____.

Continue in a similar manner up through the last month that your school is in session; then program the last two pages as shown in the illustration.

Give each child a set of the pages (or do them one page at a time as a center activity). Have each child fill in the appropriate pronoun on the page, then write something that he likes to eat in the blank. Next have him illustrate the sentence accordingly. When all of the in-school months are completed, have him illustrate what he might do on his vacation on the next-to-the-last page. On the last page, have the child draw a picture of what he thinks he might look like *next* year. Bind each child's pages together along with the cover. As each child shares his book with you, sign the last page with a congratulatory message!

Adapted from an idea by Pam Warren—Gr. K, DeSoto Trail Elementary, Tallahassee, FL

The "Ouch!" Book

This book not only encourages lots of language-arts skills, but it just might help children "heal" a little bit faster too! To make the book, glue a large construction-paper bandage to a cover. Laminate that page and another one for the back cover. Bind blank pages between these two covers. When a child is injured, help her process both her physical and emotional injuries by writing about and illustrating them.

Barbara Meyers—Gr. K
Fort Worth Country Day
Fort Worth, TX

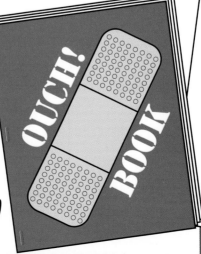

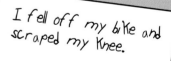

The Incredible, Hatchable Egg

With patience and careful observation, your young embryologists will witness an "eggs-traordinary" event—the emergence of newly hatched chicks! Use the information and activities in this unit to prepare for—and derive lots of learning opportunities from—the big event. Happy hatching!

ideas by Kristi Anderson and Mackie Rhodes

Project: Embryology

What a privilege to witness the awesome sight of hatching chicks! But planning for this experience requires some preliminary preparations. Use these suggestions to help make your embryology project a success from prehatch to posthatch.

- Contact your local 4-H agent to obtain information on how to prepare for and conduct an embryology project (some agencies will provide the necessary supplies). The information should include how to store, handle, mark, incubate, turn, and candle the fertilized eggs, as well as timing the incubation period, brooding the newly hatched chicks, and placing them in appropriate "homes."
- Prearrange an adequate, knowledgeable, adoptive home—and transportation there—for the young chicks.
- Prearrange a weekend schedule for turning the incubating eggs.
- Follow the directions closely for setting up the incubator and maintaining its temperature and humidity. Set up and test the incubator several days prior to your project start date.
- Post a sign warning against disturbing the incubator.
- Appoint yourself to be the designated egg-handler. Wash your hands thoroughly before and after handling the eggs. Invite youngsters to examine the eggs, but not touch them.
- Keep a video camera or camera handy to record the hatching process and other memorable moments.

The Amazing Egg

Amaze your class with information about the incredible, hatchable egg with Anca Hariton's *Egg Story* (Dutton Children's Books). In advance, set up your incubator and brooder. After sharing the book, have youngsters examine a store-bought egg, cautioning them to handle it carefully so that it doesn't break. Then gently break open the egg, and examine/discuss its fragile shell and contents. Explain that when a freshly laid egg is incubated—or kept warm—a chick may hatch from it. Then introduce youngsters to the incubator and brooder, briefly describing how and why each will be used in your embryology project. Place *Egg Story* along with other related books—such as *Egg: A Photographic Story Of Hatching* by Robert Burton (Dorling Kindersley)—near the incubator for ready references. The "egg-citement" is building!

- An *embryologist* is a person who studies living things before they are born or hatched.

- Chicks *pip*—or break—out of their shells when they hatch.

- *Embryology* is the study of a living thing's growth before it is born or hatched.

- To *incubate* an egg is to keep it warm so the chick inside can grow and hatch.

- A *candler* is a light used to check for the chick's growth inside the egg.

Hatch A Brood Of New Words

Invite youngsters to take a crack at this egg-related vocabulary.

- Newly hatched chicks are kept warm and dry in a *brooder*.

The Waiting Dilemma

The eggs are in the incubator and the brooder is set to go. Now all youngsters have to do is wait…and wait…and wait. The number of days until hatching can seem like an eternity to children! Solve the waiting dilemma with these ideas that keep students involved while waiting for that first break-out.

- Track the growth inside an egg with this class-generated timeline. To prepare, pencil a mark on the egg to be used for tracking growth. Cut out a paper egg for each incubation day and one paper chick. Each day, invite a child to tape an egg cutout and a numeral card corresponding to that incubation day on a sentence-strip length. On each candling day, have a child illustrate the egg cutout with her observations, then place it on the timeline. Chorally count the paper eggs displayed each day. On hatching day, cut a paper egg in half; then have a child tape the egg-halves and the chick cutout onto the strip. Embryologically speaking, every day counts!

- Students will learn about time concepts when they become responsible for keeping up with egg-turning times. Cut out three construction-paper eggs to represent the number of egg-turnings each day. Label each cutout with *X* on one side and *O* on the other (or with the symbols used on the incubated eggs, if different). Then post the cutouts—with all the *X*'s or all the *O*'s facing out—to correspond to the symbol on the tops of the eggs. Each day, assign a small group to remind you—at the appointed times—to turn the eggs. After each egg-turning, have one child flip one of the cutouts so that its symbol matches those on the eggs. By the end of the day, all the cutouts will be turned to the same symbol. What time is it? Egg-turning time!

The Great "Egg-scape"

It's hatching! When a chick finally makes its grand exit from its shell, youngsters will be bursting with excitement—and lots of observations to share. Record their comments and descriptions on a large egg cutout. Then—after the excitement subsides a little—give each child several half-sheets of paper. Ask him to illustrate each page with a different step of the hatching process, referring to the recorded comments as necessary. Have the child sequence, number, and bind his pages between two construction-paper covers. Help him title his booklet; then encourage the child to share his hatching story with a partner.

Now What?

Don't let the "post-hatch-em" blues drag your class down. Use these freshly hatched ideas to keep youngsters peeping with enthusiasm!

- Invite each child to role-play a chick hatching out of its egg—transforming from a wet, cramped creature into a fluffy, chirping chick.
- Ask each student to imagine she is a chick experiencing the world for the first time; then have her illustrate one of her experiences—such as the first thing she saw, ate, or heard—on an egg cutout.
- If possible, arrange a class trip to visit your chicks at their new home.
- Write and send a class-dictated letter to one of your chick's new owners—or to one of your chicks!
- If you videotaped the egg-hatching, show the tape to your class with the sound turned off. Invite students, in turn, to narrate the events being shown.
- Plan a field trip to a farm or zoo where students might observe young birds.

SOX

Batter Up!

DODGERS

Your hard-hitting sluggers will be world-class champs with these baseball-related activities covering the curriculum bases.

ideas by Mackie Rhodes and Diane Sterle

Batting Practice

Give youngsters lots of skills practice with a supply of plastic bats and these ideas.

- Outdoors, have students cooperatively form shapes and other figures with their bats.
- Invite each youngster, in turn, to arrange the bats into a pattern.
- Give a bat to each child on a small team of students; then have one player strike a pose with her bat. Have her teammates imitate her pose.
- Give a bat to each student on a small team. Invite a volunteer to tap a simple rhythm on the floor with her bat. Ask her teammates to repeat the rhythm.
- Label each of nine bats with a different numeral from one to nine. Give a bat to each child on a nine-member team. Have the team line up by sequencing their bats in numerical order; then give each child an opportunity to take a few swings at a foam baseball.

Sing A Song Of Baseball

Infect youngsters with baseball fever with a rousing rendition of the traditional song "Take Me Out To The Ballgame." If desired, share the book by the same title (lyrics by Jack Norworth and published by Four Winds Press); then break open the bags of peanuts and boxes of Cracker Jack® for traditional baseball treats.

Preseason Training

Shape up your team with these spring-training activities. To begin, gather plastic bats, foam balls, and a T-ball stand. Then set up a baseball diamond on an outdoor playing field. Begin your training session with a round of routine exercises—such as toe touches, jumping jacks, and a few sprints around the bases. Next have groups of students practice throwing and catching. Conclude your workout with a team huddle, complete with a pep talk and a cheer. Training season is over—let's play ball!

A "Sense-ible" Batter

Big-league imaginations will guide your young batters in this sensory-awareness adventure. In advance, program a sheet of paper with "I see ____," "I hear __," "I smell ___," "I feel ____," and "I taste ____." Duplicate the page for each child. Then have the students close their eyes as you describe some sensory observations that a batter might make while at the plate—such as the sight of other players, the green field, and the colorful fans; the sounds of cheers; the smell of hot dogs; the feel of warm air; and the taste of bubble gum. Invite each child to imagine himself at bat; then have him write/dictate a completion to each sentence. Encourage him to illustrate a batter on the back of his page. Ask each student to share his illustration and sentences with the class. From the batter's perspective, it all makes sense.

It's A Hit!

Teach your all-stars some baseball terms with this fingerplay. Encourage students to perform the suggested actions as they recite each line.

The **batter** steps up to **home plate**—
Raised **bat,** bent knees, high chin.
The **pitch** is thrown. He **swings** the bat.
This **hit** could **clinch** the win!

Finger-draw a box in the air.
Assume a batter's stance.
Make throwing, then batting motions.
Raise arms in cheer fashion.

A **single** may not sound like much,
But it takes him to **first base.**
A **double** earns him **second.**
He must run at a fast pace.

Hold up one finger.
Run in place.
Hold up two fingers.
Run in place.

A **triple** means he goes to **third.**
He speeds to win the race.
A **homer** sends him all the way—
A wide grin upon his face.

Hold up three fingers.
Run in place.
Hold up four fingers.
Point to smile and trot in place.

A big **grand slam**—one hit, four **runs!**
Now could it really be?
The **fans** are going wild,
For we've won the **victory!**

Swing imaginary bat. Hold up one
finger; then four fingers.
Raise arms in victory.

"Pitch" And "Hit"

Invite your sluggers to take a swing at rhyming in this call-and-response game. To prepare, position four vinyl placemats as baseball bases. Appoint a scorekeeper; then divide your class into two teams. To play, verbally "pitch" a word—such as *cat*—to a batter at home plate. When the batter responds with a rhyming word, he "hits" a single and moves to first base. If he can think of *two* rhyming words, it's considered a double, and so on. Follow suit with each batter, having the players advance as in baseball. When each team member has had a turn at bat, the other team comes to bat. Continue play as student interest dictates. Periodically play the game varying the skills being pitched—such as beginning sounds. The stretch...the pitch...and...it's a hit!

Adapted from an idea by Diane Sterle—Gr. K
St. John the Evangelist
Greenfield, WI

The Bases Are Loaded

Youngsters will hit some grand slams with this visual memory game. To prepare, gather sets of identical objects—such as teddy-bear counters, blocks, and crayons. Place the items, in sets, on a table. Choosing from among the sets, hide a different object under each of four boxes arranged in a baseball diamond. To play, give a child—the batter—a baseball cap and have her stand at home plate. At your signal, the batter travels around the bases, peeking underneath each box. She then finds and puts the matching objects from the table in her baseball cap. Rounding the bases again, she places each item on the base that covers its match. Then another child—the umpire—removes the item under each base to check for matches. The batter earns a grand slam if each pair of items is a match. If desired, increase the challenge by putting two items under one or more bases. In this game, the grand slams are really out of sight!

Red White & Blue Review

With Independence Day just around the corner, strike up the enthusiasm in your classroom with this cross-curricular red, white, & blue review!

ideas contributed by Rachel Meseke Castro

I Love Red, White, & Blue

Your little ones will be rallying around the flag after learning this upbeat song. Write the song below on chart paper. Before you teach the song, encourage students to carefully examine your classroom flag. Prompt them to talk about the colors, shapes, and patterns that they see. Then introduce the song, encouraging students to sing along as they are able.

(sung to the tune of "When The Saints Go Marching In")

Our flag is red.
Our flag is white.
And in the corner it is blue.
Oh, our flag stands for our country.
How I love red, white, and blue!

Some stripes are red.
Some stripes are white.
And in the corner it is blue.
Oh, our flag stands for our country.
How I love red, white, and blue!

Patriotic Painting

Fly those colors high in your classroom with these red, white, and blue projects. To prepare, gather several marbles, a 9" x 13" cake pan, white construction paper, and a shallow dish (each) of red and blue paint. To do this activity, have a child place a sheet of white construction paper in the cake pan. Then direct her to take a marble and roll it in the red or the blue paint. Next have her drop the marble in the cake pan and roll it around the paper by moving the cake pan. Have the child repeat this process (with red and/or blue paint) as often as she likes. When the paint is dry, mount the painted paper on a sheet of red or blue construction paper. Display the finished projects in your classroom for all to see.

Popsicle® Plot

Here's a red, white, and blue graphing activity and a cool treat all in one. In advance prepare a graph with a column each for red, white, and blue. Then give each child a red, white, and blue Bomb Pop®. As they enjoy their treats, ask children to notice which colors they like the best. Then have each child write her name on a sticky note and attach it in the appropriate column. Afterward discuss what the graph reveals. Is it red, white, or blue for you?

Stars And Stripes Forever

This red, white, and blue center provides lots of patriotic patterning practice. To make the center, use a paper cutter to cut a large supply of three-inch-long construction-paper stripes in red and white. Also cut a classroom supply of blue, 4" x 18" construction-paper strips. Then use scissors or a die-cutter to cut a large supply of white stars. Place all of the cutouts in a center along with some glue sticks. When a child visits this center, have him use the blue strip as a background. Then encourage him to arrange and glue the stars and stripes in the pattern of his choice. When each child has designed a pattern, have him share his pattern during a group time. Save all the pattern strips to use in "We've Got The Rhythm."

We've Got The Rhythm!

After your class has made the pattern strips in "Stars And Stripes Forever," use them for this activity involving movement, sound, and rhythm. As a class, decide on a movement or sound for each symbol in the patterns. For example, you might clap for each red stripe, stomp your foot for each white stripe, and say, "Hurray!" for each star. Then show one pattern strip and have your class perform it together. After your children catch on, they can change the sounds and motions as often as they like. This is great fun as a whole-class activity or even just to fill a spare minute or two.

Related Activities

For additional activities related to Independence Day, please see "Fireworks!" and "Firecracker Party Favors" on page 33, and "Independence Day Tart" on pages 298 and 300.

Recommended Reading

Fourth Of July
By Barbara M. Joosse
Illustrated by Emily Arnold McCully
Published by Alfred A. Knopf, Inc.

Henry's Fourth Of July
By Holly Keller
Published by Greenwillow Books

Hurray For The Fourth Of July
By Wendy Watson
Published by Clarion Books
Note: You might wish to avoid the small portion of text in this book that refers to political parties.

Author Units

The Wondrous Works Of
Jane Yolen

Invite your youngsters to share the fantastical world of Jane Yolen. Through stories ranging from simple concept books to fanciful legends and folktales, this talented poet and storyteller captivates and entertains readers of all ages. Jane Yolen possesses the ability to enchant an audience with her keen sense of wonder, beauty, and humor. So open a book penned by Yolen and be prepared—a fantastic flight into the world of magic and wonder awaits!

Photo by Julie Offutt

A Sip Of Aesop
Illustrated by Karen Barbour
Published by The Blue Sky Press

Help your youngsters to a delightful serving of Aesop's tales when you share selections from this collection of humorous and witty verse. To extend the tale of "The Lion And The Mouse," have the children discuss the subject of friendship. Assure students that, although they may be small, each of them can offer friendship to anyone. Encourage them to consider the many ways they can be friends to others, large and small alike. Then give each child a sheet of paper programmed with "To other folks, I may seem small, but I can be a friend to all!" Have him illustrate a way in which he can show friendship. After describing his illustration to the class, help each student mount his picture on a bulletin-board display with the title "A Friend To All."

To other folks, I may be small, but I can be a friend to all!

Piggins
Illustrated by Jane Dyer
Published by Harcourt Brace Jovanovich, Publishers

Students will be inspired to use their own problem-solving skills after hearing this story about how Piggins, a wise and proper butler, solves the mystery of the missing *lavaliere* (necklace). To prepare a lavaliere for this activity, hot-glue a plastic gemstone to a length of ribbon. During group time, explain to students that they will each have an opportunity to solve the mystery of the missing lavaliere. Invite a student volunteer to play the role of Piggins. Have that child leave the room. While he is away, invite another child to take the lavaliere and hide it in his pocket, under his shirt, or elsewhere on his person. Then have the child posing as Piggins return. Explain that there is a thief among the group, and it is up to Piggins to identify him! Provide "Piggins" with clues, one at a time, to help him identify the thief. The clues may include information such as the thief's gender, hair color, or a description of his clothing. When the thief is identified, invite him to assume the role of Piggins. Continue in this manner until every child has had an opportunity to solve the mystery of the missing lavaliere.

Dawn Spurck, Educational Service Unit #3, Omaha, NE

For additional detective fun, challenge students to embark on a search for clues to unravel an even greater mystery—the disappearance of a classroom treasure! If desired, prepare a detective badge for each student to wear during this activity. In advance, arrange for your school's principal or another staff member to pose as the thief. Set a tentative time for this person to be "caught" in possession of the missing item, which may be a stapler, tape recorder, or some other familiar classroom item. Then hide clues in various locations around your class and school. Arrange the sequence and hiding places of the clues so that each clue leads the children to the next clue. For example, the first clue may be a large tennis shoe found where the missing item would typically be located. Prompt youngsters to decide on a location in the school where a large tennis shoe may be found, such as in the gym. When they look in the gym, help them discover the next clue, such as a milk carton. Then have the class go to the location where they would most likely find a milk carton—to discover still another clue. After discovering a series of clues in this manner, have the students follow the last clue to the location of the thief. When the group arrives at that location, have the guilty party sporting some form of evidence to prove him guilty, such as wearing the matching tennis shoe. On discovering this final piece of evidence, encourage students to request that the thief return the missing treasure. Case solved!

Nancy Kriener
Fillmore Central Elementary School, Preston, MN

Detective Nancy

Owl Moon

Illustrated by John Schoenherr
Published by Philomel Books

What better time to go owling than on a cold, quiet, winter night lit up by the light of the moon? This is just what a young girl and her father do in this engaging tale about a fascinating nocturnal pastime. After reading this story aloud, encourage youngsters to practice their auditory memory skills with this listening game. Have the students form a circle. Explain that one child will produce an owl call, then will shine a flashlight at the chest of another child. That child will repeat the call made by the first child. Then the child who reproduced the call will take the flashlight, produce a different owl call, then shine the light at another student. As the children play, encourage them to produce different rhythmic patterns using the short and long "whoo" sounds of an owl. Continue play until every child has had the opportunity to produce and repeat an owl-call pattern. Youngsters will have a hooting good time with this one!

Old Dame Counterpane

Illustrated by Ruth Tietjen Councell
Published by Philomel Books

From sunrise to sunset, Old Dame Counterpane rocks and sews, sews and rocks, creating an evergrowing earth full of color and life from a ten-square quilt. But what will Dame Counterpane do when the last stitch is applied and her quilt is spread over the night? Read this colorful verse aloud to students; then invite them to help create a class quilt. To prepare, write each number from one to ten on a separate square sheet of poster board. Give each student a 9" x 9" square of white construction paper. Assign him a number from one to ten. Then have him draw a picture to depict one of the creations mentioned in the story for his assigned number. When the pictures are completed, mount each to the poster-board square corresponding to the appropriate number. Hole-punch several holes along the side edges of each square; then sequence them in a row. In quilt-fashion, attach the poster squares to one another by lacing ribbon through the holes. Display the class quilt with the title "Sew Up The Day With Old Dame Counterpane."

Mouse's Birthday

Illustrated by Bruce Degen
Published by G. P. Putnam's Sons

Mouse lives in a very small house—so small, in fact, that all his friends barely fit in it for his birthday celebration! But fit they do! And the celebration is held, with the traditional cake and candle-lighting. Oh, what a surprise for the entire party when Mouse blows out the candle! And what fun your youngsters will have as they role-play this delightful story! After reading the story aloud, spread out a parachute (or a large flat sheet) to represent Mouse's house. Have your students kneel around the edges of the parachute. Assign the role of each character from the story to a child. Have the child playing the role of Mouse sit under the parachute. Then ask each child who is assigned a character role to crawl under the parachute according to the sequence in the story. When all the children portraying the characters are under the parachute, have them call out "Happy Birthday, Mouse," then pretend to blow out a candle. As the children under the parachute blow, encourage the students kneeling around the outer edges of the parachute to simultaneously lift and release the parachute into the air. Now Mouse's house is wide—wide enough for all of his friends, and even more, to fit inside! Replace the parachute and repeat the activity so that each student has an opportunity to role-play a character.

Dawn Spurck
Educational Service Unit #3
Omaha, NE

More Jane Yolen Books

Eeny, Meeny, Miney Mole
Illustrated by Kathryn Brown
Published by
Harcourt Brace Jovanovich

Baby Bear's Bedtime Book
Illustrated by Jane Dyer
Published by
Harcourt Brace Jovanovich

An Invitation To The Butterfly Ball
Illustrated by Jane Breskin Zalben
Published by Parents' Magazine Press

Hooray For HAP!!

For more than 20 years, educators have had the fortunate influence of one of the most talented and versatile educational innovators of our times—Hap Palmer! Being a songwriter, musician, singer, dancer, and educator, Hap Palmer has the rare gift of using music for youngsters as a tool for learning, movement, creativity, and most importantly, fun! So round up a collection of Hap Palmer recordings and let the fun begin. Hip HAP hooray!

"Growing"

Learning Basic Skills Through Music: Volume 1

With the aid of this song, youngsters will learn that "there are so many things that grow, grow, grow"—including their understanding of things that grow! After hearing the song, ask students to brainstorm a list of growing things. Write their responses on a sheet of chart paper. Then divide your class into small groups. Provide each group with a sheet of poster board and a variety of magazines and catalogs. Encourage each group to cut out pictures of things that grow and glue them onto the poster board. Display the completed posters with the title "So Many Things Grow!" You'll find that, as each group's interest grows during this activity, so will the number of pictures on the collage—and your pride in your students!

Jennifer Barton—Gr. K, Elizabeth Green School, Newington, CT

"Sally The Swinging Snake"

Sally The Swinging Snake

Satisfy students' needs to slither and squirm with this snappy, snaky little song. To prepare, cut a 30-inch length of yarn for each child; then tie a knot in each end to prevent unraveling. To make a snake, have each child tape one end of his yarn to a large button. Then invite youngsters to manipulate their snakes according to the verses in the song. Afterward pair the students. Encourage one student in a pair to direct his partner in actions that require the manipulation of his snake. Then have students reverse their roles so that each child has the opportunity to both give and follow directions.

Lynne Merlino—Gr. K
James Hogg Elementary, Dallas, TX

"Parade Of Colors"

Can A Cherry Pie Wave Goodbye?
and
Learning Basic Skills Through Music: Volume 2

Line your youngsters up for an unusual event—a pillow parade—to display the colors and actions of this song! To prepare, make a classroom quantity of small pillows in the ten colors mentioned in the song (red, green, yellow, blue, orange, pink, purple, black, brown, and white), duplicating colors as necessary. Place the pillows in a large basket or box. Invite each child to select a pillow; then have the class line up in parade fashion. Explain that the class will parade around the room as the song plays, until they hear the sound of a bell. At that time, they are to stop and listen for specific directions. As each direction is sung, encourage each child with the corresponding pillow color to perform the action named. When not in use for this song, place the basketful of pillows in your reading center or have them available for rest time. During these quiet times, be sure to play some soft, easy listening music, such as that found on Hap's *Sea Gulls* or *A Child's World Of Lullabies* recordings.

Dawn Fontaine—Gr. K, The Academy For Little Children, Warwick, RI

"Walter The Waltzing Worm"

Walter The Waltzing Worm
Entice youngsters to wiggle and squirm their way into learning body parts with a worm named Walter. To make a worm puppet, hot-glue two wiggle eyes, a black oval felt mouth, a red felt tongue, and a printed fabric bowtie or hat to a green sock. Then encourage each student to make his own version of Walter using a 12-inch length of wide white ribbon. Have the child paint his ribbon with diluted green food coloring. After the ribbon is dry, help him glue wiggle eyes and a red felt mouth to one end of it. After the glue dries, invite youngsters to use their ribbon worms as the song is played. Using the sock puppet, lead students to manipulate their worms over their own bodies according to the lyrics. Then repeat the song, having each student move his worm over a partner.

Sandy Blumstein—Pre-K, Paley Day Care Center, Philadelphia, PA

"Put A Little Color On You"

Can A Cherry Pie Wave Goodbye?
Your little ones will be quite a colorful bunch by the time they complete this activity. In advance purchase blue, green, yellow, and red sticky note pads. Cut one sticky note of each color in half for every two children in your class. (If sticky notes are not available, cut a classroom quantity of 1 1/2" x 3" strips from sheets of paper of the color needed; then use a removable adhesive glue stick to rub a line of glue along one edge of each strip.) Give each child one of each color strip. Explain to students that they will stick each color strip on the body part mentioned in the song; then remove and reposition the color strip as the song dictates. To check students' skills in making color-object associations and in following directions, invite two or three students at a time to place their sticky notes on *your* body according to the song.

Kristin Kaehler—Gr. K, Bentley Elementary, Salem, MA

"Pause"

Movin'
Add an element of fun and interest to your cleanup time by having youngsters tidy up to this song. When cleanup time arrives, play the song and invite students to dance about the room as they pick up and put away. Explain to them that each time the music pauses, they should freeze in place to take a break from their work. Then when the music resumes, so should the students' cleanup activities.

Elaine Hercenberg—Gr. K, Bet Yeladim, Columbia, MD

Other "HAP-pening" Recordings

Getting To Know Myself
Easy Does It
Witches' Brew
"So Big"

...And Videos, Too!
Sammy
Steppin' Out With Hap Palmer
Follow Along Songs
Learning Basic Skills

Contact Educational Activities, Inc. (1-800-645-3739) to order the above recordings and videos, or for information on other Hap Palmer products.

237

The Exceptional
Eloise Greenfield

Your students will be lured to explore relationships, emotions, and imagination with the prose and poetry of Eloise Greenfield. Before becoming an author, Eloise had always wanted to help improve the lives of her family, friends, and neighbors. Later she became inspired to write books for and about children—specifically African-American children. Eloise Greenfield worked diligently for many long hours to learn how to be a successful writer. And her hard work and dedication paid off—since the early 1970s, Eloise has been a major voice in children's literature that celebrates family life, human relationships, and the internal strength of individuals. Share some of Eloise Greenfield's literature with your youngsters; then invite them to share some of themselves with you.

by Mackie Rhodes

Place on the fold.

Honey, I Love

Daddy   my dog

Africa Dream
Illustrated by Carole Byard
HarperCollins Children's Books

As a girl recounts her dream of long-ago Africa, she describes some of the life and culture of the African people. After reading the book aloud, return to the page on which the new-old friends sing a hello song. Encourage students to name some different words they use to greet people. Then ask any willing volunteers to lead the class in singing hello songs that they know.

Afterward explain that in Swahili—a language native to Africa—the word used for hello is *jambo.* Have youngsters greet one another with this African greeting. Then instruct youngsters to form a circle. Play "Jambo" from the recording *Jambo* by Ella Jenkins (available from Smithsonian Folkways Recordings, 1-800-410-9815). Encourage students to sing along as they greet their new-old friends in class with a song and smiles.

Honey, I Love
Illustrated by Jan Spivey Gilchrist
HarperCollins Publishers

From a child's playful, observant, and emotional perspective, this captivating poem expresses some of the things to love about life. After sharing this book, invite youngsters to create their own books to express some of the things *they* love. In advance make half-heart patterns on tagboard; then cut them out to make tracers. Demonstrate how to use a tracer by placing the straight edge on a fold and cutting out a double thickness of the pattern to make a heart shape. Then have each child trace and cut out two white hearts and one red heart from construction paper. To make booklet pages, instruct each child to align and glue one side of a folded white heart to the left side of the red heart. Repeat the process on the right side of the red heart. Then encourage each child to write about (dictate) and illustrate something he loves on each page. (Or have him glue on pictures cut out of magazines.) Then have each child write the title "Honey, I Love" on the front of his book. Invite each child to share his book with a classmate and his family members.

238

Night On Neighborhood Street
Illustrated by Jan Spivey Gilchrist
Dial Books For Young Readers

Youngsters will experience and relate to a range of emotions presented in this powerful collection of poetry depicting life and relationships. After sharing the book, revisit "Fambly Time." After discussing the poem, brainstorm a list of things that a family can do together. Write student responses on a sheet of chart paper. Then review the list, having a volunteer place a star sticker beside any activity that can also be done as a class. Discuss how your class also constitutes a type of family—a class family. Then inform children that they will have the opportunity to participate in "fambly" time every day for a predeter-mined period of time. Each day invite a different student to select an activity for the class to engage in during a designated family time. As new ideas and activities arise over time, include them on the list of student choices. And *all* the little ones can call it "Fambly Time!"

Family Time
- Eat dinner.
- Play games.
- Read books.

On My Horse
Illustrated by Jan Spivey Gilchrist
HarperCollins Publishers

An imaginary romp through the wild satisfies a child's wish to ride a horse without supervision. Read this book with your students. Then ask each child to close her eyes and imagine that she is riding a horse as she *listens* to the story again. After-ward arrange a course to represent some of the terrain mentioned in the book. For instance, a safety cone might serve as a bush, a chair might serve as a tree, and two parallel ropes could serve as a stream. In turn, invite each child to pretend she is riding a horse through the wild. Encourage her to pretend the horse is walking, trotting, and galloping as she negotiates the course. At the end of each child's turn, ask her to tell the group something special about her imaginary ride—such as a place she rode past or an animal she spied while riding.

Grandpa's Face
Illustrated by Floyd Cooper
Philomel Books

Tamika loves everything about Grandpa—especially his sturdy brown face that always tells her she is loved. But one day Tamika witnesses a very different expression on Grandpa's face—one that scares her and causes her to wonder if Grandpa could ever love her anymore. After sharing this story, guide youngsters to discuss the looks they see on the faces of people they know. Ask them to tell how each expression makes them feel. Then pass out some hand mirrors, prompting each child to observe his reflection as he practices making facial expressions to represent different moods. Afterward call on the acting abilities of your students. First choose one child to stand in front of the group. Whisper an emotion to that child and have him act it out while the rest of the class tries to guess that specific emotion. Continue playing until each child has had a turn to perform.

She Come Bringing Me That Little Baby Girl
Illustrated by John Steptoe
HarperCollins Children's Books

What a sickening feeling it gives Kevin to see all the attention his new baby sister is receiving. After all, she was *supposed* to be a boy—that's what he asked for! But Kevin's opinion of his sister begins to change as he realizes the importance of his big-brother role. Follow up this story with a class discussion to discover which students have younger siblings and to determine how they feel about being older siblings. Ask those students to share some things they do *not* like about having younger brothers or sisters. Then encourage them to tell some of the *good* things that go along with having a younger sibling. Extend the discussion by playing the song "Why Did I Have To Have A Sister?" from *10 Carrot Diamond* by Charlotte Diamond (produced by Hug Bug Music Inc. and available from Educational Record Center, 1-800-438-1637). Ask students to listen for the advantage mentioned in the song of having a little sister. Conclude the discussion by inviting youngsters to brainstorm other advantages and positive aspects of having a younger sibling.

First Pink Light
Illustrated by Jan Spivey Gilchrist
Writers and Readers Publishing, Inc.

Tyree wants to stay up all night in his hideout and surprise his dad upon his homecoming. After negotiating with his mother, they work out a comfortable compromise. Then, at the first pink light in the sky, Dad finally does arrive—but to a surprise very different from Tyree's original plan. Read this story aloud; then have students discuss some special times when they wanted to stay up late or all night. Were they allowed to do so? Did they stay awake? Then invite youngsters to make a project illustrating a similar situation. For each child, duplicate the chair pattern (page 243) on construction paper. Have the child write/dictate to complete the story starter. Ask each child to color and cut out his chair, then glue it to a sheet of construction paper. Next invite each child to draw a picture of himself, then cut it out and glue it to his chair picture. If desired, have each child glue on fabric scraps to resemble a blanket and a pillow. Mount each picture on a board titled "First Pink Light."

I wanted to stay up...

because I was trying to see when my Grandpa got to my house.
Jovan

More Literature By Eloise Greenfield

Me And Neesie
Illustrated by Moneta Barnett
HarperCollins Publishers

Grandmama's Joy
Illustrated by Carole Byard
Philomel Books

William And The Good Old Days
Illustrated by Jan Spivey Gilchrist
HarperCollins Publishers

Under The Sunday Tree
Illustrated by Mr. Amos Ferguson
HarperCollins Publishers

Literature Selections
By Other African-American Authors

The Patchwork Quilt
Written by Valerie Flournoy
Illustrated by Jerry Pinkney
Published by Dial Books For Young Readers

Mufaro's Beautiful Daughters
Written & Illustrated by John Steptoe
Published by Lothrop, Lee & Shepard Books

Shortcut
Written & Illustrated by Donald Crews
Published by Greenwillow Books

Sunday Outing
Written by Gloria Jean Pinkney
Illustrated by Jerry Pinkney
Published by Dial Books For Young Readers

Max Found Two Sticks
Written & Illustrated by Brian Pinkney
Published by Simon & Schuster Books For Young Readers

Brown Honey In Broomwheat Tea
Poems by Joyce Carol Thomas
Illustrated by Floyd Cooper
Published by HarperCollins Publishers

African Folktales...Just For Fun!
Written by Verna Aardema

Bringing The Rain To Kapiti Plain
Illustrated by Beatriz Vidal
Published by Dial Books For Young Readers

Rabbit Makes A Monkey Of Lion
Illustrated by Jerry Pinkney
Published by Dial Books For Young Readers

Jackal's Flying Lesson
Illustrated by Dale Gottlieb
Published by Alfred A. Knopf, Inc.

Anansi Finds A Fool
Illustrated by Bryna Waldman
Published by Dial Books For Young Readers

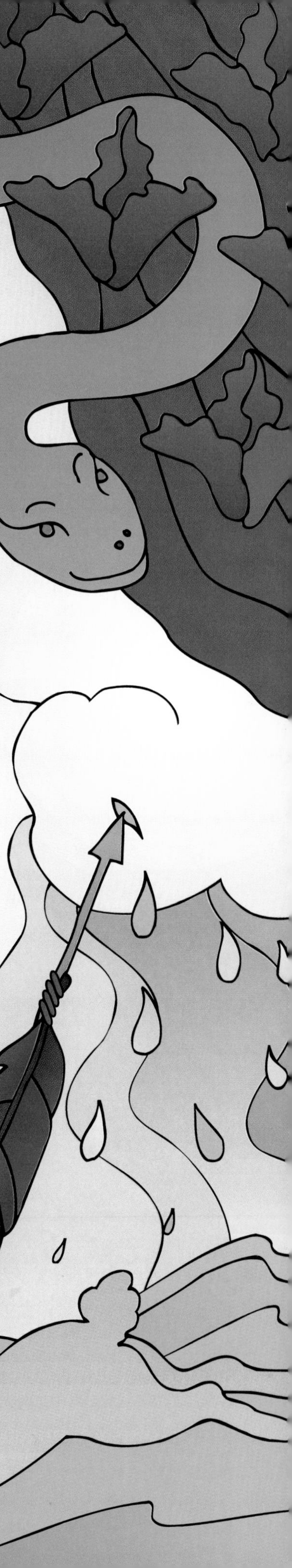

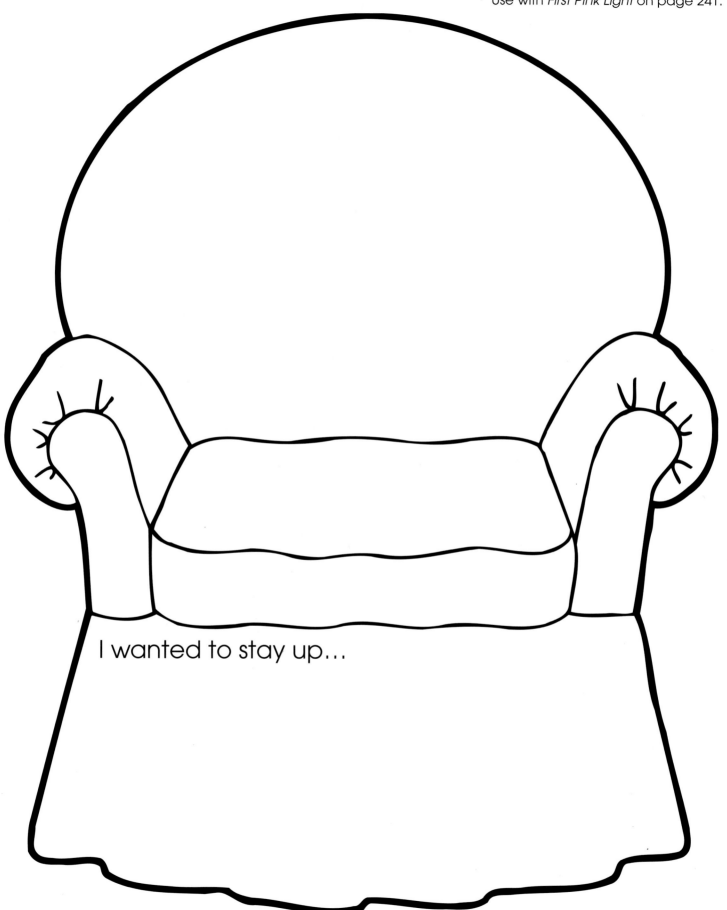

I wanted to stay up...

WELCOME TO WADDELL'S WORLD

Adventure, fun, and—most especially—emotion are the key elements in the worlds created by Martin Waddell. Although fictitious in nature, Waddell's works are inspired by the real experiences and emotions of children—separation anxiety, fear of the dark, the desire for friendship, and the joy of childhood fun. (All books mentioned are published by Candlewick Press unless otherwise noted.) Invite youngsters to journey into the wonderful world of Martin Waddell with some of these stories.

by Mackie Rhodes

CAN'T YOU SLEEP, LITTLE BEAR?
Illustrated by Barbara Firth

Little Bear's fear of the dark persists until Big Bear's loving gesture alleviates Little Bear's fear, making room for sleep. After sharing the story, explore Little Bear's fear with youngsters. Then take a turn into science by inviting students to explore the amount of light needed to expel the dark. To prepare, cut out two black construction-paper circles sized to cover a large flashlight lens. Cut a circle from the middle of each lens cover—one small and the other a bit larger. Tape the first lens cover to the flashlight. Place a masking-tape line on the floor near a sheet of black bulletin-board paper attached to a wall. Dim the lights; then have a child stand on the line and shine the flashlight onto the paper. Ask another child to use chalk to trace the ring of light onto the paper. Then replace the first lens cover with the second cover and repeat the process, helping the child center the light over the first ring. Repeat the process once more, using no lens cover. Then have youngsters compare the light-ring sizes. How much dark was expelled by the light with and without the lens covers? Which lighting situation do students think would be most comfortable for Little Bear? For themselves? The resulting discoveries will be "en-light-ening!"

I hear a woofer.

LET'S GO HOME, LITTLE BEAR
Illustrated by Barbara Firth

A carefree romp through the woods takes a fearful turn as Little Bear tunes in to the noises all around. After sharing this story, challenge youngsters to sharpen their listening skills by tuning in to the noises all around them. Ask students to stop their movements, then to listen and look—just as Little Bear did in the story. After a brief time, invite each child, in turn, to describe a noise he heard during the silence—such as *"woof, woof, woof."* Then encourage each child to illustrate and label the real or imaginary source of that sound. Compile the illustrations into a class book titled "Sounds All Around." Share the book with the class, inviting each child to tell about his page.

SAILOR BEAR
Illustrated by Virginia Austin

Lost and lonely, Small Bear unintentionally reasons himself into a dangerous adventure with a most surprising conclusion. Read the story aloud; then present each child with a situation that will prompt her to adopt Small Bear's self-inquiry, "Now what shall I do?" and his problem-solving skills. To prepare, gather a group of related and unrelated items—such as a sheet of paper, a crayon, a shoe, a block, scissors, and tape—and put them into a basket. Ask a child to think about how she might combine and use some of the items from the basket; then invite her to demonstrate her idea. For example, she might use the crayon to trace the shoe onto the paper, then cut out the shoe outline and tape it onto a wall. If desired, vary the items in the basket for each student. Now what shall *I* do? Gather, group, and get youngsters thinking!

OWL BABIES
Illustrated by Patrick Benson

When they awaken to discover their mother missing, Sarah, Percy, and Bill—the young owl siblings—anxiously speculate over her whereabouts, her doings, and her safe return. After sharing the story, liken the anxiety of the young owls to that your students might have during a separation from their parents. With warm acceptance of their feelings, guide youngsters to express and explore the emotions they experience when their parents are not present. Conclude the discussion by reassuring students that their feelings and fears are understandable and acceptable. Then ask each child to imagine that Owl Mother is his parent. Where would *she* have gone? Invite the child to illustrate his conclusion, then write (or dictate) a statement about his illustration. Display the pictures with the title "My Owl Mother Went…"

Mother Owl went to buy food.

THE HAPPY HEDGEHOG BAND
Illustrated by Jill Barton

Tum-tum-te-tum. Buzz. Click. Hum. Dickon Woods jams to the beat of Harry's drum. Infect your class with the rhythmic lines in this upbeat tale about a noise-crazy hedgehog; then invite youngsters to form a rhythm band of their own. Have each child select a rhythm instrument or choose a sound that he can make—such as clapping, humming, tongue clicking, or lip smacking. Beat a few rounds of a simple rhythm on a drum; then have the class band imitate that rhythm until you raise your drumsticks to stop the music. Begin a new rhythm with a different beat or tempo. Better clear lots of space for this activity—once youngsters get the rhythm of the beat, they're bound to get the rhythm in their feet!

SQUEAK-A-LOT
Illustrated by Virginia Miller
Published by Greenwillow Books

While searching for a playmate, a small mouse learns that there are some games he enjoys a lot—and some he prefers not! Read this delightfully repetitious book aloud; then transfer the story's word theme to a modified game of tag. Outdoors, have students role-play mice gathered in a designated safe zone. Appoint one child to be the cat and to remain outside the safe zone. To play, the cat calls out an action word with *a-lot* attached to it—such as *hop-a-lot*. The mice perform that action, scattering around the play area outside the safe zone until the cat calls out "Wham! Bam! Scram!" At that time, the mice scurry back to the safe zone as the cat tries to tag them. The cat then chooses his replacement from the untagged mice in the safe zone. This is one game youngsters are sure to like a lot!

MORE WONDERS OF WADDELL'S WORLD

Farmer Duck
Illustrated by Helen Oxenbury

The Pig In The Pond
Illustrated by Jill Barton
(Note: In this book, a character removes all his clothing. Please preview for appropriateness for your class.)

The Park In The Dark
Illustrated by Barbara Firth

Small Bear Lost
Illustrated by Virginia Austin

A Bouquet Of Books

By Eve Bunting

Eve Bunting's bountiful bouquet of literature is made up of over 100 children's books—a mixture of stories about special days, special people, and special interests. This Irish-born author jots down her seeds of inspiration on just about anything, including a play program and a small airline sickness bag! Then her fertile mind goes to work to cultivate her ideas until beautiful stories with special messages blossom. Why not share a book from Bunting's bouquet with your class? Youngsters will blossom with delight!

Flower Garden

Illustrated by Kathryn Hewitt
Published by Harcourt Brace & Company

In this story, a garden-on-the-go finds a special place in the home and hearts of a loving family. After reading the story, invite each child to create a flower-box garden of his own. To make a flower box, have the child use paint pens to decorate the sides of an empty plastic hand-wipes container (with the lid removed). After the paint dries, have him fill his box with potting soil, then transplant a few flowering plants into the box. Encourage the child to take his flower box home to give to a special person.

A Perfect Father's Day

Illustrated by Susan Meddaugh
Published by Clarion Books

Susie fills her dad's special day with treats inspired by her own favorite things. Help each child highlight special times with his dad (or a male friend) with this activity. For each child, duplicate the cake pattern on page 34 on construction paper. After reading the story, prompt youngsters to discuss things they like to do with their dads (or other significant men). Then have each child cut out a cake pattern and the number of construction-paper candles equal to his age. Have him glue the candles onto his cutout. On the back, have the child illustrate an activity he enjoys sharing with his dad, then write/dictate a sentence about his illustration. Invite each child to give his card to his dad on Father's Day. A perfect card for a perfect day!

Sunflower House

Illustrated by Kathryn Hewitt
Published by Harcourt Brace & Company

Imaginations flourish as a young boy and his friends enjoy the shelter of a homegrown sunflower house. Read this story aloud; then spark imaginations with a student-created sunflower house. To prepare, cut the top and bottom flaps off a large appliance box. Along the bottom cut a few inverted *V* openings large enough for youngsters to fit through. Invite each child to paint and initial a green, leafy stem along a side of the box. Then have her make a construction-paper sunflower to attach to the top of her stem. Put the resulting sunflower house in the dramatic-play center. Invite students to play in the house, prompting them to use their imaginations and a variety of props in their play. What blooming good fun!

The Wednesday Surprise

Illustrated by Donald Carrick
Published by Clarion Books

Anna and Grandma read together every Wednesday to prepare a super surprise for Dad's birthday. After sharing the story and its surprising conclusion, breathe some surprise into this letter-recognition activity. Explain to a small group of students that knowing the letters and their sounds is important in reading. Fog the front surface of a large, acrylic picture frame with your breath; then finger-write a letter on the fog. Challenge youngsters to name the letter before the writing disappears. Then ask them to name words beginning with that letter sound. After several rounds, invite each child in turn to write a breath letter for the others to name. Use a spray glass-cleaner and paper towel to clean the frame between youngsters' turns. What a fun way to give fresh breath to basic skills practice!

Market Day

Illustrated by Holly Berry
Published by Joanna Cotler Books

On the first Thursday of each month, the streets of a small Irish village are filled with activity, excitement, and lots of fun—it's Market Day! After reading this story, have youngsters compare the Market Day sights and events to their own shopping experiences. Then invite youngsters to create their own Market Day. Ask each child to make one or two craft items—such as a musical instrument or an animal model—using an assortment of craft materials. Display the craft goods in several areas in the room. Divide the class into small groups of students. Invite one group to shop, giving a penny to each child in that group with which to buy one item. Have the students in another group tend the market areas, collecting the pennies for purchases in small containers. Rotate the groups so that each has the opportunity to tend the booths and to shop. Then ask each group to count the pennies in a container. It's Market Day!

Our Teacher's Having A Baby

Illustrated by Diane de Groat
Published by Clarion Books

Enthusiasm and anxiety build as a class anticipates the arrival of their teacher's baby. But after the baby's birth, the students wonder if the new mother will continue to be their teacher. Read this story aloud; then lead students to discuss how a woman can be both a mother and a teacher. Ask youngsters to tell about the different roles their own mothers perform. Then invite each child to illustrate her mother on a plain, legal-size envelope. Program the envelope flap with "My mother is a mom, but she is also a…." Ask the child to illustrate one or more envelope-sized sheets of paper, each with a picture representing a different role her mother plays. Have the child write/dictate a completion to the sentence for each illustrated page, then slip the pages into her envelope. During group time, invite each child to share the contents of her envelope. Wow! Mothers can be anything!

More Bunting Books About...

Special Occasions

A Turkey For Thanksgiving
Illustrated by Diane de Groat
Published by Clarion Books

(All Illustrated by Jan Brett)
Happy Birthday, Dear Duck
Published by Clarion Books

Scary, Scary Halloween
Published by Scholastic Inc.

The Valentine Bears
Published by Scholastic Inc.

The Mother's Day Mice
Published by Scholastic Inc.

Social Issues

Someday A Tree
Illustrated by Ronald Himler
Published by Clarion Books

Going Home
Illustrated by David Diaz
Published by Joanna Cotler Books

Smoky Night
Illustrated by David Diaz
Published by Harcourt Brace & Company

Fly Away Home
Illustrated by Ronald Himler
Published by Clarion Books

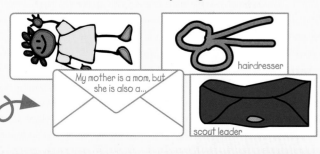

My mother is a mom, but she is also a...

hairdresser

scout leader

Cake Pattern

Use with *A Perfect Father's Day* on page 246.

For the love, for the memory, for the fun of it, too—
Here's something special I want to do with you!

Happy Father's Day!

Science Units

Color My World

Many children have elicited "oohs" and "aahs" from delighted adults by simply identifying colors at a young age. But as children grow, it becomes apparent that there's more to simple color than meets the eye! Use the ideas in this unit to discover some principles behind color and uses of color.

Before you begin, photocopy the science-journal page (page 252) for each child. Have each child color his page; then staple a few blank pages behind each cover. Encourage youngsters to write in their journals during each science activity.

Primarily Colors

Objective:
To introduce the primary colors and demonstrate that, when combined, the primary colors make up additional colors.

Introduce the primary colors by sharing Ellen Stoll Walsh's appealing *Mouse Paint* (Harcourt Brace Jovanovich) with your children. (Monique Felix's adorable, wordless picture book, *The Colors* (Creative Editions), is also a good choice.) Afterward provide the related discovery stations described below. Have children record their findings in their journals. Be sure to encourage children to share their discoveries when you gather together as a group; then record each child's findings on chart paper.

Colored Water:
Use food coloring to prepare one container each of red, blue, and yellow colored water. Provide a different eyedropper for each color and a supply of clear plastic cups. As children visit this station, encourage them to experiment with the colors by dropping one drop of color at time into their cups. What'd ya' get?

Tissue Paper:
Stock a center with a large supply of red, blue, and yellow tissue-paper squares; white art paper; water-diluted white glue; and paintbrushes. Have each child first brush a coat of the glue mixture on his paper. Next have him add various tissue-paper squares, overlapping them as desired. Then have him paint the glue over the tissue paper again and observe what happens as the colors blend.

Play Dough:
Provide one container each of red, blue, and yellow play dough. As a child visits this station, have him tear off a small portion from two colors of dough. Then encourage him to experiment by mixing the doughs together to different degrees.

Cellophane:
Cut sections of red, blue, and yellow cellophane; then store them in a basket at a center. When a child visits this center, encourage him to make predictions about how something will change in appearance when he looks at it through a colored piece of cellophane. Then have him take a look and compare the results with his predictions.

See Also "Paint Palettes" on page 41.

Pam Crane

What Are You Trying To Say?

Objective: To lead children to discover that colors can send messages.

Begin a discussion by asking children if they think colors can talk. After they respond (probably incredulously!), do the following activities to demonstrate that although colors do not *talk,* they do sometimes *communicate!* Be sure to encourage journal writing during these activities.

Are You Ready?
Present a very green banana and a ripe (yellow) banana to each small group of students. Have children examine the bananas. Ask them what they can tell by the colors of the bananas. If desired, have students taste each banana to support their discussions.

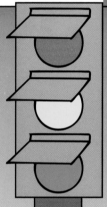

You May...
Make a large, construction-paper traffic light. Glue on the edges of construction-paper squares so that they serve as flaps to cover the colors not in use at any given time. Then show the light to your students. Ask them what drivers can do when they see each different color. How do they know? Did the colors talk?!

Related Literature: *My Crayons Talk* by Patricia Hubbard (Henry Holt And Company)

My Color Science Journal

by Jasmin Thomas

Hide-And-Seek

Objective:
To introduce children to the idea that color can help protect animals, and provide opportunities for youngsters to demonstrate their understanding of *camouflage.*

Begin this study by taking your students for a walk in a natural area. Encourage them to look for any kind of animal or insect and call out when they spot one. Have youngsters describe the colors of each of the creatures and whether they are easy or difficult to see. When you return to class, discuss how some creatures were easier/harder to see than others. Guide children in discussing how color might help protect some animals. Introduce the term *camouflage.* (Since children love to show off their new vocabulary words, have them write this big, new word on a science journal page.)

Then provide a supply of sculpting clay. Ask each child to make an animal. As he works, encourage him to think about whether he would like his animal to be camouflaged or not. Let the projects dry. Then review the concept of camouflage and have youngsters paint their animals. When the paint is dry, have each child place his animal outside somewhere. As a class, look for each animal. When all of the animals have been spotted, ask youngsters which animals are easy to see and which are more difficult. Discuss how the colors of the animals relate to their visibility. Determine which animals are well camouflaged and which are not.

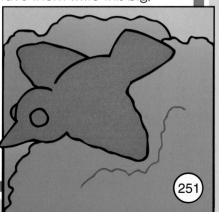

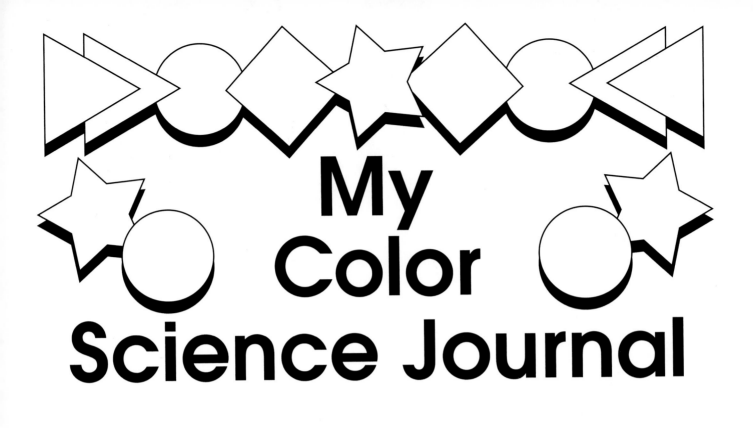

My
Color
Science Journal

by

Note To The Teacher: Use with "Color My World" on page 250–251

Wonders Never Cease

Simple Science For Young Children

The "A-maize-ing" Corn Plant

Corn chips, corn dogs, cornflakes, cornbread, corn syrup—and the list goes on and on. Corn, also called *maize,* is a very important crop in the United States as well as in the world. Use the ideas in this unit to introduce your students to corn and its many, many uses.

by Ann Flagg

Objective: Students will learn that corn is a food that comes from a plant and can be used in a variety of ways.

What's That Sound? What's That Smell?

Entice youngsters into the study of corn with a guessing game. Prepare a popcorn popper; then put it behind a screen. Gather children around; then plug it in. Explain that you'd like them to discover what they are going to study by using their senses. As the popcorn begins to pop, ask: "What do you hear?", "What do you smell?" After children have identified the popcorn, pass it out so everyone can enjoy the treat with the remaining three senses—seeing, touching, and tasting!

What Do You Know?

After an experiential introduction to the topic of corn, youngsters will be ready to brainstorm. Ask students what they already know about corn and write their responses on a large popcorn cutout. As you continue your study, corn ideas and corn vocabulary are sure to pop up. As they do, record them on your popcorn chart.

Corn cloud:
- It could be on a cob.
- You have to take the leaves off.
- It could be corn dogs!
- Corn is yellowish.
- It can be like whitish.

Corn

- It's salty and good.
- It pops.
- My grandpa grows it.
- It's good for a movie.

So, Where're Ya' From?

Ask children where they think popcorn comes from. After discussing ideas, give each child a kernel of unpopped popcorn. After examining the kernels, do youngsters have any new ideas to share? Who would think that fluffy white popcorn comes from those tiny, yellowish kernels? Explain that when a kernel is heated, steam is created inside the kernel. The pressure of the steam causes the kernel to explode and turn inside out. The result—popcorn!

Next establish the connection between the corn kernel and the cob by showing youngsters a cob of popcorn (available at novelty gift/kitchen shops). Pop out kernels from the cob and have children compare them to their original kernels.

Did You Know?

Popcorn is one of the oldest kinds of corn. It was grown by Native Americans thousands of years ago!

Corny Vocabulary

Hands-on exploration will help youngsters retain this new corny vocabulary. Give each child (or small group of children) an ear of Indian corn with the husk still attached. Encourage youngsters to examine their ears of corn and share what they observe. At an appropriate time in your discussion, introduce the vocabulary shown in the diagram.

corn silk

kernel

ear

husk

cob

I Say, It's A Seed!

Now that you've made the connection between popcorn and corn on the cob, help children understand that the little kernel is also a seed that can be planted to produce another corn plant. For each child, arrange a folded paper towel in a resealable plastic bag. Staple across the center of the bag to stabilize the paper towel (and the kernels). Lightly water the paper towel, leaving about one-half inch of water at the bottom of the bag. Then place corn kernels in a row above the staples. Tape each bag to a window or tack it to a bulletin board. Encourage children to observe their plants each day and to record changes that they see.

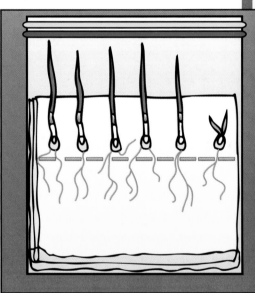

Knee High By The Fourth Of July

Have your students had the opportunity to stand right next to a cornstalk? If they haven't, you can practice a little measuring to put this plant in perspective. In the Corn Belt—the midwestern states where corn is chiefly produced—cornstalks average about nine feet tall. Divide your class into small groups. Give each group a 12-inch ruler and a supply of Unifix® cubes. Ask each child to put cubes together to match the length of the ruler. When each group has nine lengths of cubes (each one foot long), have students connect the lengths to make one long line. Next have each group slide its cubeline onto a long length of green bulletin-board paper. Draw a line loosely around the cubes; then cut on the resulting outline. This will be the stalk. Mount the stalks on a classroom wall and have children use their free time to complete the scene by adding construction-paper leaves and ears of corn. Encourage children to walk among your classroom cornfield comparing their heights to that of the cornstalks. Is your corn as high as an elephant's eye?

Corn, Corn Everywhere!

Corn has been called the most important crop grown in the United States—and it seems to be popping up all over! Challenge your little ones to search their homes to find corn products. Then duplicate page 256 for each child. Encourage each child to look around his home and copy the names of everything he can find that is made with corn. Then have him bring his page back to school. In turn, have each child share his list as you record each corny item. After each child has shared, count 'em up! How many did you get?

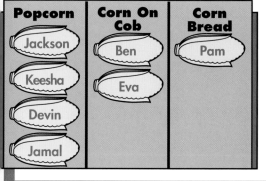

Popcorn	Corn On Cob	Corn Bread
Jackson	Ben	Pam
Keesha	Eva	
Devin		
Jamal		

How Do You Like Your Corn?

If you made the class list described in "Corn, Corn Everywhere!", choose three (or more) of the most-mentioned entries. Then make a graph using those entries. Prepare samplings of each of the forms of corn on your graph. Before tasting, photocopy the ear-of-corn pattern (below) for each child. Then have each child taste each entry. Afterwards, have him tape his ear of corn on the graph to indicate which one he liked the best. How do you like your corn?

ear of corn

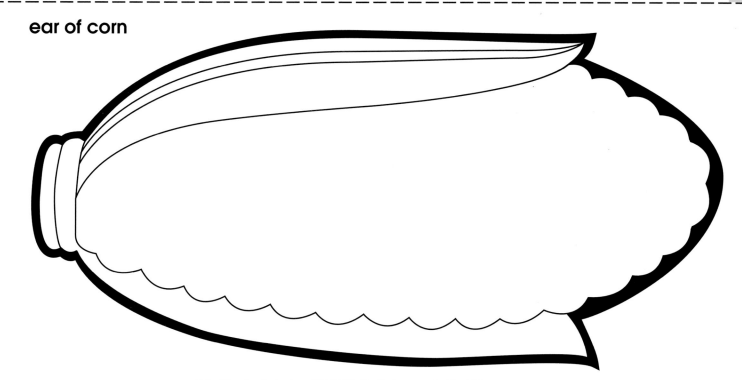

Use with "Corn, Corn Everywhere!" on page 255.

At Home With Corn

I found…

The Long And Short Of Shadows

With groundhogs popping in and out of February shadows, what better time to embark on a study of shadows? Use the ideas in this unit to help your little ones explore the long and short of shadows.

ideas by Ann Flagg

Objective:
Students will learn that it takes light and an object to make a shadow.

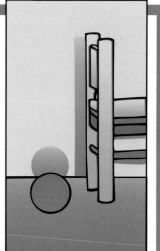

Look Around You

Begin your shadow study with a look around you! Take your students outside on a sunny morning. Instruct them to look all around for shadows. As they search, ask questions (such as those below) to help formulate ideas.

- Can you find a big shadow? Small shadow?
- Why is one shadow bigger/smaller than another?
- How are the shadows alike? Different?
- How are the shadows made? Can you make one?
- What will happen to a shadow outside at night? On a cloudy day?

Did You Know...

A shadow is a dark area that is caused when an object prevents light from shining on a surface. To make a shadow, there must be a light source and an object.

Shadow Center

This is the place for lots of discovery learning! Cover a small table or desk with a white cloth or white paper. Provide a set of one-inch blocks and a flashlight. As a small group visits this center, encourage them to build a structure with the blocks. Then have them try to make shadows by moving the light source around the structure. (If necessary, dim the lights in that section of the room.) As children freely explore, guide them to discover the facts in the following "Did You Know...."

Did You Know...

You can change the length of the shadow by changing the angle of the light. By placing the light directly above the structure, you can even make the shadow disappear. A shadow is always opposite the light source. The direction of the shadow will change if the direction of the light source changes.

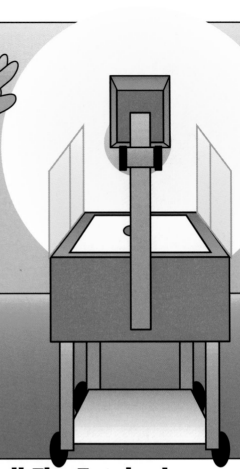

Pam Crane

Secret Shadows

To make secret shadows, you will need an overhead projector, a file folder (or two if needed), and a collection of opaque objects. In advance hide the objects in a box. Tape the file folder(s) around the base of the projector so your children will not be able to see the objects on the screen. Then gather your class. One at a time, place the objects on the screen and have children guess each object's identity based on the shadow that it casts. Begin with easily recognized items, such as a pair of scissors, a paper clip, and a key. Then progress to more difficult items, such as a button, a book, or a marble. The secret's out!

Don't Even Tell The Teacher!

Repeat the "Secret Shadows" activity with a twist—this time *you're* in the audience, too! Invite children to secretly bring in items from home. Have each child in turn place his item on the shielded overhead projector. Then everybody tries to guess the object's identity by the shadow. Youngsters will be motivated to try to stump even the teacher!

To Shadow Or Not To Shadow

Now it's time to delve further into the exploration of making shadows! To guide youngsters to discover that not all objects cast the same type of shadow, you'll need: a flashlight, opaque objects (such as a piece of cardboard and a book), translucent objects (such as a piece of waxed paper and a tissue), and transparent objects (such as a piece of clear plastic wrap and a clean transparency). You'll also need a copy of page 260 for each child. To do this activity, put all of the objects and the reproducibles in a center. Ask each child to look at the objects one at a time. Have her predict if each object will cast a shadow. Then encourage the child to see if she can make a shadow using the flashlight and the object. Have her record the results on the chart. After each child has visited the center, come together as a group to discuss the results. (If you'd like to do this as a whole-group activity, simply enlarge and duplicate page 260 to make a large chart.)

Did You Know...

An opaque *object does not allow light to pass through it, so it casts a dark shadow. A* translucent *(partly see-through) or* transparent *(completely see-through) object allows some light to pass through it, so its shadow is dimmer or sometimes not there at all.*

The Literature Link

Geoffrey the groundhog provides a whimsical look at shadows in story form. Read aloud *Geoffrey Groundhog Predicts The Weather* by Bruce Koscielniak (Houghton Mifflin Company). After discussing the story with your class, invite each child to make a groundhog (see the directions below) for some fun shadow-making practice.

Groundhog Shadows

With groundhogs of their own, your youngsters will be able to experiment with shadows in groundhog style! In advance, collect several plastic, two-liter bottles. To make a groundhog, wrap a large sheet of construction paper around a two-liter bottle; then tape the paper closed. Use art supplies (such as construction paper, wiggle eyes, pom-poms, buttons, and markers) to decorate the paper tube to resemble a groundhog. When the groundhog is complete, slide it off the bottle. Encourage children to take their groundhogs outside on a sunny day and on a cloudy day. Then have them try making different kinds of shadows by moving their groundhogs around.

Name _____

Will it cast a shadow?
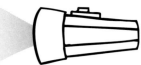

Object	Prediction	Result

Use with "To Shadow Or Not To Shadow" on page 258.

I can turn my head toward the sun.

Living And Nonliving Things

Use the ideas in this unit to enter into the study of one of the most fundamental concepts of all scientific classifications—living and nonliving things.

ideas contributed by Ann Flagg

Objective: Students will learn to identify living and nonliving things. Students will be able to identify three basic life processes of all living things—eating, growing, and moving.

The Basics

Introduce the topic of living and nonliving things to your students by reading aloud *What's Alive?* by Kathleen Weidner Zoehfeld (HarperCollins Publishers). With elementary text and charming illustrations, this title from the Let's-Read-And-Find-Out Science® series presents solid science information at a level that is just right for kindergartners. After discussing the book, guide your youngsters to verbalize the characteristics of living things mentioned in the book; then write them on the board. *(All living things take in food, grow, and move by themselves.)* With those three characteristics in mind, revisit the illustrations in the book. Call attention to random pictures in the book asking youngsters whether they are living or nonliving things and why. (For example, on pages 4 and 5 of the book, you could ask about the chair, the doll, the cat, the dog, the ball, the teddy bear, and the cut flowers. The flowers might require some interesting discussion!)

Would you like a sandwich?

Observation

Take your class on a walk around your school grounds. Prompt youngsters to look for things that are alive and things that are not alive. Carry a whistle with you and use it to call everyone together at interesting stops. Also draw youngsters' attention to contrasting items such as live leaves on a tree and dead leaves on the ground. Encourage discussion about each of these items; then return to your classroom for the next activity.

261

Pam Crane

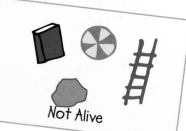

Alive

Not Alive

Recording Information

Back in the classroom, give each child a large sheet of paper and instruct him to fold it in half. Have him title one half "Alive" and the other half "Not Alive." Encourage each child to remember several things that he saw on the walk, then illustrate each of his ideas on the appropriate side of the paper. Afterward have each child share his page with the group. (If a child decides that he has misplaced one of his drawings, he can rectify the placement in "Classification.")

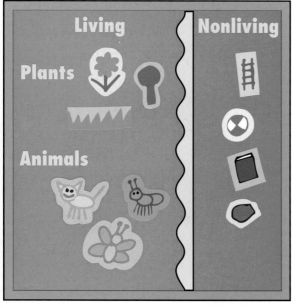

Classification

Now that your youngsters have thought about the idea of living and nonliving, go one step further into classification. Using bulletin-board border, divide a board into two vertical sections, with one side being larger than the other (as shown). Title the large side of the board "Living" and the other side "Nonliving." Then subtitle the "Living" side with "Plants" and "Animals." Have each child cut out his pictures (from the "Recording Information" activity). Then review page 30 of *What's Alive?*, asking youngsters to follow the directions in the book. Have each child pin or staple his pictures in the appropriate places on the board. (Note: If you don't have a copy of *What's Alive?*, have each child sort his pictures into living and nonliving things. Next ask him to sort the living things into *plants* and *animals*, then mount the pictures on the board.)

I'm Alive!

Delight your students with a look at some of the most "alive-ly" things around—themselves! Duplicate pages 263 and 264 for each child; then cut apart the pages. Follow the directions below for each page. Then have each child color and write her name on the cover. Complete the book by having the child sequence the cover and the pages; then help her staple the book together along the left edge. Encourage children to share these very lively books with their families.

Page 1—Read the text together. Have each child draw and label some of her favorite things to eat.

Page 2—Read the text together. Have each child trace her hand in the space provided, then write her age in the blank.

Page 3—Read the text together. Have each child illustrate herself doing one of her favorite movement activities.

I'm Alive!

by

I'm alive!
I eat...

1

I'm alive!
I am growing.

This is a baby's hand.   This is my hand at age _____.

2

I'm alive!
I can move by myself.

I eat. I'm growing. And I can move.
Yes, I'm alive!

3

The Wonders Of Watermelons

Sink your teeth into these juicy, summertime science activities that are just dripping with opportunities for students to sharpen up their science process skills.

ideas by Sharon Strickland

Objective: Students will use science process skills—the ability to observe, classify, use numbers, communicate information, measure, infer, and predict—to investigate watermelons.

Weighing In

To begin your watermelon studies, you'll need two watermelons and a bathroom scale. Start out with only the watermelons in your science center. As each child visits the center, ask her to guess which watermelon is the heavier of the two. To indicate her choice, have each child write her name on a sticky note and attach it to the watermelon she thinks is the heaviest. When you come together as a group, encourage children to talk about how they made their decisions. Did they use their eyes? Did they touch or lift the watermelons? Next ask how they think you could find out for sure. Then use the scale to actually weigh each watermelon. Discuss the actual results versus the children's guesses.

That's About The Size Of It

Divide your class into two groups and give each group one of the watermelons to use for this activity. After explaining that the *circumference* is the area *around* the watermelon, ask each child to predict what the circumference of his group's watermelon is. To do this, instruct him to cut a length of yarn that he thinks will go exactly around the watermelon, without any string left over. When everyone has cut a length of yarn, encourage him to check his guess against the real thing. How many strings were too short? Too long? Just right?

Heavy And Light

Classification skills are hard at work in this activity. Label one sentence strip with the word "heavy," and another with the word "light." Place the labels on a table. Ask children if they think the watermelon should go in the heavy or the light category; then place it on the table accordingly. Next ask children to find classroom objects that would fit in the opposite category. For example, if they thought the watermelon should go in the heavy category, ask children to find classroom items that could go in the light category. Then ask them to find (or think of) things that could also be included in the heavy category. (If an item cannot be moved to the table, encourage children to illustrate that item and place the illustration in the appropriate category.) If there is any indecision as to where a given item should go, use the bathroom scale to make the final determination.

That Makes Sense!

Immerse your youngsters in the watermelon experience by encouraging them to explore the watermelon with all five senses. In advance, post a chart labeled with the five senses. Prompt children to use all of their senses by asking questions such as "What does the watermelon look like?", "How does the watermelon feel?", and "When you thump the watermelon, how does it sound?" As children explore the watermelon, record their responses under the appropriate heading.

Next cut one watermelon in half lengthwise, and cut the other in half by width. Then ask how the watermelon looks the same as and/or different from before. Finally, give each child a small slice of the melon so they can accurately discuss how the watermelon smells and tastes! (Be sure to save two watermelon halves for remaining activities.)

| **Sight:** Round like an oval. Red, Green |
| **Hearing:** "Thump!" "Tum, Tum" |
| **Smell:** It smells like the red part. |
| **Taste:** Sweet, Drippy. |
| **Touch:** Cool, Smooth. |

Counting Seeds

Those watermelons are pretty seedy characters—but just how seedy are they? Let's see! Give each child a paper-plate wedge and a similarly sized wedge of watermelon (on another paper plate). Ask each child to color his paper-plate wedge to resemble his watermelon wedge, without the seeds. Then encourage him to guess how many seeds are in his wedge of watermelon and have him write his guess on the back of the colored wedge. As he eats the melon, have him save the seeds on his plate. When all the seeds are gathered, have him write the actual number, and then color that many seeds on the colored wedge. Encourage each child to discuss his results with the group. (Save one watermelon half for the last activity.)

What's In A Name?

If your youngsters have done the activities up till now, they might have some idea how this juicy, red melon acquired its name. But just to make sure, roll up your sleeves for this watery experience! You will need half a watermelon, a large bowl, a strainer, a pitcher, and a one-cup measuring cup. Begin by showing your students the measuring cup. Fill the cup with tap water; then ask children if they think the watermelon half contains more, less, or the same amount of water (juice). Then give each child a chunk of the watermelon. Rest the strainer over the bowl. After demonstrating, have each child use his hands to squeeze the juice out of his watermelon into the strainer. When all the chunks have been squeezed, pour the juice into the pitcher. Then, using the measuring cup, pour the liquid back into the bowl—one cup at a time—to measure the results. Well—any wonder how this melon got its name?

Did You Know...

Because watermelons grow on vines and must be replanted every year, they are considered *vegetables*?

Multicultural

Come To Cuba

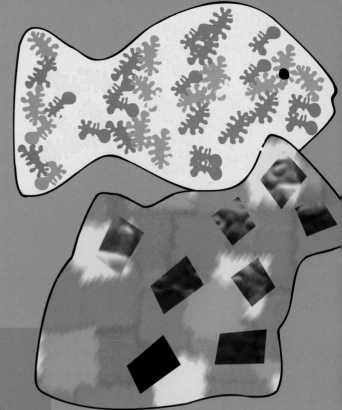

Cuba is said to be one of the most beautiful islands in the West Indies. Many Cubans call their country the "Pearl Of The Antilles." Come explore this little gem by tasting its fruits, sampling its music, playing a traditional game, and more.

ideas by Elizabeth Trautman

Has Anybody Seen Cuba Lately?

A few days before you officially begin studying Cuba as a class, set up a Search-For-Cuba center. Display a globe, a world map, or color photocopies of a section of a world map that includes Cuba. Isolate Cuba and its surrounding area by sticky-tacking a piece of thick yarn around it. Write "Cuba" on a piece of tagboard. (Be sure that you write it exactly as it appears on the map that your students will be using—for example, all capital letters—as this will be used as a reference card.) When you introduce this center, tell your youngsters that you'd like them to search for Cuba on the map. Encourage children to use the reference card to help them out if necessary.

As you wrap up center time each day, ask, "Has anybody seen Cuba lately?" Each child's interest will be piqued as more and more hands go up to indicate the children who have found Cuba on the map. Then look at the map together. Ask children to share what they notice about Cuba. Record their responses on chart paper. As you study the map together, guide youngsters in realizing the facts about Cuba listed below. Then enlarge and trace the outline of Cuba onto construction paper. Cut it out, label it, and glue it on blue paper. Mount the finished page to label your Cuba display area.

- Cuba is an island—surrounded by water on all sides.
- Cuba is long and skinny. Some people say it looks like an alligator!
- Cuba is close to part of the United States.

Swimming Pretty

Because Cuba is surrounded by tropical waters, one of the striking characteristics of its animal life can be found in the fish population. More than 500 species of fish live off the shoreline of Cuba. The many kinds of tropical fish that can be found there are of particular interest because of their beautiful colors. Your youngsters will absorb solid science information as well as use their creativity in creating large versions of tropical fish for your classroom.

To get those creative juices flowing, stock your science center with books that show a variety of colorful tropical fish (such as *Tropical Fish* by Ray Brockel and *A City Under The Sea* by Robert Wu). Have youngsters visit the center and look through the books to examine the many different types of tropical fish. Then set up your choice(s) of the fish-making stations described below. Encourage each child to make one or more tropical fish. Suspend the finished fish from the ceiling near your Cuba display area.

Crayon Melt
To make one crayon-melt fish, cut out a fish shape from a double thickness of waxed paper. Sprinkle crayon shavings on top of one cutout; then place the remaining cutout on top of that. Sandwich the fish between two sheets of newspaper. Iron over the fish with a warm iron—just a few seconds will do. When the fish has cooled, add details with permanent markers.

Color Collage
Trace a fish outline on a sheet of waxed paper. Brush a coat of white glue on the outline. Cover the fish with tissue-paper pieces. When the glue is dry, cut out the fish; then brush over it with a coat of water-diluted glue. If desired, add foil accents while the glue is still wet.

Margie Kinslow—Gr. K, Oak Park School, Titusville, FL

Make It And Shake It

Of all the art forms, Cuba has perhaps excelled most in the world of music. The music of Cuba has been so well-received that it has lilted its way past the Cuban borders into many other parts of the world. Cuban musicians use instruments that are common worldwide as well as a few that are entirely original to Cuba. One such instrument is called a *maraca*. A maraca is a round, dried fruit that has been filled with dried seeds or pebbles and is shaken rhythmically. Your students can make maracas of their own to shake to the rhythm of the beat! (If you're looking for some Caribbean-flavored music, the following recordings can be purchased from Music For Little People at 1-800-727-2233):

- *Smilin' Island Of Song* by Cedella Marley-Booker
- *Reggae For Kids: A Collection Of Music For Kids Of All Ages*
- *Positively Reggae: An All Family Musical Celebration*

Maracas
Have each child drop some unpopped popcorn kernels into an uninflated, seven-inch, round balloon. Ask adult volunteers to blow up and tie each balloon. Have each child repeatedly dip small newspaper strips into papier-mâché (recipe below), then wrap the strips around his balloon until it is completely covered—except for the knot! Let the balloon dry overnight. Cut off each balloon knot. Insert a stick or wooden dowel into the remaining hole. Stablize this handle with masking tape. Then have each child paint his maraca with bright colors of tempera paint.

Papier-Mâché
Mix one part flour to two parts water. Add the flour to the water in one-half-cup increments, continually stirring with a wire whisk. Cook the mixture over low heat, stirring continually, until the mixture thickens to a paste. After cooling the mixture, pour it into a jar until you are ready to use it.

Tempting Taste Buds

Some of our favorite fruits—such as oranges, lemons, and grapefruits—grow in Cuba. Central Cuba also produces the nation's largest pineapple crop. As a class, follow the recipe below to make a tempting pineapple taste-teaser.

Pineapple Upside-Down Cake
Melt one stick of margarine in a 9" x 13" pan at 200°. Stir in 1 1/2 cups of brown sugar. Arrange pineapple rings on the bottom of the pan. Place a maraschino cherry in the center of each ring. Make a yellow cake mix according to the package directions. Pour the batter over the pineapple. Bake for 45 minutes at 325°. Let the cake stand for ten minutes; then invert it onto a platter.

Domino Delight

The game of Dominoes is very popular among Cubans, second only to baseball—although some Cubans will even argue that! So while you're studying Cuba, how about putting a set or two of Dominoes in your game center? It's a game that can be played by all age groups, and by two or more players. And while you're dipping into the Cuban culture, you're also reinforcing counting, set-matching, problem-solving, and building strategies!

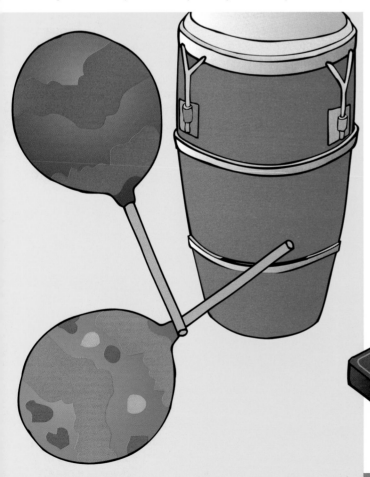

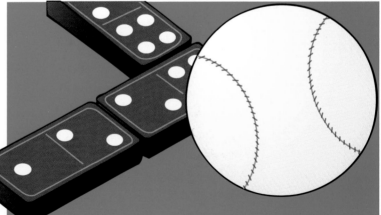

Note: See "The Magic Of Manners" on page 182 for an activity using an old Cuban folktale, *The Bossy Gallito,* retold in English and Spanish by Lucia M. Gonzalez (Scholastic Inc.).

Korea

Enrich your youngsters' view of the world with these activities designed to acquaint them with our neighbor to the Far East—Korea.

ideas by Elizabeth Trautmar

A Korean Sampler

Introduce your students to bits and pieces of the Korean culture and its language through the pages of Jim Haskins's *Count Your Way Through Korea* (Carolrhoda Books, Inc.). Show the pictures in the book as you read aloud (or paraphrase when necessary). After discussing each picture, reread the book having youngsters repeat each Korean number after you (refer to the pronunciation guide at the back of the book). Throughout your study of Korea, practice counting the Korean way!

Harvest Moon

The people of Korea celebrate many different holidays. One of the holidays is very much like our Thanksgiving. This holiday is called *Ch'usok,* or *Harvest Moon.* Harvest Moon is celebrated in the fall when most of the harvesting is over and people are ready to relax and give thanks for blessings and families. Most Koreans gather together on this day for a feast with their families and friends. At night, when the moon is high in the sky, people participate in outdoor activities such as dancing and singing.

Give youngsters the opportunity to celebrate Harvest Moon from afar with this activity. Give each child a sheet of white construction paper and light colored crayons (such as shades of yellow and orange). Encourage each child to draw and color—pressing down hard—a moon scene. Then have each child place his picture on a layer of newspaper and paint over his picture with water-diluted, black tempera paint. While the paint is drying, encourage each child to write about/dictate what he is thankful for in his family. Attach the writings to each child's picture; then display all of the projects on a board titled "Harvest Moon."

Reach For The Stars

Heavenly signs and what people say they might mean have always been important in Korean culture. One of the most widely recognized symbols of Korea is Ch'omsongdae (chom-sung-DEH), or the Star Tower (pictured in *Count Your Way Through Korea).* The Star Tower is a 29-foot-tall tower that was built to observe the stars and planets. It is made up of 365 stone blocks—one for each day of the year. This tower is often pictured on Korean stamps, guidebooks, and posters.

Challenge your youngsters to visit your block center and build star towers of their own. Prompt them to design strategies and problem-solve by encouraging them to make their structures as tall as possible. Also ask leading questions such as "How will people see out of your tower?" and "Did you use more or less blocks than there are stones in the Star Tower in Korea?"

Korean Cuisine

Although rice is a staple food in the Korean diet, a pickled salad called *kimchi* is considered the national dish and is served at every meal. Kimchi can be prepared many different ways, ranging from mild to very spicy. In the fall, Korean women have "kimchi days" when the vegetables are on sale in large outdoor markets.

Fascinating Facts:
- Can you believe that a family of five needs at least 175 heads of cabbage to supply their family with enough kimchi for the winter? Challenge your youngsters to draw 175 cabbage-sized circles on the chalkboard in their free time. Will they fit? That's a lot of cabbage!

- Kimchi is stored in a variety of clay jars—usually outdoors. Some of these jars are so large that a child could hide inside one! Provide small groups with butcher paper. Have one child in each group curl up on the paper while the others draw a jar shape around him. Then have each group cut out the jar and mount it on a wall. When you make the kimchi recipe, have youngsters imagine enough kimchi to fill up even one of those jars!

Kimchi

Prepare a batch of kimchi with your youngsters. Serve the dish with a side of rice and—if you dare—eat it with chopsticks!

1 small cabbage— cut into bite-size pieces	1/2 tsp. crushed red pepper flakes a pinch of grated ginger root
3 Tbs. salt	1/4 tsp. minced garlic
1 Tbs. sugar	1 Tbs. chopped green onion

In a large bowl, mix the cabbage with 2 1/2 Tbs. salt. Let it sit for three hours. Rinse the cabbage three times; then gently squeeze out the excess liquid with your hands. Place the cabbage in a glass bowl and add the remaining ingredients. Mix it thoroughly. Cover the mixture tightly with plastic wrap and let it sit at room temperature for a day or two. Then chill the kimchi before serving.

Makes about 2 cups after 2 days.

Pretty Pendants And A Tale

A tale that has been a favorite of Korean children for centuries is now retold by Shirley Climo in *The Korean Cinderella* (HarperCollins). After sharing the story, discuss the similarities and differences between this version and the American stories. (Refer to the notes at the back of the book for more discussion information.) After the story discussion, draw youngsters' attention to the pendants that are illustrated in the book. After explaining that these pendants were often worn with the traditional Korean dress, encourage youngsters to make their own original pendants. To make one, you will need a 3" x 6" tagboard card, paint markers, and 11 ten-inch lengths of yarn. Color the design of your choice on the tagboard. Punch two rather large holes at the bottom of the card, and one hole at the top. For each hole on the bottom, fold five lengths of yarn in half. Thread the folded end through the hole; then pass the loose ends through the loop. Attach a single length of yarn to the top for displaying.

Russia

Use the ideas in this unit to help your youngsters get a glimpse all the way across the Pacific Ocean to the largest country in the world—Russia. You'll use some beginning map skills, sample the language, design a work of folk art, and more!

ideas by Elizabeth Trautman

The Grand Scale

Set the stage for your study of Russia by introducing the largest of countries with a map activity. Enlarge and trace copies of Russia and the United States from maps with identical scales. Cut loosely around the outline of each country. Show the cutouts to your students and label each one. Then ask your class to compare and contrast the two shapes. Next demonstrate the relative size of Russia by placing the United States cutout on top of the Russia cutout. Discuss the differences and share the following facts:

- It took one man—Georgyi Busheyev—238 days to walk across Russia. That's more days than your children will come to kindergarten! At the same pace, it would take a person only 111 days to walk across the United States.

- In the continental United States, there are four different time zones. Russia has 11 different time zones!

A Book Worth Counting On

In his book *Count Your Way Through Russia,* author Jim Haskins narrates a sight-seeing tour that acquaints readers with some of the sights and culture of Russia. (Because this book was published before the breakup of the Soviet Union, there are a few references that you'll need to edit out as you read aloud.) As you travel page by page, encourage your students to try pronouncing the numbers after you (pronunciation is provided) and comment on the ease or difficulty of Russian counting compared to your youngsters' native tongues.

Nesting Dolls

One of the most popular items from Russian folk art is the set of seven nesting dolls. These dolls are called *Matryoshka* (mah-tree-OSH-kuh). Practice pronouncing that name with your youngsters; then offer each child a set of nesting dolls. To make a set, photocopy the largest doll on the page-seven spread of *Count Your Way Through Russia.* Then reduce and enlarge the pattern to make seven dolls in size seriation. Photocopy each doll for each child. Encourage children to use bright colored pencils and markers to color their dolls, then glue them to a large sheet of construction paper in size order. Display each finished, child-made Matryoshka near your Russian display area. Follow up this activity with a reading of *Matreshka* by Becky Hickox Ayres (Delacorte Press).

Rechenka's Eggs

Written & Illustrated by Patricia Polacco
Published by The Putnam & Grosset Group

Rechenka's Eggs is the heartwarming story of a lovable Babushka, an injured goose, and—miracles! After sharing this story with your youngsters, encourage each child to design a Ukranian-style egg to contribute to a classroom display. Give each child a small tagboard square—approximately 4″ x 5″. (The small size is to limit the possible size of the eggs, since youngsters' hands will tire if the eggs are too large.) To make one egg, use a pencil to draw an egg shape on the tagboard. Use a variety of bright crayons to color in the eggs, pressing hard. When the egg is colored, color again over the entire egg, pressing very hard with a black crayon. Then unbend one end of a large, wire paper clip. Use the extended end of the paper clip to scratch a design in the egg. Then cut out the egg. Arrange all of the eggs in a construction-paper basket; then place them near your Russia display area.

Picture This—Family Life

Invite your students to meet a Russian girl and her family as you read aloud *Russian Girl: Life In An Old Russian Town* by Russ Kendall (Scholastic Inc.). As you're sharing the book, encourage youngsters to discuss their ways of life compared to the people in the book. Then use the Russian recipes at the end of the book to add a tasty touch to your study of Russia.

Music, Music, Music!

Among the most popular of Russian compositions is *Peter And The Wolf*. This symphonic fairy tale was written by Sergei Prokofiev, who was a very talented Russian composer. By the age of five, Prokofiev was not only playing the piano, but he was also writing music! Offer your youngsters a viewing of a special animated version of Mr. Prokofiev's enchanting musical experience (published by BMG Video and available through your local video store.) Before watching the video, explain that the composer created characters in the story that were represented by different musical instruments. As youngsters watch the video, encourage them to listen for the different sounds that represent the characters in the story. (At the end of the story, an added segment provides a detailed explanation of the various instruments that enhances the viewers' appreciation of the work.)

Scouting Out Scotland

If your youngsters look on a map, and look very closely at the United Kingdom, they'll find one of Europe's most beautiful and interesting countries. Use the ideas in this unit to introduce and sample just a wee bit of Scotland.

ideas by Elizabeth Trautman

Where In The World Is Scotland?

Finding Scotland on a globe can be quite a challenge—but a challenge that some of your ambitious youngsters just might like to take a shot at. And while they're rising to the occasion, you'll be reinforcing map skills, visual discrimination, word matching, and cooperation. To point your scouts in the general direction of Scotland, roll a piece of clay into a long, thin line. Then arrange the clay on a globe to visually isolate the United Kingdom and, depending on your children's abilities, a few European countries. Place the globe, a class list, and a word card labeled "SCOTLAND"—exactly as it is written on your globe—in a center. Encourage children to scout around for Scotland. When a child finds Scotland, encourage him to let you know. After you verify his finding, place a check mark or a sticker by his name on the class list. (Peer tutoring can be strongly encouraged in this activity!)

Sights To See

Unless your class is able to jet over to Scotland to have a look around, try the next best thing—*Scotland* (Tintin's Travel Diaries series) by Daniel De Bruycker and Maximilien Dauber (published by Barron's Educational Series, Inc.). Through these pages, you'll travel around Scotland, pausing long enough to acquire bits of information about this land and its culture. Preview this book ahead of time; then show the pictures as you paraphrase appropriate information for your students. As youngsters look around Scotland (through the book), encourage them to compare and contrast Scotland to the area in which you live. Record their comments on a comparison chart.

Scotland	Our Area
• The people are called Scots.	• We are called Americans.
• Scotland has mountains and lakes.	• We have lots of lakes, but no mountains.
• It rains almost every day in Scotland.	• It only rains once in awhile for us.

"Thanks, Mr. Macintosh!"

If you were to take a trip to Scotland, you would have to be prepared for *a wee smirr of rain*. That's a gentle fall of rain that can happen at a moment's notice with just a puff of wind. And with another puff of wind, the clouds part and the sky is once again blue—until the next whim of weather. So it is no wonder that a Scottish man named Charles Macintosh invented what we call the *raincoat*. (The Scots call it a *waterproof*.)

The next time a wee smirr of rain is predicted on a warm day in your area, encourage youngsters to bring their *waterproofs*. Clad in rainwear, take a walk in the rain in honor of a Scottish shower and Charles Macintosh. As you walk, discuss which parts of youngsters' clothing are waterproof and which are not. And you might like to whisper a little thank-you to Mr. Macintosh!

"A Wee Cuppa Tea"

Not feeling well? Just need a little lift? According to the Scots, a cup of tea is the cure for a lot of what ails you! So take a break from your normal classroom routine and share a wee cuppa tea together. You'll be glad that you did!

To brew a large batch of tea:

- Bring one gallon of water to a boil.
- Steep five family-size tea bags in the boiled water for seven to ten minutes.
- When the tea has sufficiently cooled, serve it in foam cups. Allow youngsters to stir in sugar and milk to taste.

Pretty Plaids

The fabrics that we call *plaids* developed chiefly in Scotland. Each different plaid design, called *tartan,* served to identify which family or clan the wearer was from. Show your youngsters samples of tartans from an encyclopedia (The World Book Encyclopedia has many colorful examples). Then ask them to bring in samples of plaid clothing from home. Encourage children to examine the plaids and guide them to discover that, although the design can vary in size, it always repeats itself in exactly the same way. Then provide sheets of rich-colored construction paper and a large supply of precut construction-paper strips. Invite each child to design his own tartan by gluing the strips to the construction-paper background. Be sure that each child writes his name on the *back* of his paper. Then have each child share his tartan with the class. Afterward display all of the tartans and challenge youngsters to try to identify which tartan goes with which child.

Have You Seen Nessie!

Perhaps one of the most intriguing and well-known notions surrounding Scotland is the Loch Ness monster. Nessie, as it is called, is said to inhabit the deep waters of Loch (lake) Ness. Reporters, scientists, and tourists from all over the world have visited the shores of Loch Ness looking for this dinosaurlike creature. It is said to have flippers, one or two humps, and a long slender neck. No one has ever been able to prove or disprove the existence of the Loch Ness monster.

During your study of Scotland, stock your art center with coloring, drawing, and painting materials. Given the information in the above paragraph, encourage children to illustrate what they think the Loch Ness monster might look like. Display the pictures near your Scotland display area. Then give your youngsters a charmingly lighthearted look into the story of Nessie by reading aloud *The Ghosts' Trip To Loch Ness* by Jacques Duquennoy (Harcourt Brace & Company).

PERU

There's so much to be learned while pondering Peru! There are deserts, mountains, and rain forests...a new language, a familiar crop, and lovable livestock. Use the ideas in this unit to provide your youngsters with an opportunity to ponder Peru.

ideas contributed by Elizabeth Trautman

MAPPING IT OUT

Begin your study of Peru with this group mapping activity. To prepare, trace the Peru shape on this page onto a sheet of paper. Enlarge that pattern and trace it onto a large sheet of poster board or butcher paper. Roughly sketch in the land region boundaries as shown in the illustration. Then set that large map aside.

Gather your youngsters and identify your area of the country on a world map or globe. Trace a path with your finger to Peru. Prompt youngsters to discuss Peru by asking questions such as "Is Peru bigger or smaller than our state?" and "What direction would we travel in order to get to Peru?" Then show children the large-scale map that you made. Explain that going from west to east (or left to right), Peru has three main land regions—the *coast,* the *sierra,* and the *selva.* Provide children with each region's description (below). Then encourage them to think of ways to represent each region on the map. (For example, they might suggest sprinkling sand on glue to represent the coast, drawing mountains on the sierra, and gluing construction-paper leaves on the selva.) Then ask small groups of children to each be responsible for decorating a specific part of the map. Post the finished map as a focal point in your Peru display area.

- **The coast**—Although the coast is right next to the ocean, it is the driest desert in the world. However, people are able to live on the coast because a few small rivers run through this area, making it possible for people to get water for farming, drinking, and other needs.

- **The sierra**—The sierra is made up of mountain ranges called *the Andes.* Some of these mountains are so high that they remain snowcapped all the time!

- **The selva**—The selva is made up of green forests and tropical rain forests. In one area of the selva, rainfall averages 103 inches per year!

SPEAKING SPANISH

The official language of Peru is Spanish. Since many youngsters these days are exposed to at least a little bit of the Spanish language, they'll be eager to expand their Spanish-speaking abilities. In advance, copy the chart below on a sheet of chart paper. During a group time, find out if any of your students already know any Spanish words or phrases, or perhaps can even speak it fluently. If so, ask those students to share what they know with the class. Next introduce the words on the chart, prompting children to repeat each word or phrase after you. Encourage students to use these Spanish words and phrases throughout your study of Peru.

SI	YES
POR FAVOR	PLEASE
GRACIAS	THANK YOU
DE NADA	YOU'RE WELCOME
HOLA	HELLO
BUENOS DIAS	GOOD MORNING

Brownie

THE LOVELY LLAMA

Perhaps one of the most endearing elements in the culture of Peru is the lovely llama. South American people have been raising llamas for more than 4,000 years. Share a bit about these unique creatures by reading aloud *Love A Llama* by Colleen Stanley Bare (published by Cobblehill Books). After discussing the book, have each child use art supplies to make his own llama. Encourage him to refer back to the book to remember llama facts while he is working. When each child has made a llama, remind him of the llama names suggested in the book. Then ask him to name his own llama. Have each child share his llama with the class; then post it near your Peru display.

A PERUVIAN FOLKTALE

Share a Peruvian folktale with your youngsters by reading aloud *Moon Rope* by Lois Ehlert (published by Harcourt Brace Jovanovich). Tell students that the art in the book was inspired by the fabrics and jewelry of the ancient peoples of Peru. They believed that silver was a precious metal—the tears of the moon—and used it only to create objects of beauty. Encourage each child to make silvery jewelry to resemble the fox in the moon. For each child, you will need a silver piece of Friendly Plastic®, three rhinestones, and a safety pin. Heat a small pan of water on medium heat. Put the plastic in the pan and stir it with a wooden spoon until the plastic is moldable. Remove the plastic from the water; then cut out a circle. Cool the circle in a bowl of cold water. After a few seconds, remove the circle and wipe it dry. Using craft glue, mount the rhinestones on the plastic. Then hot-glue a safety pin to the back. Encourage children to wear these silvery pins and to share about the country that inspired them.

PERUVIAN POTATOES

Although potatoes are now common all over the world, that wasn't always the case. Potatoes originated in the mountains of Peru. And to this day, Peruvians still eat lots of potatoes. Encourage children to brainstorm a list of all the different ways they have eaten potatoes. Then, as a class, cook up and sample a batch of these Peruvian Potatoes.

PERUVIAN POTATOES

Ingredients:
10–12 medium potatoes
your favorite cheese sauce (A very simple cheese sauce can be made by cubing a block of Velveeta®, stirring in some salsa, and melting it in a microwave.)

Directions:
Wash the unpeeled potatoes. Place them in a large pot and add water so that the potatoes are completely covered with water. Bring the water to a boil; then cook the potatoes over medium heat until they are soft when poked with a fork (approximately 25–30 minutes). Using tongs, remove the potatoes from the water and let them cool. When they are cool enough to handle, slice the potatoes. Give each child a few potato slices; then pass around the cheese sauce to spoon on top.

Makes about 20 small servings.

Spain

Across the Atlantic Ocean lies one of the world's leading tourist countries. Use the ideas in this unit to give your youngsters a peek into spectacular Spain!

ideas contributed by Elizabeth Trautman

Introducing Spain

Opportunities for thinking abound when you introduce Spain and its culture through the daily life of a child. In advance read *Children Of The World: Spain* (Gareth Stevens Publishing) so that you'll be able to paraphrase the text, if necessary, when you share the book with your students. Label one sheet of chart paper "In Spain..." and label another sheet "In Our Country...." As you share the book, prompt students to verbalize likenesses and differences between Spain/Felisa and her family, and your area/your students' families (some examples are shown below). Record youngsters' responses; then discuss the resulting list. Are the lists very much the same, very different, or a little bit of both?

In Spain...
- Houses in the villages are mostly white.
- Felisa's family has nine people.
- The villagers decorate their patios with plants and flowers.
- Most people go home for a long lunch.

In Our Country...
- Our houses are all different colors. We have red, blue, brown, yellow, green, and white.
- Our class's families have two to five people.
- Six families from our class have patios. Four of them have plants and flowers.
- We stay at school for lunch. It's not too long.

Mapping It Out

Spain is often remembered as the place from which Christopher Columbus sailed when he discovered the New World. Use a globe and a sailboat cutout to illustrate this historical journey. Show youngsters where Spain is on the globe. Then explain that Christopher Columbus was trying to find a way to sail around to India—but he didn't know that what are now the Americas were out there! "Sail" the cutout across the Atlantic Ocean to the New World, thus depicting the journey of Columbus. Then put the globe and sailboat in a center so youngsters can map out Columbus's journey on their own. Wrap up this activity by sharing Laura Fischetto's whimsical *All Pigs On Deck: Christopher Columbus's Second Marvelous Voyage* (Delacorte Press).

Fiesta Flowers

To celebrate special occasions, fiestas—or festivals—are popular throughout all of Spain. People young and old dress up in colorful costumes, and streets and buildings are decorated in preparation for parades, fireworks, and dancing in the streets. For some fiestas, the people deck the roads that a parade will follow with colorful paper flowers. Adorn your classroom with the air of a Spanish fiesta by making these festive flowers. To make one flower, you will need six 10" x 7" sheets of colorful tissue paper. Stack the six sheets. Turn the stack so that your hands are along the shorter side; then accordion-fold the entire stack (at about one-inch intervals). Be sure that the folded edges have a firm crease; then staple or tie the sheets together in the middle. Layer by layer, pull the petals up toward the middle until you have a fluffy fiesta flower! Display each child's flower near your Spain display area.

Stack and accordion fold.

Staple in center.

Pull up from center.

Daily Routine

The hot summers in Spain lend a unique timetable to the daily routines of the Spaniards. Most people work or go to school during the cooler hours of the day. For this reason, school and work continues into the early afternoon; then there is a long lunch break and *siesta* (rest or nap). In the late afternoon, school and work resume until early evening. Just before their evening meals, most families participate in a *paseo*—a walk around the neighborhood or town, greeting and talking with friends. Supper typically isn't until 9:30 or 10:00 in the evening!

Enlist the help of your students to make a visual comparison between their daily routines and the typical Spanish day. Copy the schedule shown onto a sheet of chart paper; then add visual cues as desired. On another sheet of chart paper, record as your students dictate a general schedule to you. (You might like to select some students to illustrate the dictated schedule too.) When each schedule is complete, compare and contrast what each group of people is doing at any given time.

Spain—Daily Schedule

8 A.M.	Breakfast
9 A.M.	School
2 P.M.	Lunch/Siesta
4–6 P.M.	School
7–9 P.M.	Paseo
9–11 P.M.	Dinner

Our Daily Schedule

7 A.M.	Breakfast
8 A.M.	School
12 P.M.	Lunch
3 P.M.	Home/Play
6 P.M.	Dinner
8 P.M.	Bedtime

279

Spanish Tiles And Such

Many homes and shops in Spain are decorated with beautiful Spanish tiles, decorative plates, and other ceramics. Encourage your youngsters to examine pictures that display some of these crafts (such as those found on page 35 of *Country Fact Files: Spain,* on page 26 of *On The Map: Spain,* and page 103 of *Enchantment Of The World: Spain*—see the resource booklist for complete information). Then give each child a sheet of white construction paper, scissors, and an assortment of colorful water-based markers or paint pens. Invite each child to cut out and design a Spanish tile, plate, or other piece of pottery. Mount the finished projects near your Spain display.

Oh, Those Oranges!

When it comes to Spain's famous foods, Valencia oranges rank among the front-runners. Because of the dependable abundance of sunshine in Spain, the orange crop fares very well. During your study of Spain, set up an orange-juice center for those children who would like to try some fresh-squeezed Valencia orange juice. Gather a manual juicer or two, a supply of Valencia oranges, and paper cups. Cut the oranges in half and place them in bowls near the juicers and the cups. After demonstrating the process, invite each child to visit the center and squeeze a little orange juice for herself. Mmmm, there's nothing like fresh squeezed!

Resource Booklist
Country Fact Files: Spain
by Anna Selby
Raintree Steck-Vaughn

On The Map: Spain
by Daphne Butler
Raintree Steck-Vaughn

Enchantment Of The World:
 Spain
by Esther and Wilbur Cross
Childrens Press®

Folktales Of Spanish Origin
The Riddle
Retold by Adele Vernon
Dodd, Mead & Company

The Princess And The Pumpkin
Adapted by Maggie Duff
Macmillan Publishing Company

KINDERGARTEN CAFÉ

Welcome to the start of the second year of the Kindergarten Café. This special department of *The Mailbox*® magazine features recipes designed especially for the kindergarten child. Each cooking activity is seasoned with learning opportunities and generously sprinkled with fun. So read this page and the introduction on page 283; then tie on your apron and get cooking!

What's In It For Me?

The cooking recipes in "Kindergarten Café" serve up meaningful practice in language arts, math, science, social skills, and more. When you incorporate these hands-on activities into your curriculum, here are just a few of the benefits for your students:

- Oral language and vocabulary development
- Emergent reading skills
- Counting practice and numeral recognition
- Sensory experiences
- Measurement exploration
- Following step-by-step directions
- Sequence
- Developing independence

Getting Ready

If this is your first experience with "Kindergarten Café," here are a few hints to ensure that each cooking experience will be deliciously successful:

- Create your cooking center in an area that has child-height work spaces and is near an electrical outlet. Decorate (or have children decorate) this area with cooking-related pictures, such as child-drawn or cut-out pictures of homemade goodies. Mount the words "Kindergarten Café" near your cooking area.

- You also might like to host a yearly Grand Opening ceremony to equip your center and to stir up a batch of adult cooking volunteers. In advance, prepare an invitation indicating the cooking supplies needed in your cooking center. Have each child color an invitation and deliver it home to his parent. On Opening Day, display all the donated items. Serve snacks as you discuss the abundance of learning opportunities that a cooking center will provide for each parent's child.

Cooking Extensions

Extend the fun and learning of "Kindergarten Café" with the following ideas:

- Take a photo of each cooking experience. Insert the photo and a copy of the recipe in a photo album. Have students dictate about the cooking experience, and include their comments in the album.

- After each cooking experience, conduct a class survey. Label a graph as desired (such as "I loved it!", "It was OK," and "I didn't care for it"). Ask each child to write his name in the appropriate column. When the graph is complete, include it in the photo album.

- Cut out labels from products used in the cooking center. Insert these labels in the photo album, or glue the labels to a chart to add to your writing center.

- To help children with measuring and pouring skills, also provide a set of measuring spoons and measuring cups for your sand and/or water table.

KINDERGARTEN CAFÉ

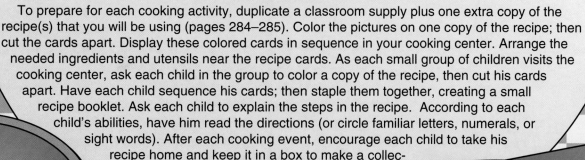

To prepare for each cooking activity, duplicate a classroom supply plus one extra copy of the recipe(s) that you will be using (pages 284–285). Color the pictures on one copy of the recipe; then cut the cards apart. Display these colored cards in sequence in your cooking center. Arrange the needed ingredients and utensils near the recipe cards. As each small group of children visits the cooking center, ask each child in the group to color a copy of the recipe, then cut his cards apart. Have each child sequence his cards; then staple them together, creating a small recipe booklet. Ask each child to explain the steps in the recipe. According to each child's abilities, have him read the directions (or circle familiar letters, numerals, or sight words). After each cooking event, encourage each child to take his recipe home and keep it in a box to make a collection of his very own cooking recipes.

AUGUST

Root-Beer Float

Ingredients For One:
1/2 cup root beer
1 scoop ice cream
1 spoon whipped topping

Utensils:
measuring cup
large, clear plastic cup
ice-cream scoop
serving spoon
straw
plastic spoon

Teacher Preparation:
Provide root beer in cans or small bottles that children can handle.

SEPTEMBER

Apple-Pie Muffin

Ingredients For One:
1/2 English muffin
butter or margarine
lemon juice (optional)
apple slices
cinnamon-and-sugar mixture

Utensils:
empty shaker
toaster oven tray
plastic knife
toaster oven
paper plate

Teacher Preparation:
If desired, sprinkle the apple slices with lemon juice to prevent browning. Prepare the cinnamon-and-sugar mixture, and pour it into an empty shaker.

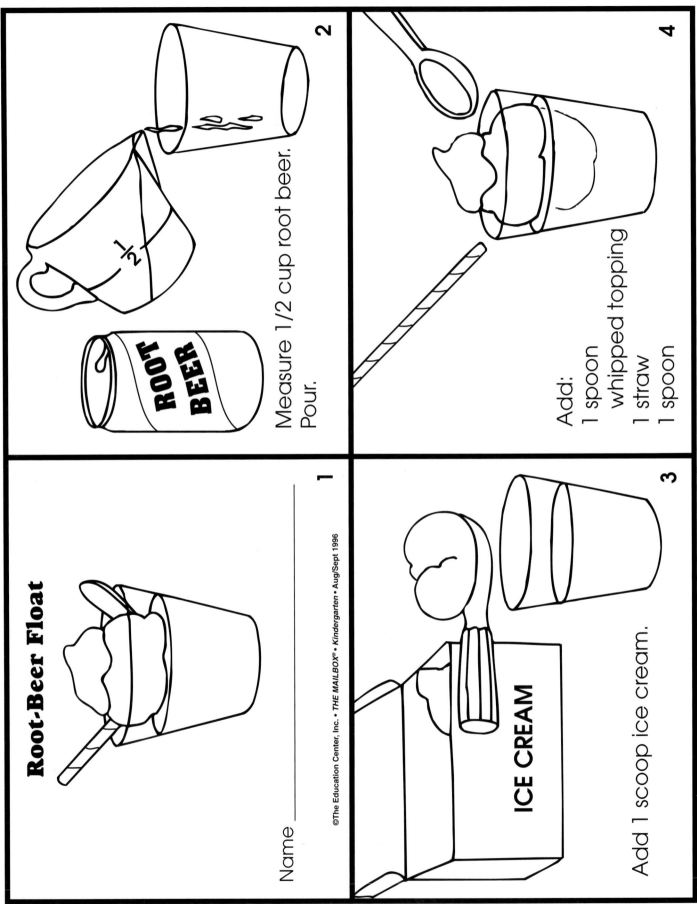

2

Measure 1/2 cup root beer. Pour.

ROOT BEER

4

Add:
1 spoon
whipped topping
1 straw
1 spoon

1

Root-Beer Float

Name _____

3

ICE CREAM

Add 1 scoop ice cream.

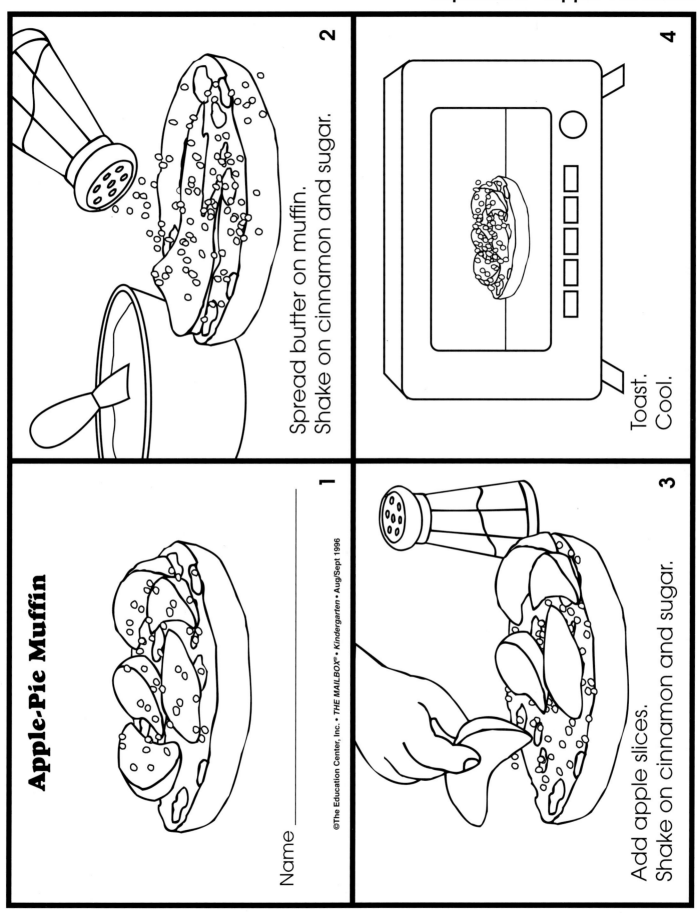

2

Spread butter on muffin.
Shake on cinnamon and sugar.

4

Toast.
Cool.

Apple-Pie Muffin

1

Name _____

©The Education Center, Inc. • *THE MAILBOX® • Kindergarten • Aug/Sept 1996*

3

Add apple slices.
Shake on cinnamon and sugar.

KINDERGARTEN CAFÉ

To prepare for each cooking activity, duplicate a classroom supply plus one extra of the recipe(s) that you will be using (pages 287–288). Color the pictures in the recipe; then cut the cards apart. Display the colored cards in sequence in your cooking center. Arrange the ingredients and utensils needed near the recipe cards. As a small group visits the cooking center, ask each child to color a recipe, then cut the cards apart. Have each child sequence his cards; then staple them together, creating a recipe booklet. Ask each child to explain the steps in the recipe. According to each child's abilities, have him read the directions (or circle familiar letters, numerals, or sight words). After each cooking event, encourage each child to take his recipe home and keep it in a box to make a collection of his very own cooking recipes.

OCTOBER

Ghost Toasties

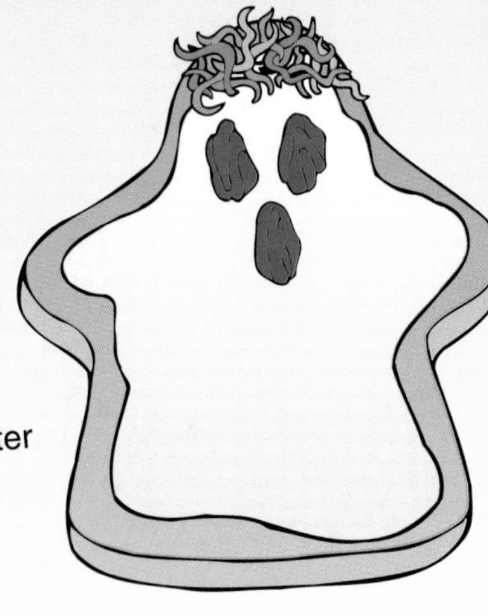

Ingredients For One:
1 slice of bread
soft cream cheese
raisins
grated carrots
shredded lettuce

Utensils And Supplies:
ghost-shaped cookie cutter
plastic knife
toaster oven
three bowls

Teacher Preparation:
Grate the carrots and shred the lettuce.

NOVEMBER

Frozen Pumpkin Squares

Ingredients For One:
two square graham crackers
1 tsp. pumpkin-pie filling
3 Tbs. whipped topping

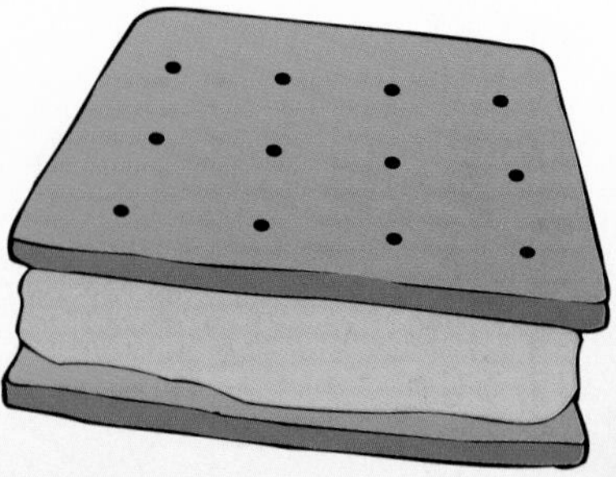

Utensils And Supplies:
measuring spoons:
tablespoon, teaspoon
bowl
serving spoons
freezer

Teacher Preparation:
Have a cookie sheet available to hold the ready-to-be-frozen pumpkin squares. Have each cook place his pumpkin square on the sheet.

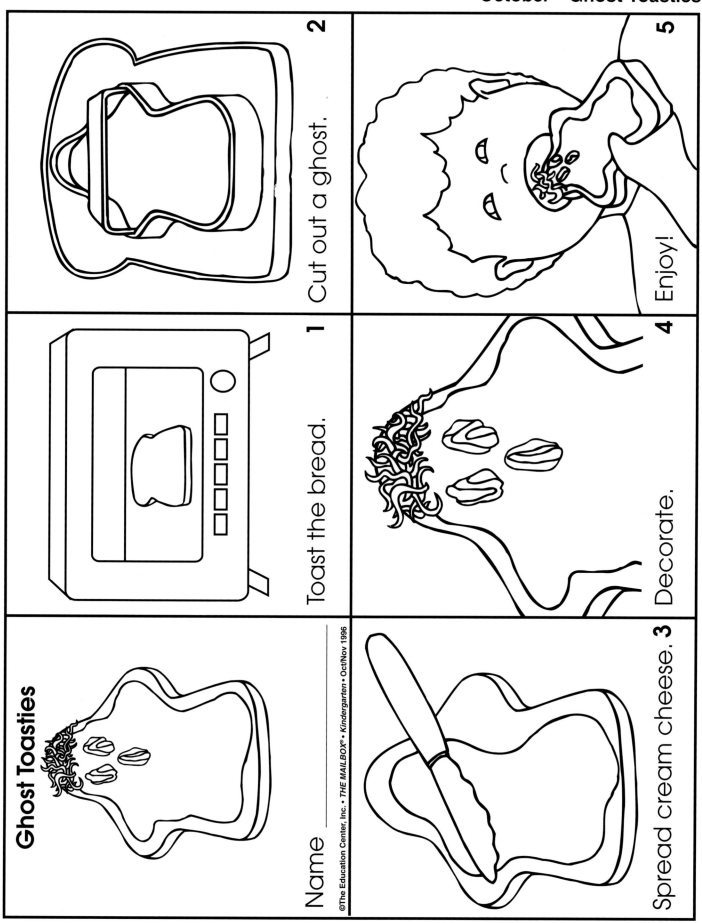

2 Cut out a ghost.

5 Enjoy!

1 Toast the bread.

4 Decorate.

Ghost Toasties

Name

3 Spread cream cheese.

Recipe Cards
November—Frozen Pumpkin Squares

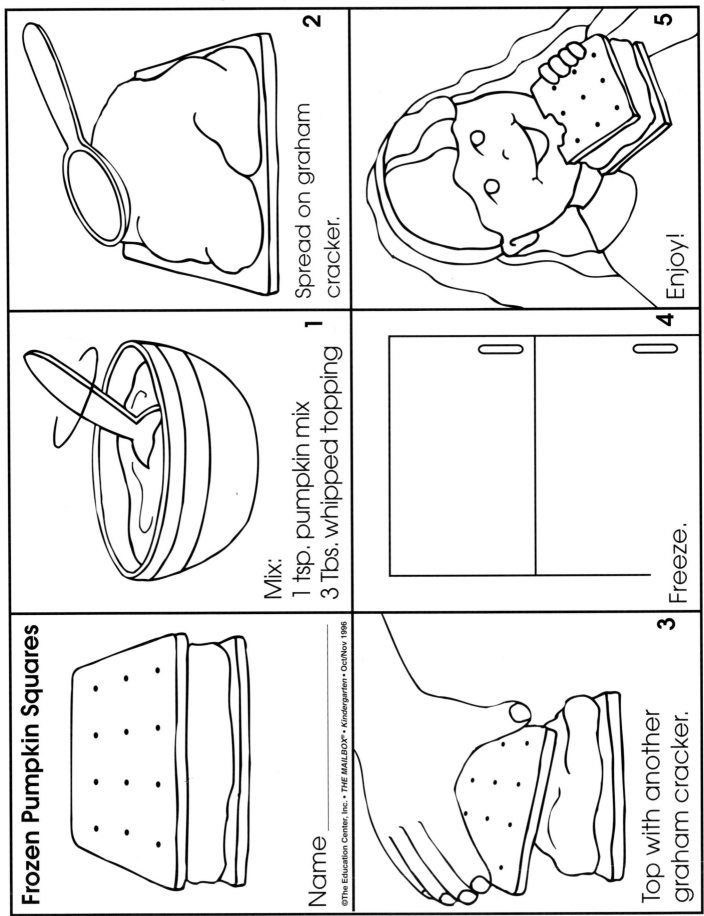

2 Spread on graham cracker.

5 Enjoy!

1 Mix:
1 tsp. pumpkin mix
3 Tbs. whipped topping

4 Freeze.

Frozen Pumpkin Squares

Name

3 Top with another graham cracker.

KINDERGARTEN CAFÉ

Sprinkles

To prepare for each cooking activity, duplicate a classroom supply plus one extra of the recipe(s) that you will be using (pages 290–291). Color the pictures on one copy of the recipe; then cut the cards apart. Display the colored cards in sequence in your cooking center. Arrange the needed ingredients and utensils near the recipe cards. As a small group of children visits the cooking center, ask each child in the group to color a copy of the recipe, then cut the cards apart. Have each child sequence his cards; then staple them together, creating a small recipe booklet. Ask each child to explain the steps in the recipe. According to each child's abilities, have him read the directions (or circle familiar letters, numerals, or sight words). After each cooking event, encourage each child to take his recipe home and keep it in a box to make a collection of his very own recipes.

DECEMBER

Yule Logs

Ingredients For One:
one-half of a pretzel log
chocolate frosting
mini chocolate chips
chopped peanuts

Utensils And Supplies:
plastic knife
2 paper plates

Teacher Preparation:
Break pretzel logs in half.
Spread the mini chocolate chips and the chopped peanuts on separate paper plates.

JANUARY

Charming Cheese Toast

Ingredients For One:
1 slice of bread
1 slice of cheese
grated Parmesan cheese

Utensils And Supplies:
toaster oven

Teacher Preparation:
If needed, assist with unwrapping cheese slices.

Adapted from an idea by Martha Ann Davis—Gr. K
Springfield Elementary, Greenwood, SC

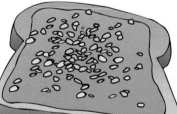

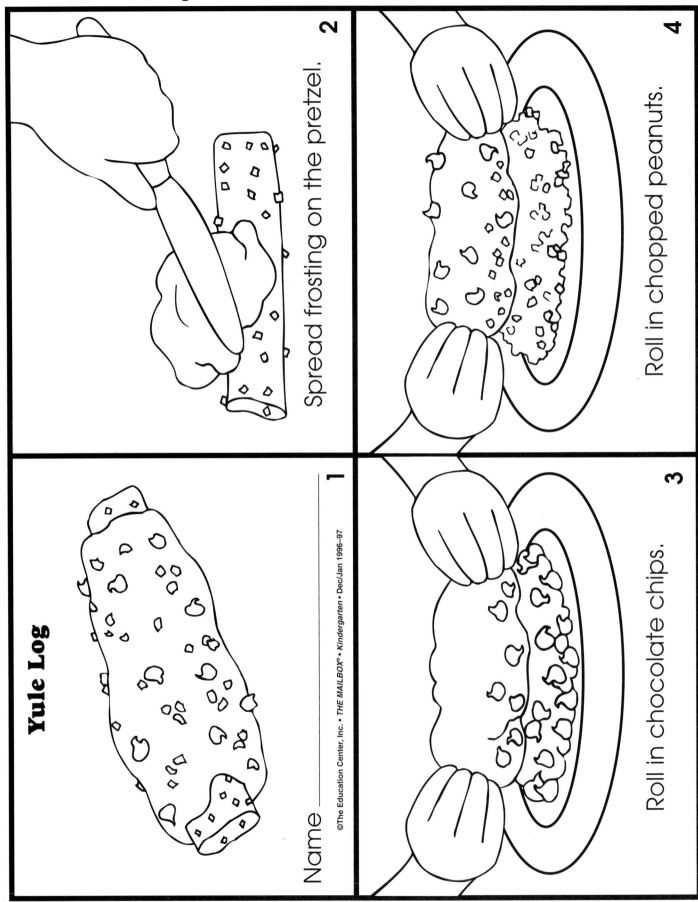

2 Spread frosting on the pretzel.

4 Roll in chopped peanuts.

Yule Log

1

Name ——————

3 Roll in chocolate chips.

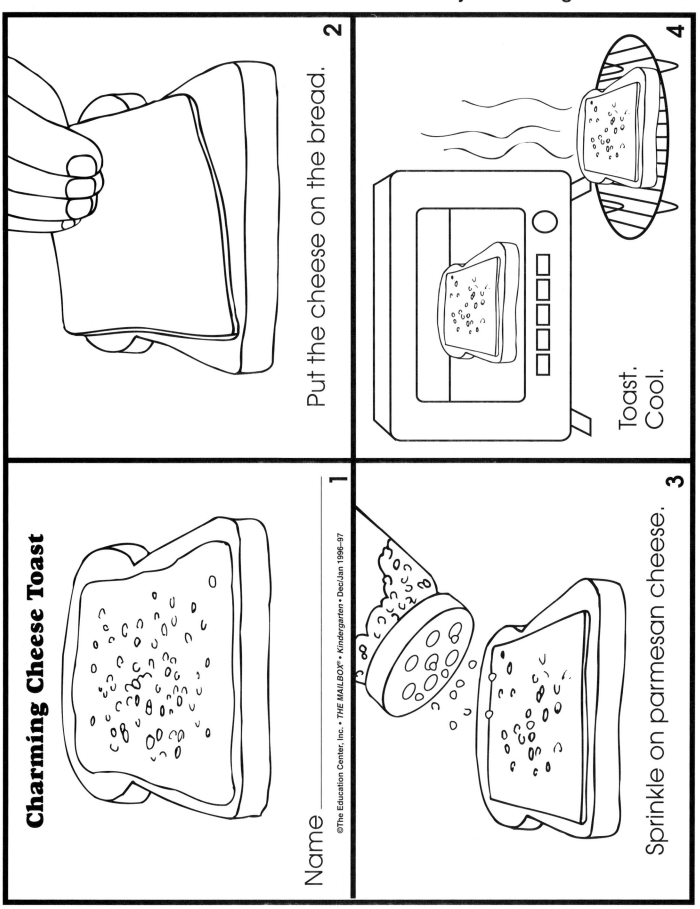

2

Put the cheese on the bread.

4

Toast. Cool.

Charming Cheese Toast

1

Name _____

3

Sprinkle on parmesan cheese.

KINDERGARTEN CAFÉ

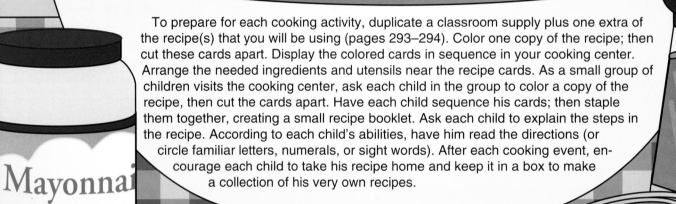

To prepare for each cooking activity, duplicate a classroom supply plus one extra of the recipe(s) that you will be using (pages 293–294). Color one copy of the recipe; then cut these cards apart. Display the colored cards in sequence in your cooking center. Arrange the needed ingredients and utensils near the recipe cards. As a small group of children visits the cooking center, ask each child in the group to color a copy of the recipe, then cut the cards apart. Have each child sequence his cards; then staple them together, creating a small recipe booklet. Ask each child to explain the steps in the recipe. According to each child's abilities, have him read the directions (or circle familiar letters, numerals, or sight words). After each cooking event, encourage each child to take his recipe home and keep it in a box to make a collection of his very own recipes.

FEBRUARY

Valentine Tart

Ingredients For One:
1 single-serving sponge cake
cherry pie filling
whipped topping
candy heart

Utensils And Supplies:
2 serving spoons
paper plates

Teacher Preparation:
Arrange the ingredients for easy student access.

MARCH

Potato Salad

Ingredients For One:
1 cooled baked potato
1 Tbs. mayonnaise
1/2 tsp. vinegar
pepper
paprika

Utensils And Supplies:
measuring spoons
bowl
spoon
plastic knife

Teacher Preparation:
Bake a medium potato for each child. Demonstrate "a pinch" of a spice.

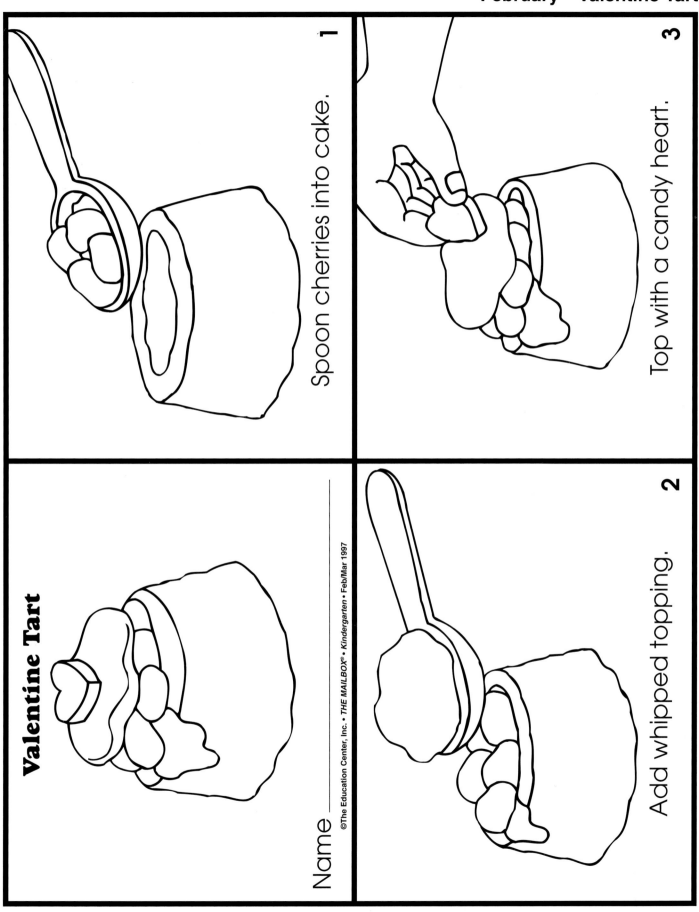

1

Spoon cherries into cake.

3

Top with a candy heart.

Valentine Tart

Name _____

©The Education Center, Inc. • *THE MAILBOX® • Kindergarten • Feb/Mar 1997*

2

Add whipped topping.

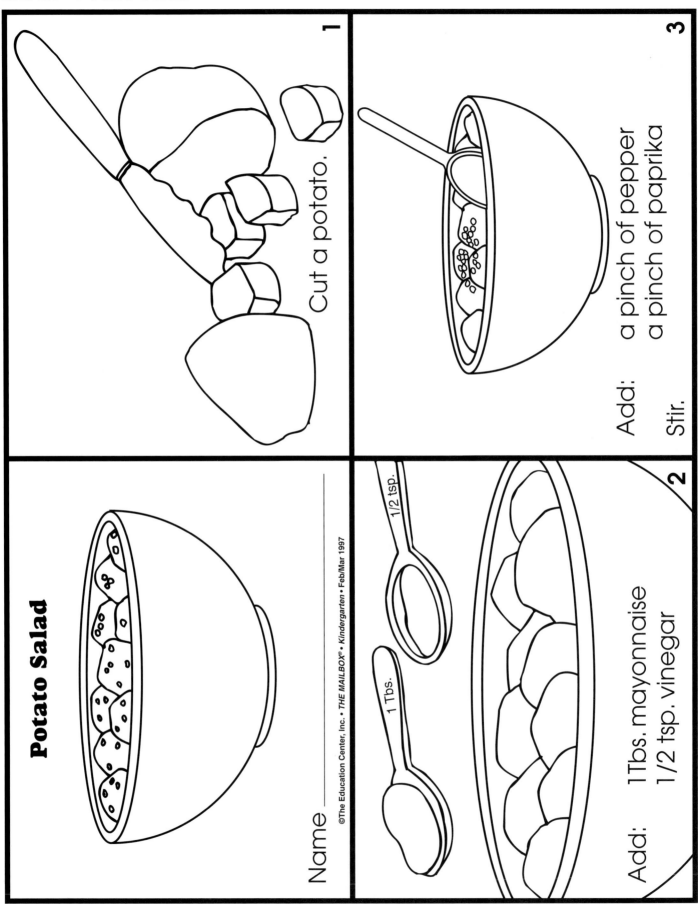

1

Cut a potato.

Potato Salad

Name _____

2

1/2 tsp.

1 Tbs.

Add: 1 Tbs. mayonnaise
        1/2 tsp. vinegar

3

Add: a pinch of pepper
        a pinch of paprika

Stir.

KINDERGARTEN CAFÉ

To prepare for each cooking activity, duplicate a classroom supply plus one extra of the recipe(s) that you will be using (pages 296–297). Color the pictures on one copy of the recipe; then cut the cards apart. Display the colored cards in sequence in your cooking center. Arrange the ingredients and utensils needed near the recipe cards. As a small group visits the cooking center, ask each child to color a recipe, then cut the cards apart. Have each child sequence his cards; then staple them together, creating a recipe booklet. Ask each child to explain the steps in the recipe. According to each child's abilities, have him read the directions (or circle familiar letters, numerals, or sight words). After each cooking event, encourage each child to take his recipe home and keep it in a box to make a collection of his very own cooking recipes.

Vanilla Yogurt

APRIL

Mitt-And-Ball Munchies

Ingredients For One:
one biscuit-dough round
cinnamon-and-sugar mixture
large marshmallow
red cake-decorating gel

Utensils And Supplies:
empty shaker
toaster-oven tray
toaster oven
timer
plastic soda-bottle cap

Teacher Preparation:
Prepare the cinnamon-and-sugar mixture; then pour it into an empty shaker. According to dough package directions, determine toaster-oven setting and cooking time.

MAY

Cuke Canoe

Ingredients For One:
1/2 cucumber, cut lengthwise
vanilla yogurt
cereal squares
Goldfish® crackers

Utensils And Supplies:
spoon
blue paper or plastic plate

Teacher Preparation:
Peel each cucumber; then cut it in half lengthwise.

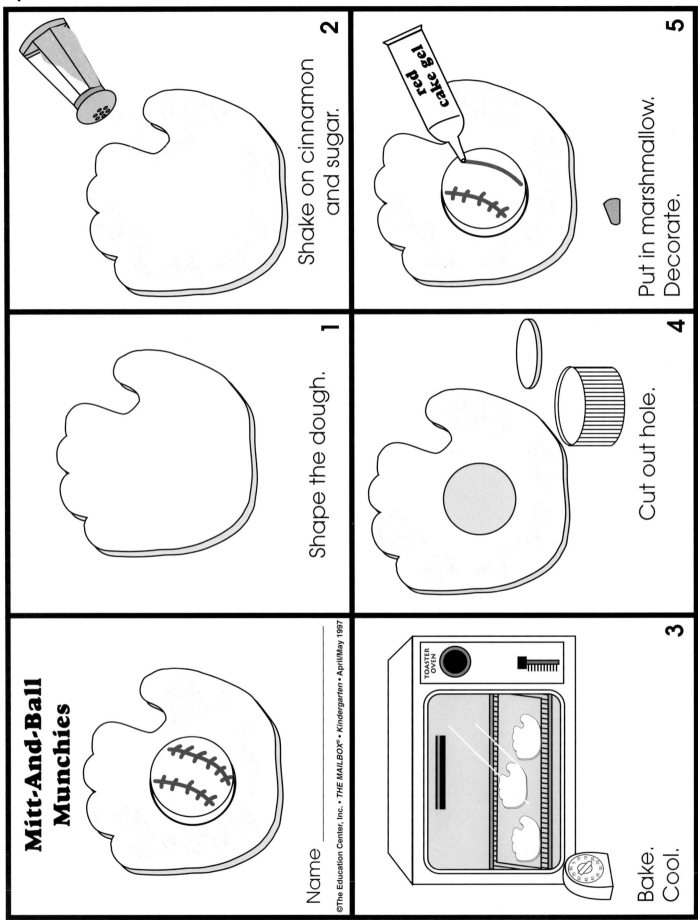

2

Shake on cinnamon and sugar.

5

red cake gel

Put in marshmallow. Decorate.

1

Shape the dough.

4

Cut out hole.

Mitt-And-Ball Munchies

Name

©The Education Center, Inc. • THE MAILBOX® • Kindergarten • April/May 1997

3

TOASTER OVEN

Bake.
Cool.

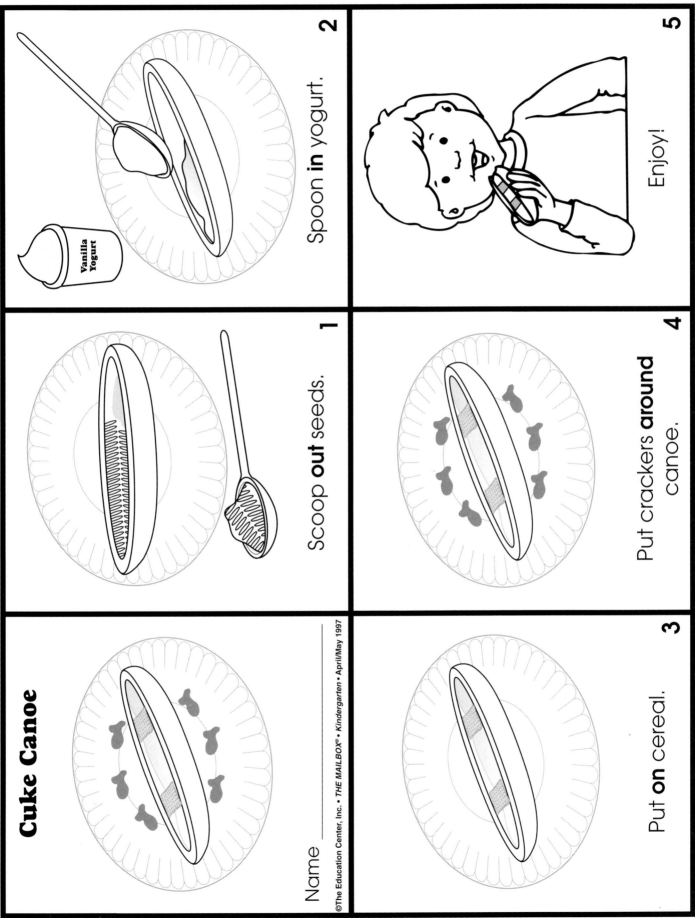

2

Spoon **in** yogurt.

5

Enjoy!

1

Scoop **out** seeds.

4

Put crackers **around** canoe.

Cuke Canoe

Name _____

3

Put **on** cereal.

KINDERGARTEN CAFÉ

Pizza Sau...

To prepare for each cooking activity, duplicate a classroom supply plus one extra of the recipe(s) that you will be using (pages 299–300). Color one copy of the recipe; then cut the cards apart. Display the colored cards in sequence in your cooking center. Arrange the needed ingredients and utensils near the recipe cards. As a small group of children visits the cooking center, ask each child in the group to color a recipe, then cut the cards apart. Have each child sequence his cards; then staple them together, creating a small recipe booklet. Ask each child to explain the steps in the recipe. According to each child's abilities, have him read the directions (or circle familiar letters, numerals, or sight words). After each cooking event, encourage each child to take his recipe home and keep it in a box to make a collection of his very own cooking recipes.

JUNE
Cheese Pizza

Ingredients For One:
one-half of an English muffin
prepared pizza sauce
grated cheese (mozzarella and/or your choice)

Utensils And Supplies:
serving spoon
aluminum foil
permanent marker
hot mitt

Teacher Preparation:
- Arrange the ingredients for easy student access.
- Line a baking sheet with aluminum foil. (After each child has made a pizza, closely supervise the baking process.)

JULY
Independence Day Tart

Ingredients For One:
1 single-serving sponge cake
whipped topping
sliced strawberries
blueberries

Utensils And Supplies:
1 paper plate for each child (for preparation)
1 spoon for each child
serving spoons for topping and berries

Teacher Preparation:
- Wash the berries. Slice the strawberries.
- Arrange the ingredients for easy student access.

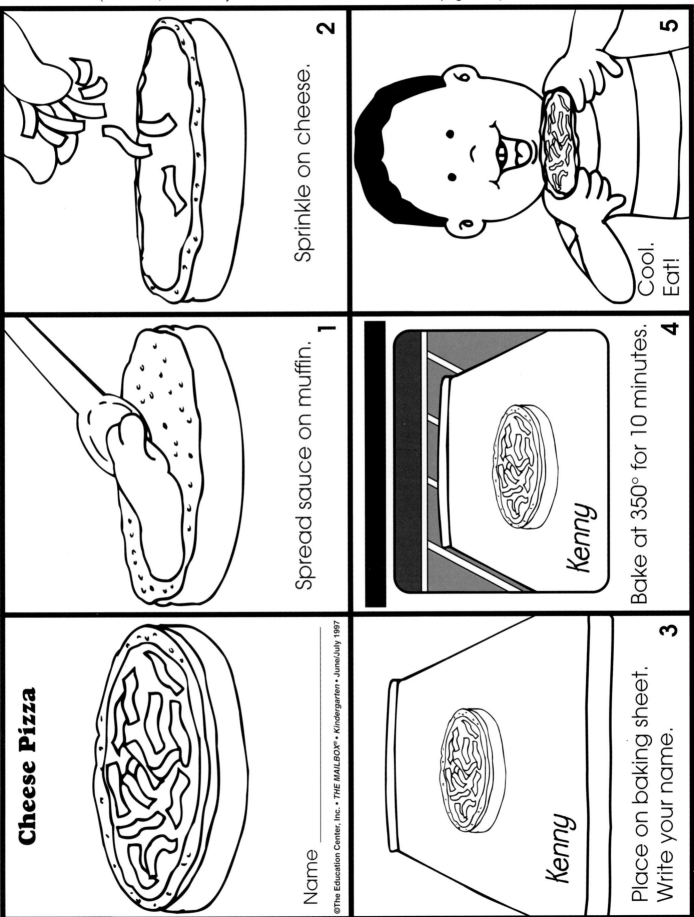

2 Sprinkle on cheese.

5 Cool. Eat!

1 Spread sauce on muffin.

4 Bake at 350° for 10 minutes.

Kenny

Cheese Pizza

Name

©The Education Center, Inc. • THE MAILBOX® Kindergarten • June/July 1997

3 Place on baking sheet. Write your name.

Kenny

299

Recipe Cards (If desired, use in conjunction with "Red, White, & Blue Review" on pages 230–231.)

July—Independence Day Tart

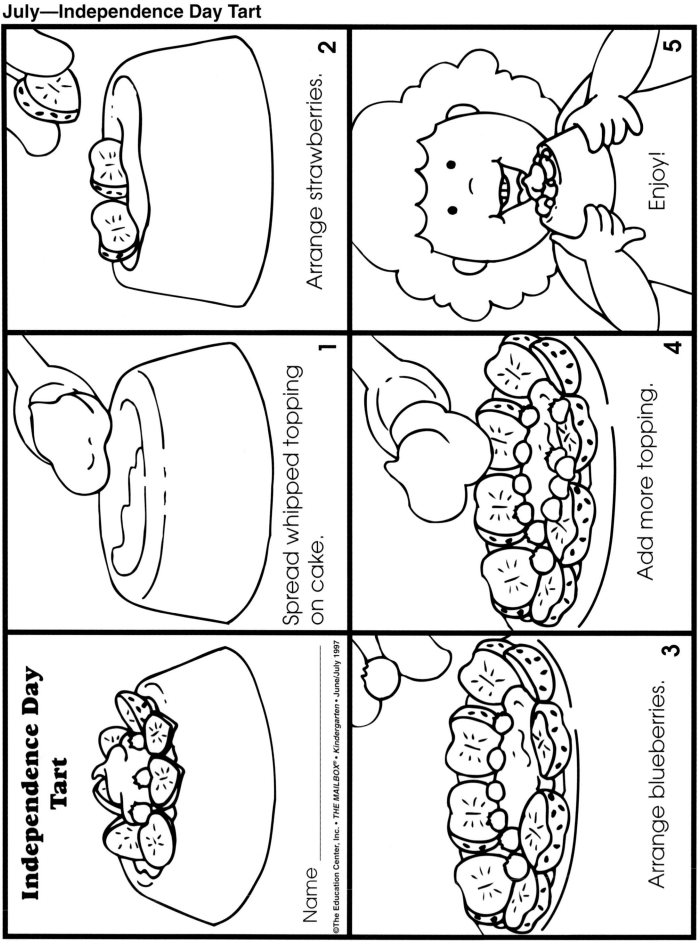

2 Arrange strawberries.

5 Enjoy!

1 Spread whipped topping on cake.

4 Add more topping.

Independence Day Tart

Name _____

©The Education Center, Inc. • *THE MAILBOX®* • *Kindergarten* • June/July 1997

3 Arrange blueberries.

Management

GETTING YOUR DUCKS IN A ROW

Name Recognition

Use this picture-perfect idea to take attendance and help your students recognize their names. Laminate a large school bus and school building tagboard cutout. Take a photograph of each child. Write his name on a photo-sized piece of tagboard. Tape each child's name card to the back of his photo. Laminate the photos. Attach the hook side of a piece of Velcro® to the top of each side of the card. Then, for each photo, attach the loop side of a piece of Velcro® to the bus and the school cutout. To use, attach each photo to the bus cutout so that the name faces up. During group time, encourage each child to find his name and have him peek at the photo to check for correctness. Then have him remove the card and attach his photo to the school.

Lisa Lieb—Special Education
Brooklyn Blue Feather Early Learning Center
New York, NY

Early-Bird Tubs

Keep your early arrivals busy with these activity tubs. Gather several large storage tubs with lids. Put several of one type of item in each tub. For instance, put a variety of books in one tub and puzzles in another. Place each tub in a designated area of the room. As children arrive, invite them to play with the items in the tubs. To clean up, simply have children put the items back in the tubs and replace the lids. Periodically change the items in the tubs.

Dianne Giggey—Gr. K, Episcopal Day School, Pensacola, FL

Nifty Nametags

For long-lasting nametags, try this nifty idea. Using the desired shape, die-cut a nametag for each student from a piece of craft foam. Use a permanent marker to write the student's name on the nametag; then punch a hole near the top of the tag with a hole puncher. Thread a length of ribbon through the hole and tie the ends of the ribbon together. These durable nametag necklaces can be used over and over again.

Judi Black—Gr. K
Beard Elementary
Fort Smith, AR

302

Color-Coded Centers

Management of center activities is quick and easy with this color-coded system. Post a different-colored construction-paper circle at each center, and a smaller corresponding-colored circle on a Peg-Board. Beside each circle on the board, clip plastic clothespins of the same color to pegs representing the number of students allowed at that center. At center time, encourage each student to select a clothespin and clip it on his shirt. Have him use the center that corresponds to the color of his clothespin. When the student is finished, have him return the clothespin to the center board and select another center.

Terri Smith—Gr. K
Blessed Sacrament School
Trenton, NJ

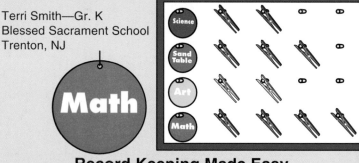

Record Keeping Made Easy

Simplify daily record keeping with adhesive labels. Write each child's name on a different label. Throughout the day, jot down anecdotal notes about each child on his label. Then transfer the label to that child's page in a loose-leaf binder. Record keeping has never been easier!

Hope Zabolinsky—Communications Handicapped
Paul Robeson Community School, New Brunswick, NJ

Center Supply Pictures

Post a picture-supply list at each of your centers to help children independently prepare for centers. Gather pictures of items that are used frequently in your classroom centers, such as glue, scissors, and crayons. Cut out and laminate each picture. Each day post the pictures of the supplies needed at each center. Have students check for, then gather, the needed supplies for their assigned centers.

Mary Langford—Gr. K, St. Agnes School, Butler, WI

Number Lineup

Teach number recognition and ordinal positions as your students line up. Attach vinyl, adhesive-backed numbers (available from office-supply stores) in sequence on the floor. When you're ready for youngsters to line up, call on a child to stand on the first number. Have him name a child to stand on the next number. Continue in this manner until all the children are in line. Encourage little ones to name the numbers and to use words to describe their ordinal positions such as *first, second,* and *third.*

Joan M. Richardson—Gr. K, Feldkirchner Elementary School
Green Brook, NJ

GETTING YOUR DUCKS IN A ROW

Cassette-Tape Storage

Keep your cassette tapes right at your fingertips with this convenient storage system. Program dividers with a different recording artist's name or the title of each cassette. Place the dividers in a decorative box; then file the cassettes in the appropriate place. Your cassette tapes will be readily available whenever you need them.

Elowese Davis—Gr. K
Bragg Elementary School
Marion, AR

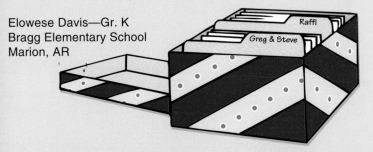

Teacher Identification Display

Do your little ones sometimes have trouble locating another teacher's room when asked to transport a note? If so, try this terrific tip. Make a different banner for each teacher that you correspond with frequently. For example, cut out a different appliqué or stencil such as a bear, car, frog, or bunny and glue it to a banner or a sheet of poster board. Have each designated teacher display her banner or poster near her door. When a youngster needs to find a specific teacher's room, just tell him what picture to look for!

Betty P. Renolds—Gr. K, Stewartsville Elementary School
Goodview, VA

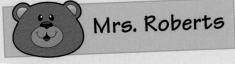
Mrs. Roberts

Trash Boxes

For an easy solution to messy tables, try this neat idea. Cut off the top portion from a small detergent box with a handle. Use Con-Tact® paper to cover the box. Place one box on each table. Throughout the day, have youngsters discard paper scraps and trash in the box. At the end of the day, designate one child from each table to empty the box. Now that's a sure way to keep your room spotless!

Terri Mack—Gr. K, Oaks Road Elementary, New Bern, NC

Easy Book Binders

If you need a quick-and-easy way to bind student-made books together, then give this idea a try. Use a hole puncher to make holes in each book; then insert a bread tie through each hole and twist the ends of the ties together. This simple alternative is a time saving way to put those books together.

Liz Mooney—Gr. K, Central Rayne Kindergarten, Rayne, LA

Rub-A-Dub-Dub!

This sweet-smelling idea will keep little fingers fresh and clean. Collect scraps of various scented soaps. Cut one nylon leg from a pair of pantyhose. Place the soap scraps in the pantyhose leg; then tie it to your classroom water faucet. When your little ones need to wash their hands, they simply rub their wet hands on the soap bag. Neat and clean!

Maria Cuellar Munson
Unity Caring Club
Dallas, TX

Bulletin-Board Borders

Now here's a display idea that's really practical. Purchase off-season borders (which are often discounted); then decorate the back side of the border in the theme of your choice. Simply sponge-paint or stencil the blank side of the border; then allow the border to dry. Mount your border on a bulletin board. Save the border and use the other side when it's in season. Two borders for the price of one!

Linda Shute, Grace Day Care, Lafayette, IN

Glue Mats

Your tables will stay neat and clean with this idea. For each child, glue a large sheet of construction paper atop a sheet of easel paper. Use a permanent marker to program the top of each sheet with "Glue Mat." Laminate the mats. Place the mats on a shelf or in an art center. Have your youngsters use the mats whenever they are using glue. No more messy tables!

Tara K. Moore
Dunwoody, GA

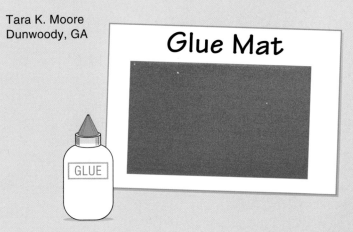
Glue Mat

GETTING YOUR DUCKS IN A ROW

Display Tip

Do you have trouble displaying children's work on your classroom walls due to high humidity or tape that peels the paint off? Here's a solution: Hot-glue clothespins to your walls where you'd like to display children's work. Then simply clip the work to the clothespins. If you mount some of the clothespins at child height, youngsters can even take responsibility for displaying their own work.

Kathy Lindsey—Gr. K
Waimea Elementary & Intermediate School
Kamuela, HI

"Egg-cellent" Attendance

Here's a springtime attendance-taking idea that involves students and also reinforces first- and last-name recognition. Gather a classroom supply of colorful, plastic eggs. For each child, write her first name on one half of the egg and her last name on the other half. Place all of the halves in a basket. As a child enters your room, have her find her first name and her last name, connect the two pieces, and place the whole egg in a different basket (or an egg carton). During your group activities, ask a child to tell the class who is absent by looking at the remaining eggs.

Shannon Bass—Gr. K
Moore Haven Elementary School
Moore Haven, FL

No More Tangles!

Here's a neat way to store skeins of yarn and eliminate those tangled messes. Cut a cross (+) in the center of a Pringles® lid. Put the yarn in the Pringles® can; then pull one section of it through the slits in the lid. Replace the lid. Then children will be able to pull out just the amount of yarn that they need without getting it all tangled up.

Valerie Cumpian—Gr. K
Windermere Elementary
Pflugerville, TX

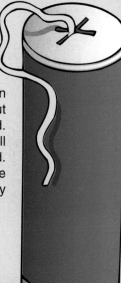

Ease The Tension

If you have students who have a tendency towards "heated debates," a mini–tape recorder can sometimes save the day. If two children are having a disagreement that you deem worthy of this technique, turn on your mini–tape recorder. At an opportune time, ask them if they are ready to hear themselves. Upon listening, some students can see a simple solution. And some just begin laughing—which eases the tension, allowing for a rational discussion.

Patrice Johnson—Gr. K, Colonel John Butler School
Niagara-On-The-Lake, Ontario, Canada

Easy Easel Cleanup

Ask cafeteria workers to save the long boxes that bulk sliced cheese comes in. Put the boxes in your easel trays; then add your paint containers. When the box gets messy, simply toss it out and add a clean one. These cheese boxes are also good for storing crayons and markers, or folded paper towels.

Marsha Feffer
Bentley School
Salem, MA

Get Organized

Here's a tip to help you get your supplies organized when closet space is limited. When your school buys soft drinks for the drink machines, ask for the cardboard flats that the drinks come in. Store your classroom supplies in these boxes, labeling each box on the sides and the front. Then stack the boxes in your closet. This helps both you and your students locate supplies in a jiffy.

Mary Kay Good
Lima, Peru
South America

Art Supplies

The Talking Stick

To keep your sharing times fair, use the Talking Stick. The stick can be a ruler, a dowel, or a piece of interesting wood. Only the person holding the stick may talk at that specific time. Be sure that the Talking Stick is passed to each child so that everyone has a chance to share.

Andrea M. Troisi, LaSalle Middle School, Niagara Falls, NY

Our Readers Write

Our Readers Write

The Kindergarten Express

Track your students' accomplishments with this train display. At the beginning of the school year, cut a large (approximately 2' x 3') train engine and ten flat railroad cars from bulletin-board paper. Label each flat car with the name of a month in the school year. Mount the train on a large wall space. Each month, as your students complete a project, tape one example to the current month's train car. Tell youngsters that when the train is full in June, it will be time to go to first grade. All aboard for kindergarten fun!

Betty P. Reynolds—Gr. K
Stewartsville Elementary School
Goodview, VA

Counting Caterpillar

Introduce students to counting and patterning with a display that will wiggle its way into your daily routine! Cut a large circle from construction paper; then add an eye and two pipe-cleaner antennae to create a caterpillar head. On the first day of school, show the children this beginning to your "Counting Caterpillar." Explain that each day you will add a numbered circle to the caterpillar's body to keep track of the number of school days. Use different-colored circles to make a different pattern each month. Make every tenth circle a little larger to facilitate counting by ten. Caution: This caterpillar may grow large enough to circle your room!

Jamie Meharry—Gr. K
Bent Elementary
Bloomington, IL

Open House Info Center

Transform a dry erase board or chalkboard into an information center for parents on Open House night. Display photos, parent notes and newsletters, art projects, and other student work. Add titles and captions to inform families about the daily routines and special events they can look forward to while their children are in kindergarten. Parents and children alike will enjoy this helpful picture of the year to come.

Alisa T. Daniel
Ben Hill Primary, Fitzgerald, GA

Have A Bubbly Day!

The first day of school is bound to be a success when it involves bubble-blowing! Provide shallow pans of bubble solution for outdoor playtime, along with toilet-tissue or paper-towel tubes for the children to use as blowers. (Have a large supply of tubes available, since some will get too wet to keep using.) Then send home a small jar of bubble solution with each child, accompanied by a note that reads "We had a bubbly first day at school!"

Sue Lewis Lein
Four-Year-Old Kindergarten
St. Pius Grade School
Wauwatosa, WI

We had a bubbly first day at school!

Helpful Hints For First-Day Jitters

Ease the first-day-of-kindergarten fears that many *parents* face with a letter sent home before school begins. Write and duplicate a short letter explaining your suggestions for how a parent might deal with separation anxiety when putting her child on the bus, dropping him off at school, or saying goodbye in the event of tears. Include some helpful tips you've found successful. For example, do your students adjust more quickly to bus routines if they begin riding the bus on the first day? Share your experience and expertise with parents—they are sure to appreciate your understanding.

Patty Schmitt—Gr. K
St. Patrick's School, Portland, MI

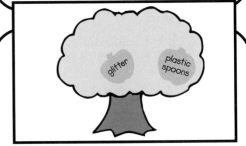

The Giving Tree

Parents will pick up on classroom supply needs when they see a "Giving Tree" display at Open House. Draw an apple tree on a large sheet of bulletin-board paper. Die-cut several apples from red, yellow, or green construction paper. Label each apple with a supply request, such as paper plates, plastic spoons, Baggies®, straws, or waxed paper—any item you may find useful for cooking or art projects throughout the year. Use a restickable adhesive glue stick to attach each apple to the tree. Display the tree on a classroom wall. During Open House, parent volunteers may remove apples from the tree and send in the requested items.

Brenda Purvis—Gr. K
Asheville Christian Academy, Asheville, NC

Home-School Communication

Encourage communication from parents when you give them postage-paid postcards at Open House. Present each family with two postcards addressed to the school. Invite parents to write you a note or request a conference. Keep your own supply of postcards handy to send home positive news about students. Everyone loves to get mail!

Carrie Richardson—Gr. K, Dr. S. A. Mudd Elementary School, Waldorf, MD

You're Invited

Little ones will enjoy making Open-House invitations for their families. A few days prior to your Open House, print a simple invitation in large letters. Duplicate a copy for each child. If desired, have each student trace over the letters with crayons. Then fold down the top of each paper and fold up the bottom to create two flaps as shown. Give each child one construction-paper square and one triangle. Have her glue the square to the bottom flap and the triangle to the top flap to create a house shape. Invite each child to embellish the invitation as desired. Who could resist such a beautiful invitation?

Robin Goddard—Gr. K
Mt. Vernon Elementary
St. Petersburg, FL

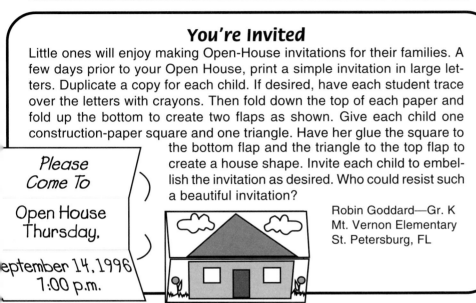

Please Come To Open House Thursday, September 14, 1996 7:00 p.m.

Name Graphing

Help little ones get to know their classmates' names with this fun graphing activity. On the first day of school, take an instant photo of each child. Mount each photo on a construction-paper square and write the child's first name below her picture. Have each child hold her photo. Then group the children by the first letters of their first names. Have each child attach her photo to a wall or bulletin board to create a graph with a column for each initial letter represented in the names of your students. Encourage the children to count the photos in each column and make comparisons. Follow up by writing an experience story about the activity.

Tammy Woodel—Gr. K, Duson Elementary, Duson, LA

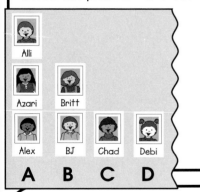

Calendar Patterns

Calendar time is the ideal time to introduce patterning concepts. For each month of the school year, create cutouts in seasonal shapes. (A die-cutting machine will be helpful.) At calendar time each day, add a cutout—labeled with the date—to your calendar grid, creating a pattern as you move through the month. For example, use a simple ABAB pattern for the month of September—schoolhouse, pencil, schoolhouse, pencil. Move on to more difficult patterns as your students' patterning prowess progresses!

Amy Allen and Lorraine Bennett
Cypress Creek Elementary
Ruskin, FL
Andrina Molina—McAllen, TX

Miss Grover

Finding Our Way

Help kindergartners and nonreaders find their way around school with colored shape signs. Assign each teacher a different color/shape combination, such as a red triangle or a blue circle. Create a sign for each teacher's door with her name and the assigned colored shape. When you need to send a student on an errand to a particular teacher's room, simply direct him to look for that teacher's color/shape combination.

Marian Goliszewski—Gr. K
Lalor School
Hamilton Township, NJ

WHAT'S YOUR FAVORITE COLOR?

Color Graph

Create a graph of your students' favorite colors during the first weeks of school. Mount a strip of bulletin-board paper in each basic color on a classroom wall. Then mount a paper bucket below each strip. Ask each child to name his favorite color, as well as an object or animal that is that color. Using a corresponding color of marker or pen, write the name of the object or animal named on an index card. Attach each card to the strip of bulletin-board paper in the corresponding color. Counting the cards on each color strip will reveal the class favorites; discussing the animals and objects named will serve as a color review.

Traci Brown Benke, Waynesburg, PA

Our Readers Write

Halloween Magic

This little project provides a unique way to help children grasp the difference between a pumpkin and a jack-o'-lantern. Give each child a half sheet each of white and orange construction paper. Have each child cut out a pumpkin shape from the orange sheet and glue it to the white sheet. Next staple a thin sheet of waxed paper to the top of the page. Instruct each child to draw jack-o'-lantern facial features on the waxed paper. (If you'd like to add word-recognition opportunities, write "pumpkin" in the lower right-hand corner of the pumpkin page. On a strip of paper cut so that it will cover the word "pumpkin," write "jack-o'-lantern." Tape that strip to the lower right-hand corner of the waxed paper so that it covers the word "pumpkin.") Fold the waxed paper back—you've got a pumpkin. Flip the waxed paper back over the pumpkin—you've got a jack-o'-lantern. Just like magic!

Marlene C. Klingeman—Gr. K
Suburban Christian School
Louisville, KY

Pumpkin Vocabulary

If you have a pumpkin in your classroom, the teachable moment for this activity is bound to pop up. As children examine the pumpkin, encourage them to use descriptive vocabulary to tell about the pumpkin. Write the words on masking tape; then attach them to the pumpkin.

Jane K. Frain—Gr. K
North Harlem Elementary
Harlem, GA

Candy-Wrapper Graph

Recycle candy wrappers for an educational experience. Ask children to save their candy wrappers and bring them to school. Collect the wrappers in a clear jar so children can see them accumulating and estimate the number of wrappers. When you have enough for everyone to participate, have small groups of children sort the wrappers. Then graph them on one large class graph. Discuss what the graph reveals.

Laura Ambrogio—Gr. K, Elizabeth Green School, Newington, CT

308

A Gift To Pass On

If you carve a jack-o'-lantern with your class, here's a neat gift idea that your youngsters can pass on to next year's kindergartners. Dry and save several of the pumpkin seeds. In May, plant the seeds. Then your new crop of kindergartners will have pumpkins to harvest in the fall!

Betty L. Gomillion—Gr. K, South Leake Elementary
Walnut Grove, MS

Estimating Never Tasted So Good

Estimating is motivating with this routine! In advance, label a clear plastic container and a notebook with "Estimation Station." Write each child's name and the days of the week on a chart; then laminate the chart. Use a permanent marker to write "Counting Mat" on a plastic tablecloth. Also draw ten circles on the cloth and label them by tens. Store all of these supplies in an estimating center.

Each week, ask a different child (parent) to stock the container with small treats such as peanuts, jelly beans, or candy corn. If the treats are unwrapped, suggest that some extras be sent along for snacking. Each day, employ a different method to estimate the contents; then have each child write his estimate next to his name on the chart. (For example: On Monday put the container in a center for visual examination. On Tuesday take out about half of the contents and count them. On Wednesday count a scoopful; then see how many scoops are in the whole jar. On Thursday look at the other estimates in the notebook [mentioned above].) On Friday during your calendar time, review all the estimates and have each child write his final guess. Then choose a child to get the counting mat and begin counting the treats. After he has counted ten treats and placed them in a circle on the mat, have him tap another child in the group to continue counting. Continue in this manner until all the treats are counted. If there are more than 100, bag the first 100 and continue counting. Reward the best guesser(s) with a certificate and the opportunity to pass out the treats at snack time.

Eva Miller, Gayton Elementary, Richmond, VA

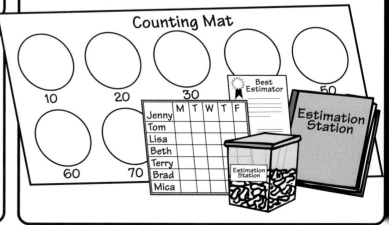

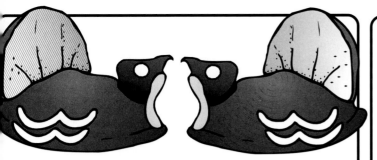

Turkey Treats

These sweet treats inspire the holiday mood. To make one turkey treat, you will need: 1 chocolate-covered marshmallow cookie; 1 candy orange slice; 1 chocolate kiss; orange, yellow, and red tube icing; and chocolate frosting. Begin by using dabs of chocolate frosting to attach the orange-slice tail and the chocolate-kiss head to the cookie body. Use orange icing for the eyes, red icing for the wattle, and yellow icing for feathers. They're almost too cute to gobble!

Sue Lewis Lein—Gr. K, St. Pius X, Wauwatosa, WI

Zippy Books

Classroom-published books can be made more durable with gallon-sized, resealable plastic bags. To make a book using this method, have each child insert his page in a resealable plastic bag. Staple all of the bags together along the sealed end. Cover that end with colored tape and you've got a bound book that will stand up to little hands.

Lynn C. Wharton—Gr. K, Baker Elementary, Mobile, AL

Election Day

With election day upon us, this activity will help your youngsters understand the concept of voting. On a given day, provide three choices for the snack. Also make a graph showing one column for each snack choice. Explain that the snack item with the most votes will be the snack for the day. Then have each child indicate his vote by writing his name in the column of his choice. Discuss what the graph reveals.

Tracey Rebock, Temple Emanuel, Cherry Hill, NJ

Friendship Friday

Since learning how to be a good friend is an ongoing practice, try this ongoing activity. Put the individual names of all of your students in a hat. Each Friday select a child to choose a name from the hat. Have the chooser read the name that he chose. Then encourage the person whose name was selected to sit by the chooser. Continue in this manner until each child has a partner. (If the name of a child who already has a partner is chosen, select another name.) Throughout the day, encourage the pairs to do activities together such as sitting together, playing together, and lining up together. At the end of the day, spend a few minutes talking about the day's events and friendship.

Terri Smith—Gr. K, Blessed Sacrament School, Trenton, NJ

Carpet-Sample Trays

Ask local carpet stores for donations of carpet-sample trays, and you'll have instant sorting trays for your classroom. Place a letter in each compartment of the tray and have students match pictures to their beginning sounds. Or write numerals on small cards and arrange them in the tray. Then have students stack Unifix® cubes and place the stacks in the appropriate compartment of the tray.

Sarah Simpson—Gr. K, Pinar Elementary, Orlando, FL

Writing Boards

These very official-looking writing boards encourage writing just about anywhere! To make a writing board, cover a piece of cardboard with adhesive covering. Clip a clothespin to the top edge to hold a sheet of paper. Students can use these writing boards in the dramatic-play area or wherever the urge to write strikes. You'll find your youngsters will be writing more than ever!

Jan Leighton—Gr. K, Searsport Elementary, Searsport, ME

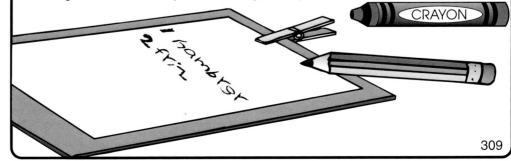

Sibling Celebrations

A baby shower for a kindergartner? Why not? The arrival of a new family member is the perfect time to hold a special celebration to boost a sibling-in-waiting's pride and ease his anxiety. To prepare, have each child in the class sign a paper bag; then fill the bag with baby items, such as a rattle, booties, and sample-sized baby products. During the event, invite the proud sibling to wear a paper banner labeled with "It's a girl [or boy]!" Serve refreshments to the class and give lots of congratulatory attention to the child. Then present the child with the bag of baby goods to take home.

Elesa Miller—Gr. K
St. Catherine Laboure
Wheaton, MD

Little Books Make It Big!

Duplicate and enlarge the little-book reproducibles published in *The Mailbox®* to make big class books. Simply mount each enlarged page on a sheet of construction paper; then follow the provided suggestions in the magazine to complete each book. If desired, laminate the pages and covers before binding the book. Share the big book with youngsters; then invite them to make smaller individual versions of the book.

Debbie Esser—Gr. K, Rome School, Dix, IL

Artistic Allure

Preserve the allure of your classroom art projects and displays with this idea. Take a photograph of each project or display. Mount each photo on a theme-related construction-paper cutout; then laminate the cutout. Display each cutout on a designated wall or bulletin board, adding new cutouts throughout the year. The ever-growing collection of pictured projects will soon be the pride of your students.

Cherie White-Helms—Primary Special Education
Wendell Phillips Visual and Performing Arts Magnet
 Elementary
Kansas City, MO

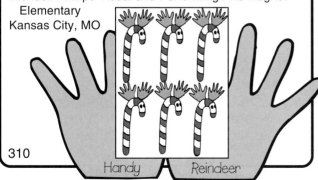

Handy   Reindeer

Unique Displays

While in grocery and department stores, do you ever think of wonderful ways to use some of their neat display stands in your classroom? If so, why not ask the store manager to donate a stand to your class? Many times store personnel are more than willing to make such a worthwhile donation, and you will have a useful, unique way to show off displays or store classroom items.

Doris Watson—Pre-K
Westview School of Rhymes
Ozark, AL

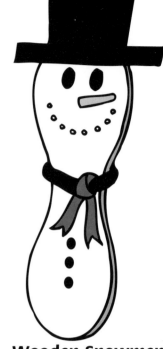

Wooden Snowmen

Invite little ones to convert wooden ice-cream spoons into adorable snowman-puppet performers. Have each child glue a construction-paper top hat to the wide end of his spoon, then use markers to draw a face and buttons on his snowman. Help him tie a length of ribbon around the neck of the spoon. Take your seats—it's show time!

Bubs Kennedy—Gr. K
Wyoming Elementary
Wyoming, MN

Napkin Ho-Ho-Holders

Santa napkin holders will add a festive, decorative touch to any holiday table setting. To make a holder, glue the ends of a bib-shaped piece of white felt together to form a ring. Glue wiggle eyes and a pom-pom nose onto the felt; then fold a red napkin into a triangular shape and fit it into the felt ring. If desired, glue a pom-pom to the top corner of the napkin.

Mary Duffy—Gr. K
Lincoln Elementary
Findlay, OH

Recycled Valentine Displays

These displays dress up your classroom and help bring back precious memories. Each Valentine's Day, cut out a large tagboard heart. Write the year in the center of the heart. When your little ones give you valentines, glue each valentine to the heart; then write the sender's name below it. Laminate the finished project and save it to display year after year. You might even find that you have long-ago students returning to your room on Valentine's Day!

Linda Garner—Gr. K
Harmony Grove
Camden, AR

Tooth Fairy Journal

When a child loses a tooth, send him home with a special notebook that you have labeled "Our Tooth Fairy Journal." At home have the child dictate/write all the events surrounding the loss of his tooth as well as details of the tooth fairy's visit. When the child brings the notebook back to school, encourage him to share his writings with the class.

Laurie Birt—Gr. K
Belinder Elementary
Overland Park, KS

Tooth Tracking

This calendar-related method of keeping track of your students' lost teeth will wiggle right into your daily events. For each month, cut out a large construction-paper tooth. Write a different month on each tooth. Post the teeth in order near your calendar. When a child loses a tooth, write his name and the date on the appropriate tooth cutout. If desired, remove the current month's tooth and post it next to your calendar for easy discussion.

Carol B. Davis—Gr. K
Garrison Elementary
Savannah, GA

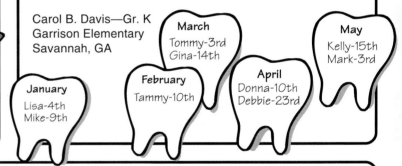

January
Lisa-4th
Mike-9th

February
Tammy-10th

March
Tommy-3rd
Gina-14th

April
Donna-10th
Debbie-23rd

May
Kelly-15th
Mark-3rd

February Surprise

Use these unique February necklaces to reinforce Valentine's Day, Presidents' Day, and penny recognition—all in one! To make one necklace, cut a heart shape from red oaktag. Punch a hole in the top of the heart; then attach a length of yarn to make a necklace. Hot-glue a penny on each side of the heart—one side showing heads, the other side showing tails. When your youngsters sport their seasonal accessories, be sure to encourage them to explain their significance.

Kathleen Miller
Our Lady Of Mt. Carmel
Tenafly, NJ

Valentine Labels

To make valentine delivery quick and easy, try using peel-and-stick labels (available at office supply stores). You can use a computer program to print out a class supply of labels, plus one. Then give each child a set of labels to take home and affix to his valentines. Use the extra set to label each child's valentine box. On Valentine's Day, each child simply matches the labels for easy delivery.

Carla Beames—Gr. K
Jefferson Elementary
Jefferson, TX

Candy-Heart Patterning

With a supply of candy hearts, tagboard strips, and glue; you've got a patterning center fit for the season! Place the supplies in a center. As a child visits the center, have her glue some of the candy hearts to the tagboard strip in the pattern of her choice. Encourage children to name and/or continue one another's patterns.

Our Readers Write

Mother's Day Memento

This piece of artwork will make a lasting imprint on each mom's heart. Write the poem shown below on a sheet of paper. For each child, duplicate the poem on construction paper. Using tempera paint mixed with a little bit of dishwashing liquid, have each child make a footprint on his page. When the paint is dry, have each child sign his page, then deliver it with love.

Stephanie Gillespie—Gr. K
McHarg Elementary
Radford, VA

> *I stepped into Kindergarten*
> *Not knowing what to do.*
> *I realized how much I had*
> *Depended upon you.*
> *Thanks for helping*
> *me through, Mom!*
> *I love you.*

MOM

LOVE
CORI

Story-Can Theater

Heighten storytime interest with this enticing idea. Select a large, empty coffee can with a lid (or an opaque, plastic lidded container). When you have a story to read to your class, collect items from your classroom that could represent characters in your story. For example, if you're going to read *The Little Red Hen,* you might put some toy barnyard animals in the Story Can. As you share the book, use the manipulatives in the can to help dramatize the story. Afterward place the book and the Story Can in a reading center; then encourage students to use the supplies during center time.

Cindi Zsittnik, Surrey School
Hagerstown, MD

Old MacDonald's Vowel Farm

This rendition of "Old MacDonald" might sound silly, but it's fun to do—and it works!
Here's how it goes:

> Old MacDonald had a farm, A-E-I-O-U.
> And on that farm he had a short *a,* A-E-I-O-U.
> With an ă-ă here, and an ă-ă there,
> Here an ă, there an ă, everywhere an ă-ă.
> Old MacDonald had a farm, A-E-I-O-U.

Continue singing, inserting a new vowel sound with each additional verse.

Christine Hunter—Gr. K, Garrett's Way, Newtown Square, PA

Big, Beautiful Bubbles

To make an extra-big bubble maker, thread string through two straws as shown. Make big, beautiful bubbles by dipping the assembly into bubble solution, then waving it through the air. Ooooooh!

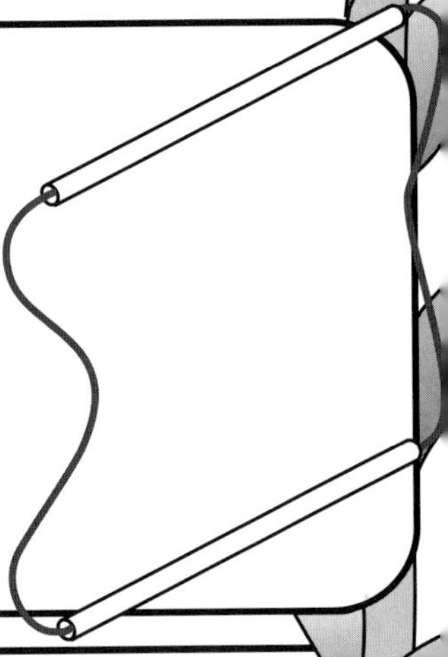

Julie Fallenstein-Johnson—Gr. K
Plymouth, MN

Wow, Mom!

For a quick and clever Mother's Day card that kids will love making, try this idea. Make a tagboard tracer—in all capital letters—for the word *MOM.* Show your students how to place the tracer on the fold of a sheet of construction paper and trace around the lettering. Then have each child cut out the pattern and an additional circle in the center of the *O.* Have each child decorate the outside of the card, then write a special message on the inside. "Wow, Mom—you're the best!"

Patricia A. Schrum
Woodside Elementary
Hartford, MI

WOW

Dear Mom, you are a wow!
Love, Adam

MOM

The Magic Of Reading

If you're reading *Jack And The Beanstalk* this spring, here's a tip to motivate all kinds of additional independent reading. After sharing the story, show students some magic (construction-paper) reading beans. Tell them that these beans have been known to sprout if they are read to. In fact, (so you've heard) the more they are read to, the more they grow! Then "plant" the beans in a pot in your reading center. If your students are reading to the beans, begin a paper beanstalk. As they continue reading, add to the length of the beanstalk. This little bit of magic grows a beanstalk—and while no one is really looking—great enthusiasm for reading!

Jill Hodder—Gr. K
Milford Brook School
Manalapan, NJ

A Special Gift

If you're a picture-taking kind of teacher, here's an idea for end-of-the-year gifts that are practically made before you know it—individual photo albums! Start by collecting a class supply of mini photo albums. As your school year draws to a close, distribute the year's collection of pictures among the albums. Also include copies of special poems or other writings that were meaningful to your children, and personal notes from you. At the end of the year, give each child his customized photo album as a long-lasting kindergarten keepsake.

June E. Maddox—Gr. K
Calvary Baptist Day School
Savannah, GA

David, Remember when you were Humpty Dumpty in our play?

Doughnuts With Dad

Dads will be delighted by this token of appreciation for Father's Day. In advance, have each child create a card of appreciation for his father or a male friend. (See "Father's Day Card" on this page for one idea.) Then send home a note inviting each father or male friend to come to school for "Doughnuts With Dad." On that day, serve doughnuts to the dads; then encourage each child to present his card to his father or friend.

Debbie Rowland
APO, AP

Pomp And Circumstance

Here's a graduation-entrance idea that is sure to touch the hearts of one and all. Have each child make a paper-plate rainbow. To make one, cut a paper plate in half. Use crayons, paint, or tissue paper to color a plate half to resemble a rainbow. Then glue puffs of cotton to each end. On that special graduation day, have your students walk in holding their rainbows while you play "The Rainbow Connection" sung by Kermit the Frog.

Bonnie Boucher—Gr. K
Tiny Tots Preschool
 And Kindergarten
Auburn, NH

Graduation Caps

Add a touch of class to your graduation ceremony with these graduation caps. For each cap you will need: a laminated 9" x 9" square of black construction paper, two 9" x 3 1/4" strips of black construction paper, one brad, and yarn in your school colors. To make the cap, cut three 1 1/2" slits into each of the black strips. Tape the strips onto the laminated square in a rounded *V* shape. Make a tassel with the yarn; then use the brad to attach it to the center of the square. (If necessary use bobby pins to secure the caps on youngsters' heads.)

Heidi Fryman—Gr. K
Beverly Elementary
 School
Beverly, OH

Father's Day Card

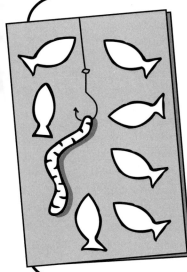

Can't you just hear your little ones saying, "Get it? *Fishing* you a happy Father's Day?" It's debatable just who will get the most enjoyment out of this card—father or child. To make a card, fold a blue sheet of construction paper in half. Glue construction-paper fish to the front of the card. Next draw a hook and line in the scene. Then glue a colorful candy worm to the hook. For the inside message, have each child copy the phrase "Fishing you a Happy Father's Day!" Add a signature; then the card is ready for a special delivery.

Debbie Rowland

Summer Surprise

Keep in touch with your old kindergartners with this little summer surprise. On the last day of school, have a volunteer take a photo of you with each child. During the summer, let each child know you are thinking about him by sending him the picture along with a little note from you. What a nice summer surprise!

Laurie Mills—Gr. K
Stevenson Elementary
Stevenson, AL

Index

318